LIVING (IN)DEPENDENCE:
Critical Perspectives on Global Interdependence

Edited by
**Bill F. Ndi, Benjamin Hart Fishkin
& Adaku T. Ankumah**

Langaa

Langaa Research & Publishing CIG
Mankon, Bamenda

Publisher:
Langaa RPCIG
Langaa Research & Publishing Common Initiative Group
P.O. Box 902 Mankon
Bamenda
North West Region
Cameroon
Langaagrp@gmail.com
www.langaa-rpcig.net

Distributed in and outside N. America by African Books Collective
orders@africanbookscollective.com
www.africanbookscollective.com

ISBN-10: 9956-550-76-0

ISBN-13: 978-9956-550-76-0

List of Contributors

Editors

Bill F. Ndi, Associate Professor of English and Foreign Languages at Tuskegee University, Tuskegee, Alabama, USA, earned his Doctorate from the University of Cergy-Pontoise in 2001. He is a poet, playwright, storyteller, literary critic, translator, historian of ideas and mentalities as well as an academic who has held teaching positions in several universities in Australia, France and elsewhere. His areas of teaching and research comprise among others English Languages and literatures, French, Professional, Technical and Creative Writing, World Literatures, Applied/Historical Linguistics, Literary History, Media and Communication Studies, Peace/Quaker Studies and Conflict Resolution, History of Internationalism, History of Ideas and Mentalities, Translation & Translatology, 17th Century and Contemporary Cultural Studies. He has published extensively in these areas. His publications include numerous scholarly works on Early Quakerism and translation of Early Quaker writings. He has also published poetry and plays in both the French and the English languages. Professor Bill F. Ndi has 22 published volumes of poetry of which 5 are in French, a play and 4 works in translation. He is co-editor of *Outward Evil, Inward Battle: Human Memory in Literature* with Adaku T. Ankumah, Benjamin Hart Fishkin, and Festus Fru Ndeh as well as co-editor of *Fears, Doubts, and Joys of not Belonging* and *The Repressed Expressed* with Adaku T. Ankumah and Benjamin Hart Fishkin. His most recent edited work is *Secret, Silences, and Betrayals.* Also, he has served as a National Endowment for the Humanities' scholar.

Benjamin Hart Fishkin, Associate Professor of English at Tuskegee University specializes in teaching Nineteenth Century British Literature. He holds a Ph.D. from the University of Alabama where he served as a Junior Fellow in The Blount Undergraduate Initiative. In his research, he has emphasized Nineteenth Century British Literature through each phase of his education. Prior to earning his Doctorate from the University of Alabama in May of 2009, he obtained a BA in English and Film from the University of Michigan, Ann Arbor, and an MA from Miami University, Oxford, Ohio where he examined the interest of Charles Dickens in the theatre and how the stage influenced his novel writing. He has published *The Undependable Bonds of Blood: The Unanticipated Problems of Parenthood in the Novels of Henry James.* He co-edited *Outward Evil Inward Battle: Human Memory in Literature* with Adaku T. Ankumah, Bill F. Ndi, and Festus Fru Ndeh, and *Fears, Doubts and Joys of not Belonging* and *The Repressed Expressed* with Bill F. Ndi and Adaku T. Ankumah. His recent research interests include, besides his growing interest in Anglophone Cameroon literature, the problems of marriage and the American family, and the relationship between the Blues and the single-parent home in the works of William Faulkner, August Wilson, and F. Scott Fitzgerald.

Adaku T. Ankumah, Interim Chair and Professor of English at Tuskegee University, received her PhD in Comparative Literature from the University of Wisconsin-Madison with a minor in drama. Her dissertation and initial research interests focused on revolutionary playwrights from the African Diaspora, such as Kenyan Ngugi wa Thiong'o, Martiniquais writer Aimé Césaire, and African American Amiri Baraka, who use their creative efforts to work for the destruction of what they consider to be the colonial/capitalist foundation of post-colonial Africa. Ngugi's play *The Trial of Dedan Kimathi,* a play that examines the arrest and trial of one of the famous leaders of the Mau Mau revolt against the British in Kenya in the 1950's, has been the subject of her published research. She has also done research on the role of women in revolutionary theatre, voicelessness of African women, and gender and politics in the works of African women authors like Mariama Bâ, Ama Ata Aidoo and Tsitsi Dangarembga.

Professor Ankumah's recent research interest includes the writings of women in the African diaspora. This includes research on memory in literature and its role in helping those dealing with painful, fragmented pasts forge a wholesome future in Edwidge Danticat's *The Dew Breaker.* She has also examined memory and resistance in the poetry of South African performer and writer Gcina Mhlophe. She recently edited *Nomenclatural Poetization and Globalization*. Also, she co-edited, with Bill F. Ndi, Benjamin Hart Fishkin and Festus Fru Ndeh, *Outward Evil Inward Battle: Human Memory in Literature*, and with Bill F Ndi and Benjamin Hart Fiskin: *Fears, Doubts, and Joys of not Belonging* and *The Repressed Expressed*.

Contributors

Hassan Yosimbom holds a PhD in Literature from the University of Yaoundé 1 Cameroon. Currently, he teaches in the Department of English, University of Buea, Cameroon. His PhD thesis explores "Identity Dynamics in Cameroon Literature". His current research interests and projects focus on the links between Postcolonial and Postmodern theories, and how their interplay shapes and nurtures multiple-layered identity formation and performance in postcolonial societies, especially Cameroon. Also, he is keen on researching Latin American epistemological foundations such as Transmodernity, Coloniality, Decoloniality, Pluriversality, etc. and how they could be used to de-/re-construct postcolonial African societies. He has published extensively in these areas.

Richard Evans is assistant professor of English at Tuskegee University in Tuskegee, Alabama. Educated in classics at the University of South Carolina, the American School of Classical Studies at Athens and Columbia University, Dr. Evans holds a Ph.D. in comparative literature with research interests in ancient and medieval literatures, theories of translation and linguistic relativity. He has published numerous academic book reviews, essays promoting the study of Classical Greek in schools, and articles on Greek and Roman authors in the Dictionary of Literary Biography and articles on various topics in classical literature.

Andrew Bonanno is a doctoral fellow in anthropology at the University of Georgia. His current work explores the effects of land tenure formalization and commercialization in northern Sierra Leone, particularly how these processes restructure social relations and individuals' range of possible actions regarding land claims and use. He holds an M.S. in Environmental Policy from Bard College in upstate New York.

Elisabeth N. M Ayuk-Etang is an academic, gender advocate and ecofeminist critic. She teaches at the University of Buea, Cameroon. She holds a PhD in Black Women's Writings from the University of Yaoundé 1, Cameroon. She has published extensively in peer reviewed journals and authored book chapters on the status of the Black woman in Africa. Her research interest is on Black Women Studies, Women and Development in Africa, Ecofeminsm and Sustainable Development in Black Communities. Some of her publications include "Cultural Redemption and Identity (RE) Construction in John Nkemngong Nkengasong's *Across the Mongolo*" (2013), "Combating Forced Labor and Human Trafficking in Africa: The Role of Endogenous and Exogenous Forces" (2012), and "Colonialism, Female Literacy and the Millennium Development Goals in Africa" (2012). She is currently working on "The Place of the Woman in Higher Education Institutions (HEIs) in Africa". She is a recipient of many award including the University of Michigan African Presidential Scholars (UMAPS), a prestigious fellowship.

Dalal Alkordi is a PhD fellow in the Integrated Public Policy and Development Program (IPPD) at Tuskegee University. Dalal obtained a Master of Science degree in Agricultural Economics with a thesis titled: "Consumer Demand and Willingness to Purchase Asian Fruits and Vegetables Produced by Local Farmers in Selected Korean Communities in Alabama and Georgia". She won the first prize in the statewide Social Business Plan Forum: "Financing Small and Limited Resource Farmer Inputs as a Business Strategy in the Alabama Black Belt." Her research interests are in international development polices and the economic development of the manufacturing companies and / or oil industries as well as foreign aid and its impact in the developing countries.

Benjamin Hart Fishkin is an Associate Professor of English at Tuskegee University, where he specializes in teaching Nineteenth Century British Literature. He holds a Ph.D. from the University of

Alabama where he served as a Junior Fellow in The Blount Undergraduate Initiative.

Zachary Peterson is a PhD. Fellow at Georgia State University. He began his odyssey toward the historical field in a city, Birmingham, Alabama, which proved pivotal in the history of the Civil Rights Movement. His interests as a student of history began with examining the movement from a traditionally national perspective. However, through his education in the doctoral program in the History Department at Georgia State University, he now explores the transnational connections of the movement, especially its many connections to the African continent. This transnational approach to history has informed his teaching and research. His teaching approaches the history of the United States of America from a transnational and global framework. He teaches U.S. history 1492-present; African history 1500-present; and Global history 1500-present; and Global history 1500-present. He has a forthcoming publication, entitled "From Sharpeville to Tlatelolco and Beyond: Apartheid South Africa, Authoritarian Mexico, and Transnational Activism around Sports in the Global Sixties," in the upcoming issue of the *World History Bulletin*, "The Whole World Is Moving: 1968 and The Long Global Sixties."

Eliot James is Assistant Professor of History and Coordinator of the interdisciplinary African and Black American Studies program at the University of Minnesota, Morris. Elliot is currently writing a book manuscript based on his doctoral dissertation, "*Sithutha Isizwe* ('We Carry the Nation'): Dispossession, Displacement, and the Making of the Shared Minibus Taxi in South Africa, 1930-Present."

A. Christson Adedoyin, (MSW, PhD.) is currently an Associate Professor of Social Work in the School of Public Health, Department of Social Work, at Samford University, Birmingham, Alabama. His research focus revolves around roles of congregations and religious institutions in addressing socio-economic and health disparities among minorities' specifically African immigrants and refugees, integration of faith and learning, and spirituality in social work.

Mary S. Jackson, (PhD, ACSW, LICDC, CCS, CFC) is professor of Social Work at East Carolina University, Greenville, North Carolina. She has published numerous journal articles on substance use/abuse and gangs. In addition, she has authored and co-authored books on Policing in America and Juvenile Delinquency. Research areas of interest are gangs, substance use/abuse/misuse, juvenile justice, juvenile delinquency and issues related to diversity.

Kayode Julius Ayeni is an independent scholar with keen interest in clinical research and management consulting. His research and practice experiences covers sectors such as business, health information management, cultural competency, and organization leadership. He is the CEO of Dominion Group LLC, and an alumnus of Western Kentucky University, Bowling Green, Kentucky where he recently graduated with a master of arts in organizational leadership.

Bill F. Ndi teaches at Tuskegee University. He has numerous scholarly publications on Early Quakerism and translation of Early Quaker writings. He has also published extensively in both the French and the English languages. These publications include scholarly articles and book chapters, poetry, and plays. Professor Bill F. Ndi has 22 volumes of poetry of which 5 are in French, a play and 4 works in translation.

Table of Contents

Introduction

> Since the 1970s, the first literature on interdependence and then in that of globalization, it has been argued that we are moving towards a more unified and cosmopolitan world, where national differences, and the nation state, will be less influential and less necessary.
>
> Fred Halliday, "Nationalism" in John Baylis & Steve Smith, *The Globalization of World Politics: An Introduction to International Relations.* (534)

The above quote excerpted from the concluding segment of Fred Halliday's studies on "Nationalism" explores multi-directional dependency purely from the perspective of international relations while ignoring other disciplinary areas. However, this leaves to wonder whether humanity is headed towards a geo-political world in which the symmetric or asymmetric effects of bidirectional and or multi-directional dependency will no longer be felt. And even if this were true to a specific discipline, viz. International Relations, will it hold true for all other disciplines? That notwithstanding, in International Relations, have we not just in recent years witnessed, in the USA, an election that was marked by heightened rhetoric of erecting walls for total appropriation of that which populists deem to be the one and only access to total independence while excluding the "parasites" or "takers"? Exclusionism seems to be the *modus operandi* and *modus vivendi* for nationalist advocates who fan the flames of autonomy within walls that will leave the rest out.

Historically, ethically, politically, psychologically, culturally, economically, philosophically, biologically, etc. human beings have striven to be free of constraints. Being free is a fundamental human aspiration and quest. As such, humans have fought wars of and for independence on the grounds that such wars are the sole guarantor of their freedom. *Living (In)Dependence* embraces a multidisciplinary approach to the interconnectedness of independence and dependence in every ramification of these words. Can people ever be if they live by excluding others? Scholars and academics from different disciplinary area have had to examine both words: "independence" & "dependence", not simply as polar opposites in their Saussurian sense. For, the freedom and dependence binary is embedded in the concept of "independence". Consequently, independence and dependence as concepts have led to zillions of pages being written, and oceans of ink being spilled in writing about them.

In addressing this issue in *Living (In)Dependence*, scholars have had challenged their perceived or preconceived notions about "Independence" and "dependence" from their respective disciplinary discursive perspectives. The word "Independence" encapsulates that which is most fought against viz. dependence, and thus warranted this close examination of the aforementioned Saussurian notion of polar opposites which, however, has not deterred proponent of interdependence. Yet, structuralists as well as theoreticians expounding on dependency have elaborated the negative effects of interdependence as if to legitimize the exclusionists' clamor for walls separating people supposedly living in a global village.

Can one intelligibly, in one or any discipline—exclusionist or inclusionist—define independence while discarding the notion of dependence? How do people, though dependent, conceive themselves independent? Can a writer or again does a writer— novelist, dramatist, poet, etc.—create a universe in which characters enjoy total independence from each other? Our world, as we know it, is one of dependence on each other, interdependence, cooperation, etc. Even if humans claim to be independent, do laws, values, traditions, customs, economics, ethics not regulate their claim to independence? And/or again, is theirs not some form of economic, diplomatic, socio-political arrangement? Furthermore, this could have prompted Ngaire Woods, talking of "International Political Economy in the Age of Globalization" to drive home the idea that "[w]orld markets and countries, local firms and multi-national corporation which trade and invest within them are all shaped by layers of **rules, norms,** laws, organization, and even habits." (qtd. in Baylis and Smith 326) Therefore, this study has had to explore the binary of life experience of independence and that of dependence—as constituent flipsides of a coin whose meaning can only be grasped by taking a closer look at each facet. Besides, Kenneth McLeish, in his *Key Ideas in Human Thoughts,* talking of Sovereignty, points out it "possesses both external and internal dimensions" (701). In addition, he submits that, "independence suggest lack of dependence" (375).

Living (In)Dependence appears at a moment when the whole world is at cross-purposes. Just a few months ago, at a NATO leaders' meeting in Brussels, the principal parties debated (among other things) whether or not the United States is independent of interdependence. A 29-member military alliance, one that exists to ensure collective defense and has done so for decades, now has to take the disruptive, disaffected, and seditious posture of arguing against its own obsolescence. The editors thus bring in such an inflammatory example because if the wealthiest and most powerful nation can stand up and question the need for a mutually beneficial alliance where does that leave the assailable nations of South East Asia, Central America, Africa and among others the Southern Cameroonian writers who chronicle theirs in the diaspora and its consequences? In this circumstance can it be said that such nations enjoy the ultimate protection and recognition of their respective group's collective identity? (McLeish 375).

Living (In)Dependence is about human beings being alone and suffering negative repercussions for someone else's actions. The authors are concerned with how living without meaningful and altruistic connection can transform, alter, and damage one's character. *Living (In)Dependence* is more than a book about political, economic, religious, and linguistic themes. The work is also about the psychology of independence/dependence. As an interdisciplinary-focused collection *Living (In)Dependence* strives to examine how theories are generated; their possible limitations; and the much needed methodological innovations when the theorization of the lived experience of dependence and independence "aims at implementing lasting change" (Michlin & Rocchi 3). How does one deal with or attempt to overcome the pain of exclusion, enmity or indifference? This need for empathy, and how it shapes, sculpts and recasts the way in which people think, react, and plan can wreak long-term havoc and make independence appear far different in reality than it does in theory. It makes life more difficult and, our study hopes to reveal, changes the resultant literature into something that no one could have predicted. A new routine of independence, loneliness, estrangement, and isolation corresponds to and throws up a new way for literature to present its displeasure with modern society. It is no surprise that as far back as the middle of the last century, Erich Kahler in his observation of the contemporary society summarizes the history of man as that of alienation (qtd. in Seeman 783). In this guise Fishkin, Ankumah, & Ndi highlight that isolation and detachment apply to more than just people, "they apply to the literary critic, the literary theorist, readers and the characters they are reading about. [...] people could, by choice withdraw from it and insulate themselves from actual hostility by reading about it" (xvii)

The publication of *Living (In)Dependence* is necessary because the dividing line between independence and dependence, just like the line between love and hate, is as thin as the edge of a razor. African nations, starting with Ghana in 1957, have allegedly become masters of their own fate and destinies. However, this description bounces back and forth between the desire to be alone or not, on the one hand, and the desire to survive in the globalized twentieth and twenty-first century's world, on the other. This group of sovereign entities remains in a permanent state of impermanence, flux, limbo and indecisiveness while battling through a terrible conundrum. A full-fledged member of the globalized world will ultimately lose its own cultural identity; an isolated, measured, and calculated emerging class of entrepreneurs will ultimately lose the financial markets necessary to maintain lasting growth. This comes as a result of the fact that the "... hegemonic ideology [would] manage to convince members of the subordinate groups to take it to heart that a potentially radical chain of events is set in motion" (Scott 106).

Mufor Atanga, the Southern Cameroonian political scientist, arranges, organizes, and orders integration in such a way that the very word implies marginalization. Pushing two sides together does not create happiness. Instead, it creates a system which satisfies no one, like a wedding ceremony that is conducted in two religious formats because the participants are from disparate backgrounds. This leaves to wonder whether the solution should be independence or forced dependence. Illustrating with the example of Cameroons with specification of the Southern Cameroons portion of that country, Piet Koonings of the African Studies Centre in Leiden argues that this "…reunification was more like a loveless United Nations-arranged marriage between two people who hardly knew each other" (qtd. In Atanga xii). Under such a system, one side controls the other, erases its past, and censors its future. Since one side of this equation, the side that makes dependence compulsory clearly has its problems, Atanga almost immediately swings in the other direction. Maybe "…the [Southern Cameroons] territory may have a future separate from Yaoundé" (xix). Stepping away from the Cameroons, the colonizer surely has cultural identity advantages. It may even help establish political order, but it simultaneously creates financial black holes. From where will one import? To where will one export? What about currency? What about the problems of autonomy once the euphoria of making such a break are gone? Problems are bound to arise with removing oneself (permanently) from the *La République du Cameroun*. This is the paradox. The problem is that we have two courses of action and both are uniquely handicapped. This is the case made by Michael Cox in his exploration of security challenges in post-Cold War Europe. He brings to the fore former communist nations in the throes of celebration, celebrating the true and whole freedom of Europe forgetting that the new Europe would generate more demands for "deeper and wider conception of Europe" to the point "when the former Yugoslavia began to implode" (qtd. in Baylis and Smith 149).

Other examples abound. Nigeria, for instance, was granted independence on October 1, 1961. This is roughly the same period of time that nations like Southern Cameroons, Senegal, Mali, Congo, Niger, and Burkina Faso got theirs. Today, Transparency International estimates that the former president of Nigeria, Sani Abacha, embezzled between $ 2 billion and $ 5 billion (Rogoff 71). This is worthy of mention because it is by no means clear in which direction a citizen of one of these nations should run. Would it be best to seek independence by running away from a traditional colonizing protector (in this case Great Britain) or would it be best to seek dependence by running away from his or her own leader? This is an extremely difficult problem to solve because kleptocracy is at both sides of the equation. Kenneth S. Rogoff, former chief economist of the International Monetary Fund, states that "Obviously, corruption predates paper currency and will live long after it is gone…those engaged in corruption and other criminal activities will find other ways to do business, and there will be even greater incentive for innovation" (72). The African, in his or her quest to be free, is placed right between Homer's Scylla and Charybdis. In a previous volume of collected essays, Ndi, Ankumah, and Fishkin have hinted in their introduction that:

> Post-colonialism has placed the African in a fog, and there is no promise that it will lift anytime soon. What is necessary is to look even farther afield. These types of problems are troublesome, and this is no time to be bashful, so wherever people feel politically or educationally limited they need a pilot for their soul to provide commentary and courage. (xix)

It is clear, in this circumstance, that neither independence nor dependence is particularly appealing. Either choice brings with it a degree of steadily narrowing alternatives. The phasing out of names and titles while replacing them with new ones in the era of independence, have not solved any of the African problems of international dimension, for example.

In theory, Franklin Delano Roosevelt and the US allies established the International Monetary Fund and The World Bank in

1944 to control economic chaos (Mallaby 2). In reality, it was just another way to do business. Just as an artist, an author, a sculptor or a painter endeavors to make order out of chaos these two conjoined organizations want things to run smoothly in Africa, Latin America, and Asia (Mallaby 2; Baylis & Smith 326). That said, the World Bank and its counterpart are not altruistic but moneymaking institutions. To echo Ngugi wa Thiong'o's sentiment, "The relation was primarily economic. The colonized as worker, as peasant, produces for another. His land and his labor benefit another. This rearrangement was also accomplished through cultural [financial] subjugation..." (108). In a sharp comparison to the Lilliputians in Jonathan Swift's *Gulliver's Travels*, the main character wakes up to find himself tied down by thread and finds himself incarcerated by people that are less than six inches tall. This argument by Sebastian Mallaby clearly has geographical landmasses like Africa in mind (although it is not the only one). The International Monetary Fund and The World Bank are protectors of the colonizing powers and despite promises, to the contrary, they constitute forces of subjugation, not to say enslavement. The promise is to eradicate and erase poverty, but this is misguided romanticism for more people suffer more exclusion in these parts of the world than ever before. We are taking backwards steps, or better still the creation of these institutions was a step taken forward and three steps taken backwards. What's more, we have seen this narrative before, "[n]ow this is still an Imperfect method of control—the enforcers are clearly identified and the coercion is too obvious (Bethke 47).

Contrary to popular belief, there are problems with being acquainted and connected. One of them is what could be styled a misdiagnosis. This term is from a William Easterly's *The Whiteman's Burden: Why the West's Effort to Aid the Rest Have Done So Much Harm and So Little Good*. Easterly, a former senior research economist at the World Bank, states, "From the beginning, the interests of the poor got little weight compared with the vanity of the West" (Easterly 23). The famous remark, encased in Easterly's book title, from Rudyard Kipling's famous 1899 poem has always brought with it a self-gratifying, masturbatory invention that this part of the world is somehow anointed. We know better or are uniquely qualified to solve complex external problems. Even James Stuart Mill, as far back as 1810, rejected independence and stated that "For the sake of the natives" in India, the British could not "leave them to their own direction" (Easterly 23). Even this phrasing does not give the alleged subaltern a say in how his or her future will be taken apart or how the psychological price to be paid to rescue the underdeveloped will be financed. Jean-Claude Shanda Tonme, in a *New York Times* Op-Ed column on July 15, 2005 had the following to say as a lawyer and journalist based in the Cameroons who can see a mile away that international currency remains unstable because Western assistance takes more than it gives. This is because as he writes, "They still believe us to be like children that they must save, as if we don't realize ourselves what the source of our problems is." This caustic criticism of the paternalistic thinking of Western powers comes at an age when it is assumed that former colonies have ascended to independence. This brings to question the whole premise of globalization making the world a global and interdependent village. Is the world in the 21st Century one marked by independent autonomous countries or one in which the hegemon lord it over weaker and failed states? Within the countries, independent or dependent, can the citizens pride themselves as part of a national whole or even part of an international whole? Is the 21st century one of Independence or one of Dependence? Is it not all too familiar that "naturally the factual sovereignty (or autonomy) [independence] of many formally recognized states may be meaningless as in the case of client state"? (McLeish 701). This all brings to mind Ngugi wa Thiong'o's portrayal of how imperialism "has distorted the view of African realities" (*Decolonising* 28). He further points out that:

It has turned reality upside-down: the abnormal is viewed as normal and the normal is viewed as abnormal. Africa actually enriches Europe: but Africa is made to believe that it needs Europe to rescue it from poverty. Africa' natural and human resources continue to develop

Europe and America: but Africa is made to feel grateful for aid from the same quarters that still sit on the back of the continent. Africa even produces intellectuals who now rationalise[sic] this upside-down way of looking at Africa. (*Decolonising* 28).

In order to elaborate on this topical concern and, without helping to rationalize any kind of "upside-down look at" any component of our global world, different scholars from various disciplines were called upon to discuss the historical, literary, political, international, psychological, economic, financial, ethical, etc. perspectives of "Living (In)Dependence" from that of their respective disciplinary discourses. Embracing still the bigger and altruistic concept of freedom/independence, each scholar drew his or her conclusion without constraints from the editors. The various scholars having challenged both dependence and independence either as polar opposites or binaries and flipsides of the same coin, leave the reader with a savory platter of treats with which to indulge mindlessly as the sequential order of the chapters was carefully arranged by the editors to allow for an enjoyable exploration of living (In)Dependence.

The Living (In)Dependence project is constraints. If there is any one problem that dominates the plight of the African, it is how he/she has limits, barriers, and obstacles to overcome. The Anglophone experience in Cameroon is denigrated and this has splintered into a myriad of problems. This drama, chaos, and disorder is delineated in Hassan Mbindzenyuy's "Francis B. Nyamnjoh's *Souls Forgotten*: Unpacking Minority Struggles". This chapter contends that in Francis B. Nyamnjoh's *Souls Forgotten*, *La République du Cameroun's* Francophones use difference as a force for subordination and the fracturing of the Cameroons. The contention here is that claims to cultural supremacy, whether made by Francophones, or on behalf of Southern Cameroonians are xenophobic. It further asserts that the "minority" seen through the prism of the University of Asieyam and the Lake Abehema Disaster, is a substantial justification of the "Living (In)Dependence" binaries that rationalize the authoritarian tendencies within the cultures of *La République du Cameroun*. In addition, regional balance and prerogatives underlie and substantiate *La République du Cameroun's* determination to enforce authoritarianism upon the minority British Southern Cameroonians/Ambazonians. The minority-majority boundaries are thresholds or vestibules of meaning that must be crossed, erased, and translated in the process of articulating equality and difference. The Janus-face of cultural boundaries transforms the problem of outsider/insider into a process of hybridity, the chapter recommends the turning of Southern Cameroons and *La République du Cameroun* boundaries and limits into the in-between spaces or zones, not only of transition but also of transaction, through which the meanings of cultural and political authority are, and must be, negotiated.

The above need for negotiation calls for improvisation and adaption to overcome. This is complemented by Zachary C. Peterson and Elliot James's "Living (In)Dependence: Bayard Rustin and Queer Pan-Africanists Overcoming the Constraints of Their Respective Societies". Here too the protagonists are not accepted. They are punished for going against the grain although the location, substance of argument is different. In both cases the government is doing everything it can to "cripple our movement and ban our leaders". Eliot James & Zac Paterson in this chapter tackle issues of Gay and Transgender individuals in many contemporary African nations. They are being persecuted for their sexual orientation or gender identities and this has led many of them to become activists challenging the mistreatment they are subjected to. The chapter ascertains that modern-day Queer Pan-Africans can draw from the example of Bayard Rustin, an African-American gay man who was also one of the most important civil rights and African liberation activists during the twentieth century. The chapter highlights escape routes that Queer Pan-Africanists must find to free themselves from the constraints their societies impose over them. The high point of the chapter is the example of Rustin who, decades ago, fought for pacifism, gay rights, civil rights, and African liberation. The writers further make clear that there are many differences between these modern activists and Rustin; thus, making it difficult for exact parallels to be drawn. Both Rustin and these Queer Pan-Africanists deal with persecution on the bases of their sexual orientation or gender identity. The chapter interrogates what Queer Pan-Africanists can learn from Rustin's lifework. Finally, the chapter draws heavily from the works of Zethu Matebeni and Elliot James for the Queer Pan-Africanists and on various primary and secondary sources for a biography of Bayard Rustin and therefore making the chapter a compelling read.

The arrangement of the chapters, once beginning with the political, now turns to the subject of gender. A big part of the Living (In)Dependence Project has do with gender. The point of view of the African female dominates the next three entries. Elisabeth N. M. Ayuk-Etang's "Women, Dependence, Independence, and Land Usage in The Cameroons: An Ecofeminist Reading of Bole Butake's *Lake God* and *And Palm Wine Will Flow*" begins to delve into the theme of the woman as entrepreneur, landowner and financial decision maker. This chapter critically examines women's dependence on and/or access to land, to land rights, and to land ownership as the essential for a society in which freedom flourishes. This topical process for attaining autonomy has raised a lot of concerns in and around the world in general and in the Cameroons in particular; to be precise in the Southern Cameroons. From a purely Afrocentric cultural perspective, land belongs to the forebears (ancestors), the living and the unborn. The chapter argues that, as constituent custodians of the land, women are not given equal access to land usage as men in the Cameroons. The study aims at demonstrating that the Cameroonian rural woman depends on the land for sustainable livelihood for her family and her community. However, given that the man has always undermined the woman in land policies and practices, Bole Butake's *Lake God* and *And Palm Wine Will Flow* (a mimicry of the Cameroonian society from which he emanates) articulate the discontented voice of the women on land discrimination. Using ecofeminism as a theoretical construct, the chapter focuses on women's access to farming land, their physical and spiritual connection to nature and their reproductive role in

xxi

community building. The woman's access to land as well as her dependence on it proves to be the bedrock of independence.

In a similar vein Benjamin Hart Fishkin's "The Stranger's Indifference of Powerless in an Unprotected Market Economy? A Critical Reading of Doh's *The Fire Within*" adds the concept of making her a single parent tossed about from side to side by the indifferent power of global markets and fluctuating currencies. The chapter "The Strangers' Indifference or Powerlessness in an Unprotected Market Economy? A Critical Reading of Emmanuel Fru Doh's *The Fire Within*" focuses upon the fact that in Emmanuel Fru Doh's Africa" tells there are no fairytales in a world dominated by globalization. The text is a post mortem of how all of this can happen and, upon further look, why it happens so often in the postcolonial development of the continent of Africa. In a continent brimming with the residue of international chaos, intentions mean nothing, and this chaos wreaks havoc with the family. The chapter pays close attention to the overall economic forces that overwhelm Mungeu' and discard her with scarcely a care. *A Fire Within* explores the story of someone who is in desperate need of help and never gets it. It is an unfulfilling look at a family that fails in its most basic duty. Integration and cultural exchange are not positives and this chapter argues that economic encroachment devastates Mungeu' via organizations such as the International Monetary Fund and The World Bank. This novel is a look back at what has happened to the individual (female) African and how she must (unknowingly) dance to a tune that is called far, far away. The chapter anchors on macroeconomic science and tells the reader that things have changed because of fiscal policy leading to the debt accumulating like a snowball in its wake.

This theme of the female in economic insecurity continues by exploring gender-differentiated "bundle of rights" to land in Africa. The notion that land formalization processes in Africa often restrict, rather than secure, land access, particularly for women, is broached and opened for discussion in Andrew Bonanno's "Formalizing Freedom: Land Tenure Arrangements from the Perspective of Social

Modes of Production". The chapter examines the pursuit of bureaucratic demarcation and titling of land claims—that is, formalization—as an economic development mechanism throughout the global south. The basic, and deceptively straightforward, argument made by mainstream development economists is that documenting land rights will secure property claims and allow individuals to leverage capital, thereby unlocking the wealth-generating potential of markets. Nevertheless, bureaucratic forms cannot engulf the complex web of social arrangements surrounding customary land tenure. By adopting an overly narrow understanding of land tenure arrangements and economic relationships, formalization proponents miss important information about human freedom—what people are actually able to do—within different social, political and economic contexts. This chapter, specifically, focuses on emerging land tenure formalization efforts in Sierra Leone, West Africa, and argues that the apparent tension in formalization impacts should be evaluated through the lens of tenure-related operational freedoms, that is, what people are actually able to do given existing physical resources and claims to those resources. The chapter draws on the capability view of poverty and wealth to include the ability to maintain dignity and to participate in community activities. However, while these capabilities, among others, are important, they are difficult to compare from society to society and the capability view alone does not provide a framework for evaluating one set of capabilities versus another. Following anthropologist David Graeber, this chapter argues that intangible, socially embedded relationships to precisely what economic activity is fundamentally about. It explores economic systems that recognize the human element of these relationships as well as systems that abstract human-based relational value into a particular commodity or credit instrument. This "social modes of production" (SMP) perspective predicts that shifting from the former to the later economic system will particularly disadvantage non-elites by restricting the socially embedded capabilities derived through human relationships. Given the relational aspect of customary tenure in

Sierra Leone (and elsewhere), the SMP perspective provides a potentially powerful, albeit hitherto largely untested, explanatory framework for future analyses on the unfolding impacts of formalization. The previous three chapters in this section, all deal with the development of women struggling to be an economic force in brand new circumstances and lead to the themes of immigration and independence.

While Migration involves movement, it is really a form of liberation. This chapter "Migration, Dependence, Freedom and Independence in Ifeoma Chinwuba's *Merchant of Flesh*" is about movement in search of freedom. The African moves to change his/her wallet, environment, and identity. Ayuk-Etang focuses on the trickery and confusion that the African faces when he/she moves to Europe. Exploring the natural tendency in every human being to improve on his welfare, this chapter dwells on the existential attitude and commitment that have transformed man to be a migratory being. Again, immigration in quest for greener pastures is at the origin of human trafficking in this context of globalization and advanced information technology. This chapter thus examines the reasons why young girls and women from Nigeria, as well as those in less privileged countries, end up as prostitutes in Europe (especially in Italy) as articulated in Ifoema Chinwuba's *Merchant of Flesh*. Aghatise contends that trafficking of persons across the globe for prostitution is "a global scourge and a worldwide problem of monumental scope." The chapter delves into and highlights the legalization of prostitution in some Western countries and the debasement of female sexuality through trafficking of poor and voiceless women and young girls as a violation of women/human rights. The central claim in exploring Chinwuba's maiden text, *Merchants of Flesh* laments on the state and estate of dehumanized young women and girls consequently pushed to involuntary "suicide" through "Human Trafficking." Voluntary and involuntary migration thus result from independent states' inability to cater for the needs of its citizens. Africans, at large, remain precarious victims of exploitation, marginalization and all sort of dehumanization. Following

Chinwuba's narrator in *Merchant of Flesh,* the chapter brings to life how Nigeria's economy has left women and the have-nots to become the victims of repression on the stage of (In)Dependence binaries.

Also, this chapter set out to demonstrate that the inability of most African states to provide the necessary tools for independent/autonomous survival to their citizens push the people to move in search of a more fulfilled life and a sense of independence. The socio-economic and political situations in the world of the *Merchant of Flesh* remains the push factors to both the migrants and immigrants. Nigeria, like most postcolonial societies, is confronted with political, economic and social challenges which have resulted in poverty and the culture of dependence on foreign aid. This insufficiency is at the center of the characters' displacements and Human Trafficking as highlighted by Chinwuba. However, these victims experience diasporic realities, which like a curve ball, unveil their search for independence and better livelihood to dependency. The immigrants, represented by Faith et al become victims of human trafficking meanwhile their 'employers' are the traffickers (Pimps) From the migrant perspectives, the pimps attract attention through affluence and investments back home. A postcolonial reading of the text served as an analytical tool making migration a fundamental issue in the study of literature from the global South in the 21st century.

Expanding on the theme of migration is Christson A. Adedoyin, Mary S. Jackson and Kayode Julius Ayeni's "African Immigrants in the United States: Perspectives on Acculturative Stress and Religiosity". These authors are concerned with spiritual problems that come about when someone leaves Africa and moves to America. This text, unlike the previous by Ayuk-Etang, is more a query into the African psyche. The stress of being suddenly ripped from the African continent causes stress, anxiety, and psychosis. There is a medical component to "African Immigrants in the United States: Perspectives on Acculturative Stress and Religiosity" that no other work in the "Living (In)Dependence project" has. This chapter provides a panoramic view of the intersections of health and religion of African immigrants in the United States. As one of the fastest and most educated immigrant groups in the United States, African immigrants have been identified as demonstrating an unassailable and tenacious hold to their religious beliefs, practices, and communities in diaspora. The chapter further unveils the understudied role of spirituality particularly in the health, and other daily endeavors of African immigrants. There are debilitating factors, which confront immigrants irrespective of country or continent of origin. These factors include stress caused by culture shock, inadequate health, socioeconomic information, and most recently anti-immigrant sentiments. Nonetheless, spirituality and religion, as highlighted, play a large role in addressing the stressors that accompany the acculturation, assimilation, and identity challenges that assail African immigrants in the United States. The chapter concludes with a call for more research to better understand the role of religion in providing health and social services to African immigrants in American society. Implications for practice, social work education, and policy are also delineated.

The human being, or a patient, never appears more than a step or two from the hospital bed. Bill F. Ndi spends his time discussing how people are demented and tormented by "…social, political, cultural, psychological…" repression. The environment withholds pleasure from circulation or expression. The raw, tyrannical, forceful and inconsistent subjugation dominates "Emmanuel Fru Doh's *Boundaries*: Pre-emptive Framing of Freedom and or Autonomy and Independence". Ndi's text is an assessment of a novel where love ultimately triumphs, but that is not always the case. Restraints, constraints, and exclusion come in all sorts of forms and almost never are they resolved satisfactorily. In this chapter, Bill F. Ndi takes the reader, in his exploration of Emmanuel Fru Doh's *Boundaries*, through the inward narrative journey from the microcosm of Southern Cameroons within *La République du Cameroun,* to a macrocosm of Africa and the entire world. The chapter draws on the various forms of restrictions—linguistic, physical, social, cultural, political, emotional, spiritual, and psychological—in Emmanuel Fru Doh's universe to elucidate the intricate and oftentimes inexplicable inward/outward dependence binary for freedom. The chapter shows how Emmanuel Fru Doh frames the freedom/subjugation, and the independence/dependence binaries to safeguard their fruitful symbiotic interaction. Over and above the chapter reveals *Boundaries* as a multi-layered holy experiment akin to a spiritual odyssey of freedom, independence, autonomy, and sovereignty in their journey from subjugation, dependence, imperial domination, and colonization. By pre-emptively framing freedom, autonomy and independence, this chapter underscores *Boundaries* is a syncretic piece written with the enthusiastic excitement, the enchanting commitment and dynamic verve of a poet and not forgetting its novelistic descriptive grip as well as its dramatic enthralling and captivating character representations.

Dalal Alkordi discusses finance on the world stage and financial aid that often masquerades as domination. "Foreign Aid Dependency and the African Continent" is a text about transactions where "...repayment would be an advantage to the donor..." "Aid," Alford says, "does not encourage economic development in Africa." This is how, to borrow from Walter Rodney, "How Europe and the Underdeveloped Africa." The contact between the two societies has caused this problem of "unevenness" via the IMF and the World Bank. What is the position of the foreign aid? Does it demolish state institutions in Africa? If this is the situation, does aid dependency contributing to state failure in Africa? In addressing the topic of foreign aid, scholars' point of views divided into two groups. On the one hand, African states currently well governed should not be dependent on financial assistance to conduct basic government operations and providing public goods. Additionally, multinational companies critiqued that extensive multinational business activity will create a hierarchical structure of economic activity on a global scale. However, the intentions of contributing to *Living (In)Dependence* are to find answers for the above questions as well as examining the relationship between aid receipts, politics and economic autonomy. On the other hand, the evidence seems consistent with a positive relationship between aid and the state performance. Nevertheless, in this situation, the decision of the international community on reducing foreign aid will have enormous effects on how African states can maintain and improve their performance with less foreign assistance. Although, governments decide that foreign investment can be useful under some conditions, the effects cannot be optimized without developing explicit policies. Moreover, developing countries treat multinationals as capital and technology suppliers. Yet when these multinationals come along in their resources and technology, it doesn't help the host country. In fact, an increasing number of multinational firm activity involves changes in the organization of production so that portions of a previously included activity can be done elsewhere. By this activity must be understood "outsourcing". It is true that multinationals can have range of positive and negative impacts on host country workers. Moreover, there are economic effects of the direct investment that focus on the economic gains or losses of particular elites and interest groups in the home and host countries. These gains and losses will be determined by the product and income resulting from the investment upon global efficiency and growth effects as well as the distribution of that income. Any consideration of economic effects will be under: global efficiency and growth, international equity, and national equity.

While money is an important commodity education is, inarguably, more important. Any nation is defined by its universities. Unfortunately, the foundational structures of Cameroon have been Westernized. This Francophone dominated system illustrates just how powerful (and unAfrican) the university system in Africa is and this is the emphasis of Hassan Mbindzenyuy's "Bate Besong's *Disgrace: Autobiographical Narcissus and Emanya-nkpe Collected Poems*: Unmasking Francophone Cameroon's Epstemicide". The political and academic gaps of the university are not confined to this nation but extend to all fifty-four countries on the continent. This chapter argues that in Bate Besong's *Disgrace*, the *La République du Cameroun*/British Southern Cameroons (Francophone/Anglophone) asymmetry in the Cameroons has resulted in a Francophone stifling and strangulation of British Southern Cameroons social, economic, political, and cultural forms of knowing and wisdoms. Part one, questions Francophone imperial epistemology by countering its 5 monocultures. It takes a critical look at the monoculture of knowledge, the monoculture of linear time, the monoculture of the naturalization of difference, the monoculture of the universal, and the monoculture of criteria of capitalist productivity and efficiency as well as their resultant 5 forms of annihilation of the British Southern Cameroonian/Ambazonian within the *La République du Cameroun* polity. This Francophone hegemonic epistemology and rationality account for the obliteration of the British Southern Cameroonian/Ambazonian.

Through such forms, the Francophone of *La République du Cameroun* projects the British Southern Cameroonian/Ambazonian as ignorant, residual, inferior, limited, and non-productive. He further situates them in five ecologies viz. the ecology of episteme, the ecology of temporalities, the ecology of recognitions, the ecology of trans-scales, and the ecology of productivities. Part Two of this chapter, discusses the sociology of emergences as an embodiment of signals, clues or traces of future possibilities of understanding that have been ignored by the Francophone hegemonic and arrogant theorization of "knowledge", regarding its methods, validity, and scope, as well as the distinction between Francophone justified belief and opinion. In effect, the chapter proposes an alternative way of understanding and knowing. The alternative is one that replaces the one-dimensional Francophone approach to understanding and knowing with bionetworks and political frameworks of understanding – in a way that Francophones and Anglophones in a diversity of understanding would maximize each other's equal contributions towards the building of a Cameroonian world in which another approach to knowledge is always possible beyond Francophone and Anglophone epistemologies.

Richard Evans talks about and discusses some of these flaws in relation to whether or not the curriculum should be an African curriculum or a Classical one. The university system in Malawi struggles with what direction the very soul of the university should follow. "Classical Studies at the University of Malawi 1982-2018: Evolving (In)Dependence". The Classics Department is not something that the administration is sold on or even tolerant of. Can the fields of classicism and colonialism intersect? Leaning on Francis B. Nyamnjoh's article: "Potted Plants in Greenhouses" A Critical Reflection on the Resilience of Colonial Education in Africa (*Journal of African and Asian Studies* 2012, 47) Richard Evans in this chapter takes on Nyamnjoh's claim that "African universities have significantly Africanized their personnel, but not their curricula or pedagogical structures to any real extent...." He illustrates his point with reference to the Kamuzu Academy, a British-style classical school, founded by Hastings Banda, in Malawi, and focusing on the teaching of Greek, Latin and ancient history. From his lived experience, having had to be in Malawi as part of the early hires to develop the program in 1985, just shortly after the founding of this program at the University of Malawi, Evans explores how Africans have appropriated the classics and made it "[a] classic example of excellence at relevance in education", to subvert Nyamnjoh's assertion.

Unfamiliar with "neo-colonialism" at the time of his arrival in Malawi, he worked toward building the best academic program that he could put together, especially adding ancient Greek to the Latin and classical culture courses already in place in the curriculum. Discussions within the faculty about the relevance of Classics instruction to a poor African country spurred much criticism of this expensive "Eton of the Bush", teaching selected students A-level Greek and Latin. This made of Classical Studies in Africa, the epitome of Western educational colonialism and neo-colonialism. This chapter therefore, problematizes this anti-classics polemic by tracing out the evolution of the discipline of Classics from extreme Eurocentrism in the 19th and early 20th centuries to a more historically realistic, contemporary multiculturalism that includes the dialogue of Greece and Rome with Africa and the Near East, which now offers the African student much relevance to their African experience. To crown the African appropriation of the Classics, this program recently produced its first local Ph.D. graduate in 2016.

The intricate ways in which the chapters, herein, are woven permeate time and space. It is the editors' hope that the authors' respective understanding and usages of the Dependence cum Independence binary, have permitted the reader to reconsider the symbiotic and peaceful co-existence of Independence and Dependence, the nemeses which this volume addresses. The respective authors, through the exploration of different lived experiences and using different theoretical and disciplinary considerations, have drawn attention to the historical, ethical, political, psychological, cultural, economic, philosophical, biological, etc. constraints that put to question the whole notion of independence and/or dependence. *Living (In)Dependence* has thus endeavored to shed light on the Janus face nature of dependence and independence, a concept which, to understand, call for more than a mono-focal lens.

Bill F. Ndi
Benjamin Hart Fishkin
Adaku T. Ankumah

Works Cited

Atanga, Mufor. *The Anglophone Cameroon Predicament* Langaa Research, 2011

Baylis, John & Steve Smith. *The Globalization of World Politics: An Introduction to International Relations.* OUP. 2005.

Easterly, William *The Whiteman's Burden: Why the West's Effort to Aid the Rest Have Done So Much Harm and So Little Good* Penguin, 2006

Elshtain, Jean Bethke. *Real Politics at the Center of Everyday Life*, John Hopkins UP. 1997

Fishkin, Benjamin H., Adaku T. Ankumah, and Bill F. Ndi. *Fears, Doubts, and Joys of not Belonging,* Langaa Research & Publishing, 2014

Mallaby, Sebastian *The World's Banker: A Story of Failed States, Financial Crises, the Wealth and Poverty of Nations,* Penguin, 2004

McLeish, Kenneth. *Key ideas in Human Thoughts.* Prima, 1995

Michlin, Monica and Jean-Paul Rocchi. *Black Intersectionalities: A Critique for the 21st Century,* Liverpool UP. 2013

Ndi, Bill F. Adaku T. Ankumah, and Fishkin. *The Repressed Expressed.* Langaa Research & Publishing, 2017

Rogoff, Kenneth *The Curse of Cash* Princeton UP, 2016

Scott, James C. *Domination and the Art of Resistance: Hidden Transcripts* Yale UP. 1990.

Seeman, Melvin. "On the Meaning of Alienation" *American Sociological Review* 24.6 (1959): 783-791. *JSTOR.* Web. 13 Sep. 2018.

wa Thiong'o, Ngugi. *Something Torn and New: An African Renaissance,* Civitas, 2009.

_____. *Decolonising the Mind: The Politics of Language in African Literature.* Heinemann, 1997.

Chapter 1

Francis B. Nyamnjoh's *Souls Forgotten:* Unpacking Minority Struggles

Hassan Yosimbom
University of Yaoundé

Introduction

Cameroonians hoped that the end of colonialism would lead to a more egalitarian Cameroonian world. Instead, the ideological conflict between the colonizer and the colonized has been replaced with an upsurge in socio-economic, cultural and political conflicts between the Francophones and the Anglophones. Anglophone minorities and Francophone majorities clash over ideological issues such as bilingualism, federalism, political representation, regional autonomy, and even outright separation and restoration of the Independence of the Southern Cameroons, a country which at independence chose to unite with East Cameroons or *La République du Cameroun*. This Chapter examines the Francophone majority/Anglophone minority debate in Francis B. Nyamnjoh's (FBN's) *Souls Forgotten (SF)* by arguing that the Anglophone minority and Francophone majority are not natural entities but are Mimbolandian constructions. This construction is seen through the Francophonization of Mimboland education in the University of Asieyam (UA) and the Anglophonization of the Lake Abehema Disaster (LAD). The Francophone majority suppresses the Anglophone minority on the bases of the idea that in Mimboland, the Francophone weltanschauung is the norms to which every other Mimbolander should aspire. When compared to the Francophones, the others are still the "minors" for whom the Francophones, the "adults" of the Mimbolandian world, have to continue to take charge. In Mimboland, the worldview and constructions of the Anglophone

1

have remained "minor" in the sense that their very incorporation into Mimboland historical narratives marginalizes them *vis-á-vis* dominant Francophone understandings of Mimboland canonical history. Anglophone experiences are assigned inferior or marginal positions as they are translated back into the canonical historian's language of domination. These Anglophone experiences and constructions, this essay contends, are treated as instances of backwardness on the part of the Anglophone agent. *SF* attests that it is by working through, or living through, the processes of minoritarianization and majoritarianization – their tensions and contentions; incompletions and emergencies; shuttling between antagonisms and alternatives, between rule and exception – that Mimbolandian minorities derive a more appropriate measure of global conflicts. Thus, *SF* attests that Mimboland minoritarian-majoritarian fault lines should be acknowledged as thresholds and their limits turned into the in-between spaces or zones, not only of transition but also of transaction, through which the meanings of cultural and political authority are negotiated.

Conceiving Minority and Minority History: Deleuze & Guattari, and Chakrabarty

Deleuze and Guattari (1987) and Chakrabarty (1998) argue that there is a link between minority and minority histories. Deleuze and Guattari opine that

> we must distinguish between: the majoritarian as a constant and homogeneous system; minorities as subsystems; and the minoritarian as a potential, creative and created, becoming...there is no becoming-majoritarian; majority is never becoming...all becoming is minoritarian (105).

They further assert that "[m]inorities...are objectively definable states... with their own ghetto territorialities, but they must also be thought of as seeds, crystals of becoming whose value is to trigger uncontrollable movements and deterritorializations of the mean or

2

majority" (105-6). To them, the minority-majority opposition is not simply quantitative; minorities are not necessarily defined by the smallness of their numbers, but rather by becoming or by the gap that separates them from the axiom constituting a majority. A minority can be small in number; but it can also be large in number. What defines a minority, then, is not the number but the relations internal to the number. A minority can be numerous, or even infinite; so can a majority. What distinguishes them is that in the case of a majority the relation internal to the number constitutes a set that may be finite or infinite, but is always denumerable, whereas the minority is defined as a "nondenumerable" set, however many elements it may have. Minorities constitute "fuzzy", nondenumerable, nonaxiomizable sets, "masses", multiplicities of escape and flux (461, 469 and 470). The majority assumes a state of power and domination over the minority and not the other way around. Thus, it is not, for instance, by using a minor language as a dialect, by regionalizing or ghettoizing, that one becomes revolutionary; but rather, by using a number of minority elements, by connecting, conjugating them, one invents a specific, unforeseen, autonomous becoming. In *SF*, the Anglophone community is a numerical and socio-economic and politico-cultural minority. Most of the Anglophone characters in the text are revolutionaries fighting against the Francophonization of Mimboland education in the UA and the Anglophonization of the LAD. They are articulating forms of exclusion and possibilities for inclusion and arguing that wherever a dominant Francophone culture creates disadvantages for legitimate cultural minority practices, Mimboland public policies ought to accommodate and compensate minorities.

Chakrabarty concurs that minority histories proceed by processes that express the struggle for inclusion and representation. He says that "'minority histories' are oppositional chiefly in the early part of their careers when they are excluded from mainstream historical narrative" (15). Begun in an oppositional mode, "'minority histories' can end up being additional instances of 'good history'" (15) because minorities and majorities are constructions. Like Deleuze and Guattari, Chakrabarty affirms that even though the popular meanings

3

of the words "majority" and "minority" are statistical, "numerical advantage by itself is no guarantor of a majority status because sometimes, a group can be larger than the dominant one, but its history could still qualify as minority history" (18). Deleuze's and Guattari's definition of a minority and Chakrabarty's delineation of minority histories converge because minority histories express the struggles of minorities for inclusion and representation; they record the fight by minorities to insert hitherto neglected identities into the politics of social justice. In *SF*, the characters who decry the marginalization of Anglophones are producers of minority history; they argue that in the Cameroons, "good" minority history should be about expanding the scope of social justice and representative democracy, about struggling for non-statist forms of democracy that are constantly being envisaged in postcolonial Cameroons. They contest genealogies of origin that lead to claims for Francophone cultural supremacy and historical priority and invoke a worldliness and situational consciousness where the telling of the Francophone and Anglophone stories and experience ultimately involves the telling of the Mimboland collectivity itself.

Drawing on the Deleuzean-Guattarian-Chakrabartyan conception of minority and minority history, it could further be argued that the power relations in the novel are defined in terms of the inequality between the presumed Francophone center and the assumed Anglophone periphery while identity is often articulated according to the binary logic of Francophone oppression and Anglophone opposition. As various communities – *Francophones Anglophones, North Westerners, South Westerners, Bamis, Sawas, Betis, Graffis, Came-no-goes* – accommodate themselves to a heterogeneous society, the boundaries of the Francophone and Anglophone worlds are becoming increasingly blurry as capital and production move to the "periphery," while the movement of labor to the metropolitan centers leads to the peripheralization at the core. Using the UA and the LAD as sites of engagement the minority history, represented by the Anglophone community in *SF*, is in principle an important critical-conceptual resource that should rather be reconstructed than jettisoned. The novel reveals distinct facets that problematize the false promises of university education and disaster management in *SF* and propose some strategies for Cameroonians to respond to the challenges of diversity. The overall aim is to re-politicize the false promises of *La République du Cameroun's* canonical history so that minority history can recover its critical edge and its political capital and keep faith with its original promise to contribute to struggles for emancipation. The Francophonization of Mimboland education in the UA and the Anglophonization of the LAD are instances of minoritarianization that involve two processes (Francophonization and Anglophonization) that in turn peripheralize Anglophones and centralize Francophones. These processes assert that even though the Anglophone minority as a subsystem has its own ghetto territorialities, it must be thought of as a crystal of becoming whose value is to trigger uncontrollable deterritorializations of the Mimboland majority. This chapter has two parts. Part one focuses on the UA and the Francophonization of Mimboland education while part two discusses the Anglophonization of disaster management and the plight of the forgotten victims of the LAD.

The UA and the Francophonization of Mimboland University System

In *SF*, Nyamnjoh chooses a fairly, aggressive presentation of familiar socio-political elements in which differences are highlighted. One of such elements is his presentation of the educational system epitomized by the UA. The educational system in the UA is neither educational nor systematic. It is not educational because, as a moral idea, its recognizable organizational form spells dystopia. It is not systematic because it seems to have very little to do with social relations, spatial intimacy, or long-term moral amity. Yet there is something compellingly real about this misnamed object. That reality lies in its failed moral promise. The central problem is that the UA seems to increasingly ignore transnational loyalties, regional polities, and global economic regimes. The UA is a dangerous reference point for the naïve like Emmanuel Kwanga. Its connotation of sociability and intellectual commitment invites unwise reliance by those who must ultimately fend for themselves. Its diffusion of responsibility

5

excuses both students and lecturers who have no intention of doing their jobs. The concept amounts to a moral hazard, inspiring imprudent behavior by lecturers and administrators who expect that someone else will pull their fat out of the fire. When the novel opens, Emmanuel Kwanga recalls the euphoria that marked his departure to study in the UA: "[t]he journey to the Great City was long but thrilling.…. I wanted to miss out on no detail in the various stages of initiation. I stayed awake until we arrived Nyamandem at night. A marvelous sight, a spectacular revelation" (11). When Kwanga wakes up the next morning, all the promises and euphoria have disappeared and he now begins to see the Great City of Nyamandem and the UA differently: "[t]hough I had qualified for both the scholarship and university accommodation, I was only awarded the former. Nyamandem had changed, from a garden of blooms to a jungle" (12). Also, "[t]hough the accommodation officers were supposed to give priority to students from the provinces, the sons and daughters of the rich urban influential men and women received the lodging allotments" (12) because the officers are a "microcosm for a government and public service that subsists on graft, greed and corruption [and so], secrets, silences and betrayals exact an imperceptible cost that no one is exempt from paying" (Fishkin, 2015: 180).

The disorder and corruption that deprives Kwanga of his accommodation, affirms that the UA is shaped by the conflicting Nyamandem identity trends that are shaking institutions, transforming cultures, creating wealth, inducing poverty, and spurring greed, while simultaneously imposing hardship and instilling despair. The students of the UA are living in confusing times where the intellectual categories cannot grasp what is new by referring to the past. The urgency for a new approach to understanding the kind of economy, culture, and society in which the inhabitants of Nyamandem live is heightened by the crises and conflicts that characterize the social and cultural exclusion of large segments of the population of Mimboland, from the country's networks that accumulate knowledge, wealth and power. Kwanga and the Abehema/Anglophone community that he represents, lacks knowledge, wealth, and power and has come to the UA to benefit from the government's promise of a befitting higher education to all. Regrettably, this dream is not fulfilled because the UA seems to have abandoned its proper functions because the scholarship and accommodation officers minoritize/marginalize Kwanga. By refusing Kwanga what he qualifies for, they have failed to realize that the UA should play a major role as an ideological apparatus, expressing the ideological struggles present in Mimboland. It should also generate knowledge; be a mechanism of selection and socialisation of dominant elites and train skilled labour force (Brennan, King and Lebeau (2004); and Castells (2001)). Drawing from Brennan's, King's and Lebeau's, and Castells' arguments, the major role of the UA should be the transformation of Mimboland economically by responding to external pressures; and politically by distinguishing between the stages of removing the old, building the new in political change and providing protected space in which critique and opposition could ferment. Also, the institution should contribute to social reproduction by transforming and differentiating the varying roles between public and private sectors. Culturally, it should provide both a route for the entry of external ideas and experiences into otherwise closed societies. In other words, the US should transform the economy through the formation of human capital; and democratize the polity through the creation and sustenance of civil institutions; the selection and socialization of political and social elites. It should pluralize social structures through the creation of pluralistic societies, including the relationships between, and opportunities for, diverse social and ethnic groups. It should promote cultural diversity through the production and dissemination of ideas, exerting influence upon and providing critiques of the economy, the polity, and the social structures.

Unfortunately, the Francophonization of the education in the UA stifles its economic, political, social, and cultural functions. Kwanga captures this dysfunctionality and the dystopia it instills in students by graphically describing the publication of results:

The Dean comes out… still in his robes of academic hangman….
We all gather around him…. He pastes up the list and rushes back to
his office…. He knows his crime, he and his colleagues. They are…
learned sadists…. There is no doubt it's catastrophic, judging from the
repeated shouts of: 'C'est mauvais.' 'Ouais!' 'On m'a tue.' 'On est mort.'
'C'est incroyable!' 'Masa, man don die!' 'They have killed us!' (12).

The multilingual wails (in French, English and Pidgin English) of the
students indicate that the UA guillotine respects neither the linguistic
nor cultural boundaries of the Francophone majority and
Anglophone minority. The image of the UA in *SF* is a continuation
of the same image of the minoritarized Anglophone that Nyamnjoh
has painted in *Mind Searching* (1991), *A Nose for Money* (2003), *Souls
Forgotten* (2008), *The Travail of Dieudonné* (2008), and *Married But
Available* (2009).

In all these novels, the UA guillotinizes Anglophones more than
it does Francophones because lectures and pedagogy are
monolingually Francophonecentric. Though under a different name,
the "University of Besaadi", Nkengasong captures the same image of
the UA in *Across the Mongolo* (2004) where both politicians like
Monsieur Abeso and intellectuals like Docteur Atebba (176) ensure
that Anglophone students like Ngwe will never graduate; and
Anglophone intellectuals like Dr. Amboh will never teach major
courses even though they have terminal degrees. Kwanga records the
disintegration and dysfunctionality of the system in the UA in the
simple present tense, thereby capturing its perenniality.

The Dean and the lecturers have failed to nurture the minority
group's minds into substantial interventions into those justifications
of binarity that rationalize the authoritarian tendencies within
Mimboland/Cameroonian cultures in the name of the
regional/ethnic prerogative. To paraphrase Achille Mbembe (2001),
the UA has been wrapped in a cloak of impenetrability and has
become the black hole of reason thus condemning
Mimboland/Cameroonian politics and economics to appear in social
theory only as the sign of a lack. The discourse of political science
and development economics has become that of a quest for the

causes of that lack. Considering the social function of the university and the promise of education to all, one would have expected that the UA should have recognized its social commitments and obligations to the students and society, and explored new ways of meeting them. By so doing, it will become more socially relevant and valuable, achieving tangible benefits for its extended community and for society in general and thus ensuring its sustainability.

In the rapidly growing Nyamandem cityscape that surrounds the UA (just like many others in the developing world), important and pressing problems need to be addressed with creativity and with the engagement of the scientific community. Ironically, the lecturers and administrators turn out to be specialists in social and academic marginalization, ensuring that a high percentage of young people, especially Anglophones, are excluded from higher education. One would have further expected that opening the university system to those who need it – rather than to those with the means for it – would present an important benefit to society in general. However, the UA has been transformed into a guillotine. Even though Naidoo (2003) notes that in the contemporary social context, some of the cultural, political and social functions of higher education have been eclipsed by the developments associated with globalization and the knowledge economy, the argument in this section concurs with Nandy's (2000) contention that: "[d]ominance is now exercised mainly through categories embedded in systems of knowledge... the war cry of our times is now: 'define or be defined.' ... Universities have come to share this new power, for they specialize in handling categories" (115-16). In line with Nandy's arguments, the political transformation and nation-building role of the UA has been brutally sacrificed at the altar of domination. The dominance perpetuated by the UA is directly connected to the seizure of political power because in the end, Kwanga fails to become the Divisional Officer of his community's (Abehema's) dream. The university has become a place where Kwanga is brutally defined in terms that run contrary to his ambitions to become a great politician like President Longstay. If one of the university's roles is the processing of information, then the quality, effectiveness and relevance of the UA would have been directly related to the ability of Cameroonian people, society and institutions to develop. In the context of a technological revolution and in the context of a revolution in communication, one would have expected the UA to become not only a central actor of scientific and technological change, but also a trainer of a labor force adequate for the new conditions of production and management.

But by training students to fail their exams perennially, the UA sacrifices technological change, the labor force and production and management. Considering The Cameroons' socio-political and cultural diversity, the UA should have become the critical source of equalization of chances and democratization of society by making possible equal opportunities for *Francophones, Anglophones, North Westerners, South Westerners, Bamis, Sawas, Betis, Graffis, Came-no-goes* etc., not only as a contribution to economic growth but also as a contribution to social equality or, at least, lesser inequality. In so doing, it would have fostered a politics of equality and difference but unfortunately, difference, symbolized by the Kwangas, is being used as a force of subordination. As Professor Moses Mahogany points out, the absence of equal opportunities gives the Great City of Nyamandem and the UA the type of "cosmetic appearance" which, as the narrator states,

> is likely to deceive the foreign tourist, but not the native who has learnt to distinguish between gold and golden, and who knows no one ever makes any valid judgment about a country from a flying plane, from within a luxury car, or through the windows of a five-star hotel (12).

The multilingual wails of the students constitute a hybrid haven from which the university could develop new cultures; that is, become a source of cultural renewal and cultural innovation which are linked to the new forms of living which we are entering. Yet, in spite of all the above challenges, possibilities, and opportunities for the university system, the UA continues "to be corporatist and bureaucratic, defending [its] own interests – particularly in terms of the professors – and extremely rigid in their functioning in terms of their administration" (Castells, 2001: 206). By priding on its ability to mystify examinations, the UA has failed to demolish the philosophical foundations of Francophonecentrism. It has neither deconstructed dominant Francophone knowledge structures nor constructed a body of work in Mimboland ethics, political philosophy and political economy that will be nationally influential.

Considering the village origin of the students such as Kwanga and his girlfriend, Patience, the dysfunctionality of the UA seems to be part of the larger problem of postcolonial Mimboland/The Cameroons i.e. inadequate linkage between the concept of the institution and local communities. Emmanuel Kwanga's parents, Pa Peaphweng Mukong and Ma Ngonsu are peasant farmers in Abehema who have no organic linkage, let alone awareness of the disciplinary divisions of a university. The least the administration could have done would have been to make available agriculture and agricultural economics as academic disciplines in which "gifted individuals" like Kwanga (their son) are given equal opportunities to acquire new knowledge with relevance to their daily lives. Likewise, there is a lack of organic connection between academic disciplines like veterinary medicine and the economics of pastoral production in Abehema and the "mixed economies" (livestock keeping combined with peasant agricultural production) of the country. By failing to provide such connections, the UA still functions on the "colonial" notion of the generalist universities, universities that came to elevate the level of education of the population at large, especially the propertied classes; universities as mass teaching centres not meant to provide training but to provide degrees. The absence of such awareness, and its irrelevance for their economic interests, among the peasant communities of Abehema gives the UA a crucial detachment from their supervision and guidance and transforms it into a guillotine. The Dean's and the lecturers' concepts and practices of academic excellence, teaching and research as well as critical attributes of a university are denied ownership by the local communities.

The terrible consequence of this condition is that adherence or non-adherence to it remains a matter of indifference by the vast majority of the public that consider themselves academic orphans. The status of academic orphans is more aggravating for Anglophones whose Anglo-Saxon culture and language, English, identified in the novel as Tougalish, is considered inferior to the Francophone culture and language, French, identified in the novel as Muzungulandish. Testimony of this bifurcation is that when the Anglophone lecturer, Professor Moses Mahogany says that Anglophones need people committed to the cause of their crippled, wretched and panting runners-up of life (5), he is brutally murdered, and his books are censored (5-6); thus, peripherializing the Anglophone culture. In a conversation with Diawara (1998), the Guinean writer, Williams Sassine, confirms this peripherilization of minorities by arguing that the leadership in postcolonial Africa has created three types of mutants: the "flatterers", the "floaters", and the "deflated" (50). The *flatterers* say anything the president wants to hear and thus become the ministers, general managers, and ambassadors in every regime; the *floaters* barely survive between governments; and the *deflated* constitute a race unto themselves; not the unemployed because a *flatterer* and a *floater* can both become unemployed. A *deflated* person is someone beyond good and evil, beyond feeling the blows of unemployment (50). Sassine concludes that African presidents (like President Longstay) and their flatterers (like the UA students Pius, George and the Marxy Wang and Minister Tchopbrokpot) are constantly gripped by the fear that the floaters and the deflated will be tempted to *emigrate* and invade their *natural* geopolitical spaces. Kwanga salutes Professor Mahogany's bravery because even though Mahogany is a "floater" who has control neither over his employment in the UA nor over his own life, Mahogany refuses to become a "flatterer" who says anything the president wants to hear so that the president may make him a minister, general manager, and ambassador in the president's regime. He is thus a veritable organic intellectual.

The discussion on the UA questions hegemonic geopolitical mappings of intellectual territories and exchanges (knowledge, land and people) within "Anglophone-Francophone" relations. This discussion has attempted to recenter the Anglophone culture in the productions of Mimboland politics. It suggests a multicultural approach to a politics of equality and difference that calls into question some of the fundamental ideologies, theories, methods and histories, conversations, debates and knowledge re-productions of Anglophones and Francophones. Segregations and connectivities of systemic and interpersonal power within Mimboland knowledge exchange and political practice about Anglophone–Francophone/minority-majority relations at the UA. The key argument highlighted has been that knowledge, especially university knowledge, is a way of ordering the Mimboland world. It is inseparable from social organization. We all come to the university classroom from different locations and diverse epistemological approaches to understanding the world around us. The university classroom should be a meeting place for cultural traffic and we are supposed to utilize that vital space for collective intellectual examination and growth that is attentive to the multiple workings of power within academia and Mimboland state policy frameworks. Particular attention should be paid to the ways knowledges are disseminated, mobilized and reproduced in various historical contexts through course readings, lectures and discussions. The UA should focus on multicultural critical practices to develop effective global communication skills and to further explore approaches in understanding Anglophone-Francophone inequalities and their position, complicities and accountabilities within national structures. The real university demands that we grapple with historical issues and contradictions that emerge throughout the country in relationship to the country's social and political realities and locations. It should encourage us to articulate these connections in various formats. It is only through this that the UA can cease to produce "flatterers/floaters" like the lecturers and the Dean; and the "deflated" like Kwanga and the students who perennially fail their exams. By ceasing to produce *flatterers, floaters* and the *deflated*, the university will stop dominant groups from defining their own subjectivity as dynamic, flexible, plural and complex and the subjectivity of the others as traditional, unproblematic, unsophisticated and transparent. By promoting critical agents of knowledge such as Professor Moses Mahogany, the purpose will not

13

be to herald the arrival of an authentic other, but to help destabilize and disrupt assumptions of stereotypical representation that flow from the history of majoritarian power to stifle attempts to write minority history.

The Anglophonization (Minoratarianization) of Mimboland Disaster Management and the Plight of the Forgotten Victims of the LAD

Since independence, different types of disasters have exacted a heavy toll on Cameroonian societies, polities and economies, robbing her of her developmental and democratic possibilities. The causes of such disasters have been as difficult and complex as the challenges of resolving them. The magnitude and impact of these disasters have been lost between hysteria and apathy. The distortions that mar discussions and depictions of Cameroonian disasters are rooted in the long-standing tendency to Anglophonize or Francophonize them. This section seeks to examine the consequences of the Anglophonization of the LAD by President Longstay's government. In *SF*, the inhabitants of Abehema claim that the Lake Abehema toxic gas disaster needs to be rethought and the facts modified. Emmanuel Kwanga, for example, goes on to dispute the very existence of a natural gas in the lake because he suspects the white man, Monsieur Ravageur's intermittent visits to the lake. The disagreements over the manner in which the government of Mimboland handled the disaster affirm that the Abehema imaginary and Mimboland leadership are phrases in dispute. In that moment of crisis, the parties concerned present their case in a language and through sets of maneuvers unacceptable to the other. The narrator tells us that:

> [f]our years have gone by since the disaster struck the villages of
> Abehema, Tchang and Yenseh [but life] has not returned to normal for
> most of the survivors now scattered all over Chuma Division and
> beyond…. They are resigned to being ignored when they complain of

14

heartburn, eye lesions, nerve problems, dying muscles, and paralysis. They have waited long for resettlement, rehabilitation... in vain (341).

The refusal by the government of Mimboland to resettle and rehabilitate the victims of the LAD underscores its failure to recognize that socio-economic politics is the struggle for, rather than against, representation. That minoritarian politics does not seek to take its place in big politics; rather, the minority insists upon their diffference with representational politics. The villagers of Abehema, Tchang, and Yenseh respect external authorities, they do not seek to speak for themselves as autonomous subjects communicating with other autonomous subjects. They seek to respond to those authorities and expect the authorities of Mimboland to respond to them in times of need. The conflict between the people of Abehema, Tchang, and Yenseh and the government of Mimboland is not a simple opposition between us and them, the postcolonial and the nation-state, or the colonizer and the colonized; rather, it is a consequence of a phrase regimens endemic to a deprived world that advocates the radical practice of heterogeneity where difference is not affirmed but suppressed. The narrator further informs us that: "The bulk of the victims were temporarily accommodated in camps and tents in Abeghabegh, Kakakum River, Pukafong and Hepalem, while men of science competed with one another to divine the causes of the disaster.... To them, Wabuah and his likes were simply much too superstitious and illiterate to have anything to contribute" (341).

The Mimboland leadership is unable to scientifically assess the disaster priority and grant an objective history. They use the disaster as an instrument of scientific totalitarianism and injustice shunning and deriding the victim's testimony baseless. This leads one to argue that the history (rationality) is really unjust in cases of the politics of equality and difference and this calls for counter-hegemonic positions. In all this the urgent demand of the people of Abehema, Tchang, and Yenseh, is that difference should be valorized. The Abehema, Tchang, and Yenseh imaginary is that which defies social assimilation with ease. If and when that assimilation occurs, Abehema, Tchang, and Yenseh will disappear. Until then what

Mimbolanders have to adopt from an Abehema, Tchang, and Yenseh perspective – as a matter of minoritarian justice – is the radical politics of heterogeneity. As a postcolonial "differend", Abehema, Tchang, and Yenseh propose strategies of resisting homogenization. The people of Abehema, Tchang, and Yenseh are struggling to engage with issues of empowerment and disempowerment and the ideas of development and progress as connected to understandings of minority and/or subalternity. Their minority-resistance front includes all kinds of counter-hegemonic heterotopias or spaces of hope. That front contests hegemonic centers of disaster management power, working towards a truly decentered, de-imperialized Mimboland world. Donohue, Masilela, and Gear argue that:

> [d]isaster management encompasses all aspects of planning for and responding to disasters, including hazard analysis, vulnerability reduction (preparedness), prevention, mitigation, response, recovery and rehabilitation…. Mitigation is action to reduce the consequences of a disaster…. Early responses are rescue and relief; later responses are rehabilitation and reconstruction (457).

Unfortunately, the LAD responses in Mimboland are clouded in apathy and confusion. There are severe deficiencies in communication and information systems. These distortions from a rational response are caused by political and media factors: corruption, inadequate resources, and various local as well as foreign agencies working at cross-purposes. The responses often focus on short-term, high profile rescue operations and neglect the bigger, long-term issues (Donohue Masilela, and Gear 457). Cases of madness and loss of memory amongst adult survivors keep multiplying. Mr. Tangh-e-keh, a cattle farmer, after waiting in vain for the compensation of his cattle, has taken to the streets of Kaizerbosch and "from sunrise to sunset, he roams about in nakedness, making strange noises and absurd accusations, defying attempts by his family to re-domesticate him, and by police to shackle him" (343).

The narrator explains that some people have heard Mr. Tangh-e-keh "accuse the government of recruiting mercenaries to dispossess harmless villagers" (343). The mysterious Ravageur and Vanunu are the suspects, for the story that has spread, since it was first featured in the critical *West Mimboland Post*, that Ravageur—French for Ravager—and Vanunu had been agents testing nuclear and chemical weapons for foreign governments too powerful to name (343). The Abehema community has concluded that Mr. Tangh-e-keh's "madness has been induced by the government's failure to fulfil its own pledges of rehabilitation and compensation, thereby denying him reconnection with his soul of existence" (343). Four years after the LAD, management is still limited to early responses and later responses and mitigation have been ignored completely. That explains why victims are still accommodated in camps and tents in Abeghabegh, Kakakum River, Pukafong and Hepalem. Men of science are still competing with one another to divine the causes of the disaster. Life has not returned to normal for most of the survivors now scattered all over Chuma Division and beyond, but they all seem resigned to the abnormal way of life. They are resigned to being ignored when they complain of heartburn, eye lesions, nerve problems, dying muscles, and paralysis. They have waited long for resettlement, rehabilitation or return from living and partly living, but they have waited in vain and have become the victims of the false promises of 50 years of Mimboland's history of equality between Francophones and Anglophones. To borrow from Fishkin (2014), Mimbolanders have been sweating in earnest because they are having excruciating betrayals from everyone who should be taking care of them and the reader sweats "because of the thorny, irrational, crazy and absurd problems" (57) that independence has continued to bring. Independence has continued to create an exclusionary status for the marginalized "nouveau pauvre" of the Abehema community, rendering them "voiceless and powerless in a society where the leaders and the 'nouveau riche' exploit them" (Ankumah, 2014: 85) making them feel estranged and disenfranchised but giving them the courage to "subvert the negativity of their exclusion, alienation and

17

marginalization, by empowering themselves and taking control of their lives" (85).

Mimboland is entrapped within the existing bias-confirmation matrices of research and journalism underpinned by Eurocentrism and coloniality (Ndlovu, 2013b: 332). According to Amin (2009), Eurocentrism consists of a bundling of Western prejudices about other people. It is a form of ethnocentrism informed by a discursive terrain of racism, chauvinism and xenophobia underpinned by ignorance and mistrust of others that has been used to confer on Europeans the right to judge and analyze others (177–178). Eurocentrism is "expressed in the most varied of areas: day-to-day relationships between individuals, political formations and opinion, general views concerning society and culture, social science . . ." (179). In line with Amin's postulations, Maldonado-Torres (243) and Grosfoguel (219) argue that in postcolonial societies like Mimboland, there is need for more critical ways of understanding "independence" that in turn shape our understanding and analysis of Eurocentrism and coloniality as crucial discursive processes for the breaking or fulfilment of the promises of history. One person who researches the causes of the LAD is a Muzungulander (French man), Fardeau—French for Burden—Westview, an African Correspondent for *Muzungu International News Services*. In his report titled "Socio-cultural Beliefs of Victims of the Killer Gas Disaster", Westview draws conclusions that reveal his Eurocentrism and coloniality. To him, the "survivors of the afflicted villages of Tchang, Abehema, and Yenseh are asking journalists and scientists what causes we are investigating when the answer is so obvious" (301). He further says that, "winning or losing elections is not a simple matter of the ballot [but] how well one harnesses spiritual and mystical powers." He also writes that "in Mimboland, newspapers are the prerogative of the urbanites [and] witchcraft and occult animate life and discussion in urban spaces and among elite Mimbolanders"; and fianally that, "African journalism in practice is at variance with the professional cannons of objectivity and empirical evidence that characterize[sic] our Muzungulander journalism" (301, 302). His views echo his name Westview i.e. Western Point of view.

Even though Fardeau's conclusions demonstrate his awareness of the fact that "knowledge and thoughts can transform things, move mountains and make ephemeral power appear permanent" (Mulgan, 27). He is also cognizant of the fact that

> [p]ower is the relational capacity that enables a social actor to influence asymmetrically the decisions of other social actor(s) in ways that favor the empowered actor's will, interests, and values [and] is exercised by means of coercion and/or by the construction of meaning on the basis of the discourses through which social actors guide their action (Castells 10).

Therefore, his assertion that "African journalism in practice is at variance with the professional cannons of objectivity and empirical evidence that characterize our Muzungulander journalism" (304) is ridiculous and ironical. His coloniality of knowledge report has nothing of any of the professional cannons of objectivity and empirical evidence.

His kind of research (which reminds one of the Francophonization of education and knowledge in the UA) and journalism are central to encouraging the government of Mimboland to ignore the responses to the disaster. In order to stop this, both the victims and more importantly the government of Mimboland, need a decolonial turn, a shift in knowledge production of similar nature and magnitude. Such a shift will introduce questions about the continuous effects of colonization on Mimboland subjectivities and forms of life as well as the contributions of Abehema, Tchang, and Yenseh subjectivities to the production of knowledge and critical thinking. It is a way of trying to look at the pathology of the world from the position of those regarded as most pathological and, in some way, non-human. The decolonial shift demands responsibility and the willingness to take many perspectives, particularly the perspectives and points of view of those, like the people of Abehema, Tchang, and Yenseh whose very existence is questioned and produced as insignificant because they are Anglophones. The decolonial turn is about making visible the invisible and about analyzing the mechanisms that produce the invisibility or distorted visibility of such disasters in light of a large stock of ideas that must necessarily include the critical reflections on the invisibility of Abehema, Tchang, and Yenseh people themselves. There is need for a fundamental shift in perspective that leads one to see the Mimboland world anew in a way that allows one to target its evils (such as the bias-confirmation journalism of Fardeau) in a new way and that gives us a better sense of what to do next. This will promote a shift away from the imperial attitude of Anglophonizing disasters instead of Cameroonizing them.

Given the government's Muzungulandcentric and Francocentric attitude towards the LAD in Mimboland and the tradition of neglect that weighs on the entire Mimboland, a new, broader and more reflexive understanding of politics, and a new style of thinking that makes it possible to think politics through Mimboland's problems is needed. Through such thinking, the government of Mimboland ought to help Mimbolanders read culture politically, to read difference concretely, and to problematize their ideas of the disaster and the bias-confirmation scientific and journalistic reporting on it by working at the margins of a knowledge system that is still logocentric and eurocentric. This fight against eurocentrism would engender struggles against coloniality of power, coloniality of knowledge and coloniality of being as constitutive elements of global coloniality (Ndlovu, 2013a: 183).

Thus, the possibility of the villages of Abehema, Tchang, and Yenseh creating their own future, taking charge of their own destiny, and mapping out their own autonomous development trajectory and ceasing to be marginalized reminds that such and endeavor would be one of the major steps towards de-Anglophonizing disasters. This implies that Mimbolanders have to struggle ceaselessly against the shibboleths of global coloniality represented by Fardeau's journalism and research and, by extension, the UA. Only after defeating global coloniality can the government of Mimboland ensure that Mimbolanders create a sustainable developmental future for Abehema, Tchang, and Yenseh. One of the agents of Anglophonization that needs to be surmounted is Mr. Tchopbropot, *ministre plénipotentiaire*, whose nonchalant attitude towards the victims of the disaster is valorized by President Longstay's political culture of hegemonics. Under the instructions of Minister Tchopbrokpot, the District Officer once in a while appoints someone to oversee life in the camps of Kaizerbosch and the appointee leaves with a lorry of assorted foodstuffs. Each time the appointee gets to the temporary camps of Abeghabegh, Kakakum River, Pukafong and Hepalem and the victims ask him when they shall stop living in tents, the appointee tells them that the answer lies somewhere well above him (344-45). The appointee's declaration the answer lies somewhere above him affirms the debilitating hierarchization of Mimboland leadership. As an auxiliary of the administration, the appointee is being dominated and forced to participate in the system that alienates him from decision making. He, Tchopbrokpot and the D.O. are compelled to perform actions contrary to their nature and historical essence. Decision making on the LAD is fetishized and President Longstay's totality is made absolute, closed and divinized.

The victims' demand for resettlement demonstrates that Mimbolanders need an alternate political culture that is not simply something outside the system; it should be a domain from which a language and a dialogic can reveal Longstaycentrism in all its modes of thought control. As a network, that alternate political culture should be a framework for political autonomy that speaks in terms that the Mimboland subject-object or Francophone-Anglophone paradigm can hear and respond to its expectations. It will need to be a cultural framework in order to resist all efforts to reduce it to a subject-object paradigm again, and to commodify it in the manner in which the disaster management has been commodified and consumed as a fetish by Mimboland ministers and Divisional Officers. It has to be political in order to critically address the structures and ideological frameworks of the coloniality of power represented by the District Officer and his special representative.

In addition, it has to be alternate to contest Majoritarianism as the enemy without falling into the language of binarism in the process of doing so. Such a decolonial turn that will de-minoritarize Mimbolanders will not refer to a single combative strategy but will rather point to a Mimboland family of diverse positions (Gautam and Luitel 97) that share a view of Anglophonization as the fundamental problem in the Mimboland world, and the de-Anglophonization of natural disasters as a necessary task that remains unfinished. De-minoritarianization of Mimbolanders therefore requires a systematic restructuring of Mimboland governance into a complex mix of egalitarianism, communalism, tension, competition, co-operation, clan and family intimacy, Anglophone and Francophone alliance and mutual assistance. The political process of de-Anglophonization will be to run its course in the national social periphery of the rural and working classes if the LAD victims are resettled. Only in the resettlement of these people of the Mimboland periphery is there the possibility of a future Mimboland world culture that can bring about a qualitative leap to newness. If the Mimboland center continues to sanction the biological or cultural genocide of peripheral peoples of Abehema, the Mimboland center will continue to feed itself on the Francophonecentrism it has ingrained within itself.

Ndlovu (2013a: 198), argues that coloniality of power, coloniality of being and coloniality of knowledge constitute formidable majoritarian practices that stand as a bulwark on the path of African people's struggles and initiatives to create African futures. These three forms of coloniality are represented in *SF* by the manner in which the disaster funds are mismanaged. The narrator reminds us that:

> [i]t is rumoured that Mr. Tchopbrokpot, *ministre plénipotentiaire*, and director of the Disaster Fund, is contemplating retirement to a quiet life in Muzunguland, where he has bought a whole street in an upper-class residential area of the capital city, for himself and his childhood friend and kinsman, President Longstay. (346).

Tchopbrokpot's coloniality of power is a symbolic representation of Mimboland forms of domination, control and exploitation (power). His coloniality of knowledge is about epistemological colonization of the mind and imagination through a Tchopbrokpot-sponsored-song that has taken the citizens and Radio Mimboland

International by storm; and his coloniality of being is about Tchopbrokpot's denial of the very humanity of the victims of the LAD, their inferiorisation and dehumanisation. Like the Dean in the UA, he has used difference as a force for subordination and the fracturing of the Cameroonian society. In short, Tchopbrokpot's coloniality of power, being and knowledge reinforce each other in the production and sustenance of a Mimboland coloniality of the Anglophone. Following Sassine's categorization, Mr. Tchopbrokpot by buying a whole street in an upper-class residential area of the capital city of Muzunguland/France, for himself and President Longstay, confirms his status as a "flatterer" who is afraid of becoming a "floater".

Fortunately, Emmanuel Kwanga has decided to start an NGO to do for his "dead and alive what the government and Tchopbrokpot have failed to do with the Disaster Account" (354). It shall be called "Foundation for the Forgotten Victims of the Lake Abehema Disaster - FOVILAD" (354). Kwanga explains that it shall be totally owned and controlled by the victims themselves; with its headquarters in Kaizerbosch, and branches throughout Mimboland. Kwanga's aim is to initiate FOVILAD, raise funds at the beginning, and allow villagers themselves to run it (354). Kwanga's initiative is a de-minoritarianization turn predicated on making visible the Mimboland imperial designs that work to keep Mimbolanders in a subordinate position. The initiative also marks the beginning of thinking of another world of equality. As a de-minoritarianization turn, FOVILAD promotes a shift away from the delusions of a world naturalized by Mimboland majoritarian designs. It marks the definitive entry of Abehema, Tchang, and Yenseh subjectivities into the realm of thinking and imagining another Mimboland world. This involves pushing forward the frontiers of the distorted and unfinished project of the politics of equality and difference, simultaneously with the unfinished project of deminoritization of the underprivileged groups and demajoritization of the overprivilegded groups.

FOVILAD aims at creating a world of equality, development and freedom, as well as a Mimboland "democracy" that is the product of actions deployed by and from the Abehema, Tchang, and Yenseh as primary epistemic sites of struggle. FOVILAD is a strategic reminder that the Eurocentric, which is a classic Longstaycentric and Tchopbrokpotcentric perspective of knowledge, operates as a mirror that distorts what is reflected. It is an affirmation that when one looks in the Mimbloand Longstaycentric mirror, "the image that one sees is not composite but partial and distorted" (Moraña, Dussel, and Jáuregui, 2008: 204). The Mimboland tragedy is that most Mimbolanders have been led, knowingly or not, wanting it or not, to see and accept that image as their own; thus, being what we are not (Quijano 204). If the LAD is natural disaster that has dismembered the Abehemaians from their land, Mimboland power and memory; thereby destroying the base from which they could launch themselves into the world, then FOVILAD can be understood as Kwanga's overarching project of re-membering aimed at addressing problems of alienation and fragmentation caused by the Francophonization of education and the Anglophonization of LAD.

At the center of FOVILAD's re-membering process is a restorative recovery project that is ranged against dismemberment and Francophonism because FOVILAD belongs to the victims. FOVILAD is an attempt to assert that a dismembered people can re-member themselves by re-launching themselves from the world of "non-being" into the world of "being". And that, they can re-capture their lost land, power, history, being, language and knowledge by rethinking their subjectivisation, domination, control, and exploitation. This is attainable by searching for better ways of theorizing and explaining the meaning of liberation and freedom. Kwanga's attempt to use FOVILAD to correct the distorted images of Tchopbrokpot's Eurocentric mirror is a living testimony that the LAD victims prefer "disparity and dislocation than reconciliation under duress of subject and object" (Said, 1994: 41). It captures an awareness that "a belligerent intelligence is always to be preferred over what conformity offers, no matter how unfriendly the circumstances and unfavorable the outcome" (Edward Said 43-44).

Conclusion

This essay set out to demonstrate that from an educational and natural disaster management point of view, Anglophone Mimbolanders have been minoritarized. It argued that in Mimboland, publicly provided education systems such as the UA are increasingly being seen as unable to address the specific educational needs of the poor and marginalized groups such as Abehema that symbolically represents the Anglophone community. I have advocated an emphasis on pluralism in educational provision and alternative schooling systems for such groups and a reassessment of the functions of university education as part of the process of their de-minoritarianization. The Mimboland government's process of managing the LAD ironically orphanized the victims. The failure of the *mitigation* (structural and non-structural measures taken to limit the impact of the disaster), *preparedness* (the construction of shelters, installation of warning devices, creation of back-up life-line services and rehearsing evacuation plans), *response* (the search and rescue of victims, fulfilling the basic humanitarian needs of the affected population and assistance by national or international agencies and organizations), and *recovery* (reconstruction) processes of President Longstay's government leave the fate of the victims in the hands of Emmanuel Kwanga's NGO, FOVILAD.

Like most NGOs, FOVILAD runs the risks of a lack of coordination which will lead to duplication of effort, limited understanding of local circumstances, the sustenance and extension of neocolonial relations. It could likely become the "new compradors" reviving and acting as the agent of international capitalism against the interests of local peasants and workers. Kwanga's decision to take "no managerial or executive role in particular" (354) and his insistence that "the idea is to initiate, raise funds at the beginning, and allow villagers themselves to run the show" (354), is quite promising. For these promises to materialize, the past 50 or more years of false promises will have to demand little so that the future can come closer. Through FOVILAD, Mimbolanders will travel the crude maps of de-minoritarianization.

Between the theories and actions of FOVILAD's de-minoritarianization, there may be correspondence, but there will be no sequence. All the minorities of Mimboland will not necessarily reach the same place, and many of them will not even reach any recognizable place, but with FOVILAD, they share the same starting point, and that is enough. The victims of the UA guillotine and the victims of the LAD are not all headed to the same address, but with FOVILAD, Kwanga as a victim of both, believes they can walk together for a very long time. Even though a few of them speak French and English and the vast majority of them speak other languages and therefore do not have a voice, Kwanga, the multilinguist, is their ventriloquist, a rearguard intellectual who will always look back.

This is not to downplay the diversity of the formation and performance of Mimboland de-minoritarianization. Some Mimbolanders are headed toward *Francophonization,* others to *Anglophonization,* others to *Sawanization,* others to *Graffinization,* still others to *Baminization,* others to real and true *Betinization,* others to *South Westernization,* and others to *North Westernization,* but their journeys will converge at the pluriethnic plurilingualism and transculturality of FOVILAD. Then and only then, could Mimboland acknowledge minority-majority boundaries as thresholds or vestibules of meaning that must be crossed, erased, and translated in the process of articulating equality and difference. Mimbolanders know that most emancipatory concepts tend to become conceptual monsters but Kwanga and his followers and all Mimbolanders are not afraid. The times of de-minotarianization are not flat or concentric; they are passages between the "no longer" and the "not yet" (Santos 2014) of Mimboland marginalization.

Mimbolanders are not victims. They are victimized, and they offer resistance. In line with Kwanga's idea of FOVILAD, de-minotarianization has neither leaders nor followers and its spontaneity will disorganize the Mimboland status quo only to the extent that it will organize itself in order not to turn itself into a new status quo. Abehema, Tchang, and Yenseh will translate into one another reciprocally and need to be very careful lest some engage

26

more in translation than others. It will not be important for them to agree on what it means to change the Mimboland world, but it will be enough for them to be in agreement about their actions that contribute to changing that world as envisioned in FOVILAD. Translation will help FOVILAD define the limits and possibilities of collective Mimboland action. Through FOVILAD, the Anglophones of Mimboland will de-minoritarize their kind by turning Anglophone and Francophone boundaries and limits into the in-between spaces or zones, not only of transition but also of transaction, through which the meanings of cultural and political authority are negotiated. In refusing Mr. Tchopbrokpot and President Longstay the monopoly of agency to describe and define Mimboland, Kwanga transcends the dominating and limiting parameters of the Mimboland government. In making FOVILAD a subaltern counter-discourse and an act of insurgency Kwanga participates in the re-invention of Mimboland and achieves what Ali Mazrui (2005), has called "whistle-blowing against ideologies of Otherness" with the sole goal of Living Independence.

Works Cited

Amin, Samin. (2009). *Eurocentrism: Modernity, religion, and democracy: A critique of Eurocentrism and culturalism*. New York: Monthly Review Press.

Ankumah, Adaku. "Out of the Circle: United Margins in Francis B. Nyamnjoh's *The Travail of Dieudonne*", in Benjamin Fishkin, Adaku Ankumah and Bill Ndi eds. *Fears, Doubts and Joys of Not Belonging*. Langaa Research & Publishing. 2014.

Brennan, John, Roger King and Yann Lebeau. (2004). "The Role of Universities in the Transformation of Societies: An International Research Project Synthesis Report." London: Association of Commonwealth Universities. Available at www.open.ac.uk

Castells, Manuel. (2001). "Universities as dynamic systems of contradictory functions." In J. Muller et. al. (eds) *Challenges of globalisation. South African debates with Manuel Castells*, Cape Town: Maskew Miller Longman. 206-223.

_____. (2009). *Communication Power.* Oxford, New York: Oxford UP.

Chakrabarty, Dipesh. (1998). "Minority Histories, Subaltern Pasts" *Postcolonial Studies,* vol. 1, no. 1, pp. 15-29.

Deleuze, Gilles and Felix Guattari.. *A Thousand Plateaus: Capitalism and Schizophrenia.* Translation and Foreword by Brian Massumi. U of Minnesota P. 1987

Diawara, Manthia. *In Search of Africa.* Harvard UP. 1998

Donohue, Steven, Thulani Masilela, and John Gear. "Disaster Management" http://www.healthlink.org.za/uploads/files/chapter24_00.pdf 1998

Fishkin, Benjamin. (2014). "Names, Power Relationships and influences in Francis B. Nyamnjoh's *Married But Available*", in Adaku Ankumah ed. *Nomenclatural Poetization and Globalization.* Langaa Research and Publishing. 2014

_____. A. "Chaos, Concealment, and Duress in Human Relationships in th Mimboland of Francis B. Nyamnjoh's *Married But Available*", in Bill F. Ndi ed. (2015). *Secrets, Silences, and Betrayals.* Langaa Research and Publishing 2015.

Gautam, Suresh and Bal Chandra Luitel. "A Third Space Research Methodology Through the Metaphor of Mokshya". *Journal of Education and Research.* August 2013, Vol. 3, No. 2, pp. 96-116, DOI: http://dx.doi.org/10.3126/jer.v3i2.8400

Grosfoguel, Ramon. "The epistemic decolonial turn: Beyond political–economy paradigms". *Cultural Studies, 21*(2–3), March/May, 2007, pp. 211–223.

Maldonado-Torres, Nelson. "On the coloniality of being: Contributions to the development of a concept". *Cultural Studies, 21*(2-3), March/May, 2007 pp. 240-270.

Mazrui, Ali. "The re-invention of Africa: Edward Said, VY Mudimbe, and beyond", *Thinking Africa*, 36, Autumn 2005, pp. 45-55.

Moraña, Mabel, Enrique D. Dussel, and Carlos A. Jáuregui (eds.). *Coloniality at Large: Latin America and the Postcolonial Debate.* Durham and London: Duke UP.,.2008

Mulgan, Geoff. *Good and Bad Power: The Ideals and Betrayals of Government*, 2nd edn. London: Penguin. 2007

Naidoo, R. "Repositioning Higher Education as a Global Commodity: Opportunities and Challenges for Future Sociology of Education Work". *British Journal of Sociology of Education* 24 2, 2003, pp. 249-259.

Nandy, Ashis. "Recovery of Indigenous Knowledge and Dissenting Futures of the University." In Inayatullah, S. and Gidley, J. (eds.) (2000) *The University in Transformation: Global Perspectives on the Futures of the University.* Westport, CT: Bergin & Garvey. pp. 115-123.

Ndlovu-Gatsheni, Sabelo. "Global Coloniality and the Challenges of Creating African Futures". *Strategic Review for Southern Africa,* Vol. 36, 2 (2013a): pp. 181-202.

_____. "The Entrapment of Africa within the Global Colonial Matrices of Power: Eurocentrism, Coloniality, and Deimperialization in the Twenty-first Century." *Journal of Developing Societies*, Vol. 29, 4 (2013b): pp. 331–353.

Nkengasong, John Nkemngong. *Across the Mongolo.* ANUCAM. 2004

Nyamnjoh, Francis. *Souls Forgotten.* Langaa Research & Publishing. 2008

Quijano, Anibal. "Coloniality of Power, Eurocentrism, and Social Classification." In Mabel Moraña, Enrique Dussel, and Carlos A. Jáuregui eds. *Coloniality at Large: Latin America and the Postcolonial Debate.* Duke UP, 2008.

Said, Edward. *Representations of the Intellectual.* Pantheon. 1994.

Santos, Boaventura de Sousa. *Epistemologies of the South: Justice against Epistemicide.* Paradigm 2014.

Chapter 2

Living (In)Dependence:
Bayard Rustin and Queer Pan-Africanists
Overcoming the Constraints of
Their Respective Societies

Zachary C. Peterson
Georgia State University
&
Elliot James
University of Minnesota

This chapter asks if 21st century artist scholar-activists across the African Diaspora might look to Bayard Rustin's papers as part of a growing Queer Pan-Africanism archive.[1] Queer Pan-Africanism draws from the early-mid-to-late 20th century global, transnational, heteronormative, and often quite misogynist black solidarity movement (i.e. Pan-Africanism) to bring lesbian, gay, bisexual, transgender, and intersex (LGBTI), or queer Africans and people of African descent together to advocate for gender- and sexuality-based human rights. At first look, Rustin's papers do not fit. After being outed as gay (and "perverted") by Cold War era McCarthyites, Rustin separated his U.S. Civil Rights and Pan-African activism from his gay sexual orientation. While Queer Pan-Africanists, like Zethu

---

[1] We would like particularly to thank Dr. Bill F. Ndi for inviting us to contribute to this collection. Work on this essay follows the Southeastern Regional Seminar in African Studies 2017 conference at Auburn and Tuskegee Universities, on the theme of "American in Africa, African in America: Ties that Bind or Blind." We would also like to thank the other conference organizer, Dr. Daren Ray for bringing the authors together in the panel "Pan-Africanisms, Past and Present." This essay builds on this ongoing collaboration between the authors. For more on the Queer Pan-Africanism archive, look for Elliot James, "The Ancestors Are Here and They're Queer: Queer Pan-Africanism and Afrika's Archive," in *Turning Archival*, eds. Daniel Marshall, Kevin P. Murphy, and Zeb Tortorici, under review (Durham and London: Duke University Press, 2018).

Matebeni, Zanele Muholi, Neo S. Musangi, Stella Nyanzi, and Jabulani Pererira, make explicit claims to their LGBTI and queer identities to fight injustice, and work across Africa's borders to do so, Rustin kept his sexuality private. Only in the 1980s, in the twilight of his life, did Rustin make associations between his being gay and gay Civil Rights.[2]

Bayard Rustin spent a lifetime fighting for his rights and those of countless others while living in a society that persecuted him for his race and his sexual orientation. These Queer Pan-Africanists are likewise fighting for their rights to live in the societies they were born into and to be recognized as African as opposed to be persecuted as outsiders for their lifestyles. Another thing that Rustin shares with these Queer Pan-Africanists is that they both found or are finding ways to overcome the constraints placed on them by their societies by refusing to accept their persecution and struggling against those constraints to force their societies to accept them for whom they are. Rustin passed away in 1987 after a lifetime of largely successful activism towards the causes he supported whereas these Queer Pan-Africanists are currently dealing with persecution in contemporary African societies in Uganda, Zimbabwe, Gambia, Nigeria, Kenya, etc.; and must deal with traditional African customs that regard "queer" as outside of African concepts and an unwelcome "Western" import. This essay will examine these figures and draw comparisons and contrasts between Rustin and these modern Africans.

Bayard Rustin dedicated his life to human equality. In Rustin's own words, "My activism did not spring from my being gay, or for that matter from my being black. Rather it is rooted…in my Quaker upbringing…Those values are based on the concept of a single human family and the belief that all members of the family are

---

[2] The works from what we call "Queer Pan-Africanists" are drawn primarily from Zethu Matebeni, ed., *Reclaiming Afrikan: Queer Perspectives on Sexual and Gender Identities*, (Athlone: Modjaji Books, 2014). The collection was the first to bring together LGBTI artist scholar-activists from Africans from all over the continent to theorize what it means to be queer in 21st century Africa, where the criminalization of sexual and gender non-conformity remains an ongoing human rights issue.

equal."[3] Also, must be noted that as a Quaker, he "belonged to a Christian sect… persecuted for the libertarian ideas and ideals."[4] Over a forty-year period, Rustin dedicated his life to nonviolence, peace, civil rights, African liberation and gay rights. Rustin lived within the constraints of a society during the early Cold War that viewed his sexuality as an aberration and persecuted him for it. Rustin struggled to keep his sexuality and identity as a gay man private and separate from his public activism. For example, in 1953, while on a lecture tour for the American Friends Service Committee (AFSC) in California, Rustin took a lover and had sex in public in defiance and refusal to submit to established order.[5] The lovers were caught, and this led to their arrest on a morals charge. J. Edgar Hoover, the head of the FBI, took note of this arrest and used it to blackmail Rustin to embarrass the Civil Rights Movement on several different occasions.[6] This arrest damaged relationships even with Rustin's closest allies who feared his behavior could harm the movements they all worked towards. Rustin resigned from the Fellowship of Reconciliation in 1953. And in 1960 and 1963, Hoover leaked proof of this arrest in order to damage the Civil Rights Movement. Rustin struggled to free himself from those constraints so that he could work on those causes liberated from the prejudice that chained him.

Rustin was born in 1912 in the Quaker community of West Chester, Pennsylvania. Rustin's grandparents, Janifer and Julia who raised him, were pillars of the African American community. Despite

---

[3] Letter, Bayard Rustin to Joseph Beam, April 10, 1986, in *I Must Resist: Bayard Rustin's Life in Letters*, edited by Michael C. Long (San Francisco: City Lights Books), 460-61.

[4] Bill F. Ndi, "Quakers, Memory & the Past in Literature" qtd. in Benjamin Hart Fishkin, Adaku T. Ankumah, Festus Fru Ndeh & Bill F. Ndi, *Outward Evil, Inward Battle: Human Memory in Literature* (Langaa Research and Publishing 2013), 3-35

[5] Bill F. Ndi, "Unwavering Insubordination: Rebellion and Memory in *the Letters* of Elizabeth Hooton" spells out "Quaker defiance and refusal to submit to established order in spite of the cruel persecution directed against Quakers" qtd. in Benjamin Hart Fishkin, Adaku T. Ankumah, Festus Fru Ndeh & Bill F. Ndi, *Outward Evil, Inward Battle: Human Memory in Literature* (Langaa Research and Publishing, 2013), 89-108

[6] Merl E. Reed, "The FBI, MOWM, and CORE, 1941-46," *Journal of Black Studies* Vol. 21, No. 4 (June 1991): 465-79.

its location above the Mason-Dixon Line, West Chester had *de facto* segregated public accommodations. Bayard's consciousness of the racial tensions in his community was instilled in him by his grandmother. Julia established a local branch of the NAACP in their hometown shortly after that organization's founding in 1909. As a result, luminaries like W.E.B. Du Bois stayed at the Rustin home when they visited the local area. After high school, Rustin left his home town. He eventually moved to New York City and in the largely anonymous confines of that great metropolis, there was a thriving gay/queer scene where he found it easier to express the latent homosexual feelings that he had repressed during his adolescence. He would call New York his home for the rest of his life. Rustin also joined the Young Communist League (YCL). Rustin was impressed with the Communist Party's (CPUSA) attention to race relations particularly in the Scottsboro Boys case. However, in 1941 when Germany invaded Russia, the CPUSA wanted him to stop the Committee Against Discrimination in the Armed Forces he had started; this policy change caused Rustin to forever lose faith in the Communist Party.[7]

In 1941, Rustin began working with A. Philip Randolph and his March on Washington Movement (MOWM). Randolph, the head of the Brotherhood of Sleeping Car Porters (BSCP), the most significant African American union, and one of the preeminent leaders of the civil rights movement, became a life-long mentor for Rustin. Beginning in January 1941, Randolph threatened to march with tens of thousands of African Americans on Washington, D.C., unless President Roosevelt guaranteed equal employment opportunities for African Americans in the defense industries and in the federal government. On June 25, 1941, when Roosevelt caved in with Executive Order 8802 which created the FEPC, Randolph called off the march which infuriated the youth division of the march, of which Rustin was a part.[8]

---

[7] John D'Emilio, *Lost Prophet: The Life and Times of Bayard Rustin* (University of Chicago Press, 2003), 7-38.

[8] Ibid., 56-61.

Later that summer, Rustin joined the staff of the Fellowship of Reconciliation (FOR) under A.J. Muste, who was a celebrated pacifist and veteran of using the sit-down strike in labor disputes. At FOR, Muste tasked Rustin with touring around and speaking to audiences to recruit more people to become pacifists against the war effort and to conduct workshops in non-violent direct action. Rustin worked with James Farmer and George Houser on the FOR Committee on Non-violent Action. In the spring of 1942, Houser established a Committee of Racial Equality (CORE), devoted to using non-violent direct action against Jim Crow in Chicago, whereas Rustin and Farmer, on their speaking tours, established new branches in other cities in the Mid-west, Northeast and Upper South. In 1943, at the first convention, CORE became a national organization that lasted through 1970 as a force in the field of civil rights.[9]

Also, in 1943, Rustin exercised his pacifist principles in defiance of the draft board. For that defiance he was sentenced to jail.[10] During his years in jail, he protested the segregated conditions of the prison.[11] His release from jail, in June 1946, corresponded with the Irene Morgan Supreme Court case, in which Morgan refused to give up her seat on a Virginia bus traveling interstate to Maryland and was arrested. The Supreme Court ruled that Jim Crow statutes on bus travel interfered with interstate commerce.[12] Rustin and Houser, under the joint auspices of CORE and FOR, planned to test compliance with the ruling. This Journey of Reconciliation involved eight white and eight black men riding buses and trains throughout the Upper South. There were a few arrests and only one instance of violence. In Chapel Hill, North Carolina, the police arrested Andrew Johnson and Joseph Felmet because they were sitting interracially in the front. After they were arrested, Rustin and Igal Roodenko moved

---

[9]August Meier and Elliot Rudwick, *CORE: A Study in the Civil Rights Movement, 1942-1968* (Oxford University Press, 1973), 6-24.

[10] Bayard Rustin, "Letter to the Draft Board [1943]," in *Time on Two Crosses: The Collected Writings of Bayard Rustin*, edited by Devon W. Carbado and Donald Weise (San Francisco: Cleis Press, 2003), 11-13.

[11] For an example of Rustin's resistance to segregation in the federal prisons, Cf.: Letter, Rustin to Warden Hagerman, March 30, 1944, *I Must Resist*, 15-18.

[12] *Irene Morgan v. Commonwealth of Virginia*, 328 U.S. 373 (1946).

up in their places and were also arrested. As this was happening, a mob of cabbies developed outside the bus. James Peck, a CORE member sent to witness the arrests was beaten over the head. George Houser placed their bail bond and Charles Jones, a local Presbyterian minister, drove the men to his home. Two taxies full of cabbies menacingly pursued them. A few minutes after the group reached his home, Jones received a threatening phone call, "Get those damn niggers out of town or we'll burn your house down. We'll be around to be sure they go."[13] The group decided to leave town before nightfall. Besides Chapel Hill, the Journey was largely successful as most bus drivers complied with the ruling once they were aware of it.[14] However, Chapel Hill did presage the violence that the Freedom Riders would face when they went into the Deep South in 1961. For this arrest, Rustin served twenty-two days on a chain gang.[15] In 1948, he and Houser received the Jefferson Award from the Council Against Intolerance for the Journey of Reconciliation. Furthermore, in 1948, Rustin worked with Randolph again, this time on a Committee to End Jim Crow in the Armed Forces which mirrored what he had done as part of the YCL nearly a decade ago; but this time it was successful and led to Executive Order 9981 on July 26, 1948.

In 1951, Bill Sutherland, an African American officer in the AFSC working on African liberation, happened to be in London when he ran into the editor of *The Bantu World* who informed him that the African National Congress (ANC) and the South African Indian Congress (SAIC) planned a civil disobedience campaign to

---

[13] James Peck, *Freedom Ride: The Civil Rights Movement and Non-Violent Resistance* (New York: Simon and Schuster, 1962), 23.

[14] Bayard Rustin and George Houser, "We Challenged Jim Crow!: A Report on the Journey of Reconciliation, April 9-23, 1947," Papers of the Congress of Racial Equality, 1941-1967, Series V, Departments and Related Correspondence, reel No. 25, No. 117; For a detailed play by play from Bayard Rustin's point of view, see: Bayard Rustin, "Log on Journey of Reconciliation," Fellowship of Reconciliation Records, DG-013, Section II, Sub-Section D-Program Staff, Bayard Rustin, Box 51, Journey of Reconciliation, Swarthmore College Peace Collections, Swarthmore, Pennsylvania.

[15] Bayard Rustin, "Twenty-Two Days on a Chain Gang [1949]," in *Time on Two Crosses*, 31-57.

coincide with the 300th anniversary of the Dutch landing in South Africa. Since Defiance Campaign Against Unjust Laws utilized the same Gandhian non-violent direct action that the FOR and CORE had been utilizing in the US; on his return to the States, Sutherland informed Houser, Muste, Farmer, Randolph, and Rustin and they formed the Americans for South African Resistance (AFSAR).[16] This organization raised funds for the campaign and circulated a bulletin through FOR and CORE's extensive mailing lists informing the American public about the Defiance Campaign. Z.K. Matthews, an ANC officer who worked with AFSAR while teaching abroad at Union Theological Seminary in New York; had this to say about their contributions, "I cannot close this letter without thanking you and through you Americans for South African Resistance for all you did and are doing for our cause. The government is doing its best to cripple our movement by banning our leaders and making it difficult for us to meet."[17] In the midst of the campaign, Rustin made a trip to Ghana and Nigeria where he met with the likes of Kwame Nkrumah and Namdi Azikiwe and was excited to see that these leaders were practicing non-violence in their independence struggles.[18] In 1953, after the Defiance Campaign came to an end, the officers of AFSAR formed the American Committee on Africa (ACOA) which was dedicated to all the emerging independence movements throughout the African continent.[19] While Rustin was

---

[16] Bill Sutherland, "Biographical Sketch, Southern Africa Representative, American Friends Service Committee," found at:
http://africanactivist.msu.edu/document_metadata.php?objectid=32-130-16BA; George Houser, interview by Author, Session 3, Santa Rosa, CA, May 4, 2012; George Houser, *No One Can Stop the Rain: Glimpses of Africa's Liberation Struggle* (The Pilgrim Press, 1989), 10-12; Bill Sutherland, Interview with Bill Sutherland, by Prexy Nesbitt, 2004, No Easy Victories Project; George Houser, Interview of George Houser, by Lisa Brock, 2004, No Easy Victories Project.
[17] "Thanks to U.S. Supporters," AFSAR Bulletin 15, November 6, 1953, Americans for South African Resistance Collected Records, CDG-A, Swarthmore College Peace Collections, Swarthmore, Pennsylvania.
[18] Fellowship of Reconciliation Papers DG-013, Section II, Series D-Program Staff, 1941-1984, Box 52- Bayard Rustin, Trip to Africa (Gold Coast/Ghana), 1952, Swarthmore College Peace Collections, Swarthmore, Pennsylvania.
[19] Homer Jack Papers, DG-063, Series VI: organizational work, projects travel and interests, Box 14 - American Committee on Africa, 1953-55, Swarthmore

more concerned with civil rights during these years, he often came back and worked with Houser at the ACOA.

Rustin's 1953 arrest for having gay sex in public was the third such incident and Rustin had previously agreed that if he got caught again he would resign from the FOR. This incident damaged the relationship between Muste and Rustin; though they continued working with each other in other organizations and causes. Rustin also resigned from the Executive Board of the War Resister's League (WRL), but not only did they refuse to accept his resignation they sought to promote him to the position of Executive Secretary. Further still, under Rustin's leadership of the WRL, they began to underwrite Bill Sutherland's travels to Ghana which aided in insuring that Ghana's independence struggle remained non-violent.[20] Rustin's activism towards civil rights continued. In December 1955, Rosa Parks refused to give up her seat and the Montgomery Improvement Association started the Bus Boycott. In 1956, Martin Luther King, Jr., who had no experience with Gandhian non-violent direct action, sought the aid and advice of the FOR. Rustin recommended that the leaders of the Movement go down to the station and seek arrest. From that point forward, Rustin became an adviser to King on non-violence and strategy.[21] On June 9, 1960, King and Randolph issued a joint statement penned by Rustin which threatened that there would be a march of thousands of African Americans at the Democratic and Republican nominating conventions.[22] In response, Adam Clayton Powell, Jr., issued a press release claiming that King and Randolph were under the undue influence of Rustin. He also issued a private threat that if Rustin did not resign from his position

---

College Peace Collections, Swarthmore, Pennsylvania. These papers described the very earliest foundations of the ACOA and included numerous mentions of Rustin.

[20] In *I Must Resist*, Chapter 9 focuses on this episode of Bayard Rustin's life in a series of letters involving the principal participants. Bayard Rustin, *I Must Resist: Bayard Rustin's Life in Letters* edited by Michael G. Long (City Light Books, 2012), 149-63.

[21] Bayard Rustin, "Montgomery Diary [1956]," in *Time on Two Crosses: The Collected Writings of Bayard Rustin* edited by Devon W. Carbado and Donald Weise (Cleis Press, 2003), 58-65.

[22] Letter, Rustin to the Press, June 8, 1960, and Rustin to Marin Luther King, Jr., June 15, 1960, in *I Must Resist*, 234-37.

that Powell would fabricate a lie accusing King and Rustin of having an affair.[23] Powell was, no doubt, informed about Rustin's sexuality by the FBI, which had been keeping track of Rustin since at least his arrest for draft resistance in 1943.[24] As a result, Rustin publicly cut ties, but King continued to rely on Rustin behind the scenes.[25] In 1963, Rustin was once again called to serve; this time as the leader of the March on Washington for Jobs and Freedom.[26] Hoover once again tried to derail the movement by exploiting Rustin's past. Hoover told Strom Thurmond, who spent thirty minutes on the floor of Congress ranting about how a gay, communist, draft dodger was leading the march that served as the culmination of the civil rights movement. While they did appoint Randolph in Rustin's place, Rustin still remained as Randolph's deputy and was the *de facto* organizer of the march. So, instead of abandoning Rustin, the leaders of the movement published a statement in which they expressed their "complete confidence in Bayard Rustin's character, integrity, and extraordinary ability."[27]

Rustin's Pan-African activism continued after his participation in the founding of the ACOA. In 1957, Rustin was one of the supporters of the ACOA initiated Declaration of Conscience Campaign which was an international protest campaign against Apartheid South Africa. Eleanor Roosevelt and Martin Luther King, Jr, were cosponsors of the Campaign.[28] In 1958, Rustin wrote an essay on the ongoing African liberation movements and how they were using Gandhian nonviolence.[29] In 1959, Rustin participated in

---

[23] Ibid., 237-41.

[24] "Bayard Rustin, 1910-87," in *Black Americans: The FBI Files* edited by David Gallen (Carroll & Graf Publishers, Inc, 1994), 382-423.

[25] Bayard Rustin, Press Release, June 27, 1960, Bayard Rustin Papers, CDG-A, Bio Material, 1943-79, Swarthmore College Peace Collections, Swarthmore, Pennsylvania.

[26] Bayard Rustin, "Preamble to March on Washington [1963]," *Time on Two Crosses*, 112-15.

[27] Letter, A. Philip Randolph to the Press, August 12, 1963, in *I Must Resist*, 262-64.

[28] "Declaration of Conscience Campaign," Records of the American Committee on Africa, part 2-Correspondence and Subject Files on South Africa, 1952-85, reel 5, 102/22-27, frame 752-896.

[29] Bayard Rustin, "African Revolution [1958]," *Time on Two Crosses*, 306-13.

a protest against the French detonating an atom bomb in the Sahara Desert; A.J. Muste, Michael Scott, Bill Sutherland and others also participated.[30] In 1962, Rustin again participated in an ACOA sponsored initiative known as the Appeal for Action Against Apartheid; Martin Luther King, Jr., and Chief Albert Luthuli were the co-sponsors.[31] In 1966, Rustin was part of the Committee of Conscience Against Apartheid, which was an ACOA collaboration with other NGOs involving a bank campaign against investment and financing of Apartheid.[32] In that same year, Rustin signed a letter that the ACOA sponsored. The letter called for the continued banning of South Africa from the Olympics.[33] After 1966, Rustin continued his activism in civil rights, arguing for the integration of African Americans in American society.[34] Because of his hard-won skepticism of Communism, Rustin in his later years supported liberation movements in Africa which were anti-Communist or did not have the direct support of the Soviet Union, such as UNITA. This stance put him at odds with the ACOA, and many others, who supported FRELIMO and the MPLA. He seemed to conclude that those movements were the puppets of the Soviet Union. Rustin came from a context where the CPUSA had been puppets of the politburo

---

[30] The Bayard Rustin Papers, reel 1, African Affairs—Sahara Protest Team, 1959, frame 0001-0049; A.J. Muste, "Africa Against the Bomb," *Liberation* (January 1960).

[31] Albert John Luthuli, "Appeal for Action Against Apartheid," 1962, found at: http://africanactivist.msu.edu/document_metadata.php?objectid=32-130-B73 [accessed on October 27, 2017]; ACOA, "A Brief Review of Action Taken On and Around Human Rights Day, December 10, In Connection With The Appeal For Action Against Apartheid Campaign," Records of the American Committee on Africa, Part 2-Corr. and Subject Files on South Africa, 1952-85, reel 3, 100/44- Appeal for Action Against Apartheid—Reports, Fact Sheets, Lists of Suggested Sponsors, 1963; "Group to Seek U.S. Curbs on Regime in South Africa," New York Times, December 2, 1962.

[32] "Committee of Conscience Against Apartheid," Records of the American Committee on Africa, part 2-Correspondence and Subject Files on South Africa, 1952-85, reel 3, Bank Campaign, 101/10-12, frames 0896-1027.

[33] ACOA, "Americans Call for Continued Suspension of South Africa from Olympic Games," May 8, 1966, found at: http://africanactivist.msu.edu/document_metadata.php?objectid=32-130-FED [accessed on October 27, 2017].

[34] Bayard Rustin, "The Failure of Black Separatism [1970]," *Time on Two Crosses*, 217-36.

in the 1940s and had only exploited the issue of civil rights to win over African American converts.[35] In 1983, Rustin toured South Africa and published a report entitled, "A Way Out: Solutions for South Africa," which made suggestions in how the people of South Africa could settle the crisis of apartheid without the situation devolving into a race war; and until his death, in 1987, he also continued to support the dismantling of Apartheid.[36]

Rustin's activism for gay rights began in the 1980s. In his essay, "From Montgomery to Stonewall," Rustin makes the connections between how civil rights are like gay rights and vice versa. He argues the humble beginnings of Rosa Parks occupying a seat in the white section of the bus and a group of gay men refusing to tolerate a police raid on the Stonewall bar; each led to a resistance movement, to a revolution. He argued that the goal of the gay rights movement should not be to convince the people that hate you to love you; "Our aim was to try to create the kind of America, legislatively, morally, psychologically, such that even though some whites continued to hate us, they could not openly manifest that hate."[37] In his essay, "The New 'Niggers' Are Gays," Rustin argued that gay people have replaced African Americans as the "litmus test by which this democracy is to be judged. The barometer for social change is measured by selecting the group which is most mistreated."[38] He argued that for gay rights to be respected gay people needed to argue for an embrace of human rights for all; according to Rustin, gay

---

[35] Episcopal Churchmen for South Africa, "Missions and Movements," Number 1, November 3, 1979. The issue claims that Social Democrats, USA, whose national chairman was Bayard Rustin was hosting Jonas Savimbi, leader of UNITA, who was recognized, at this time, by most mainstream liberal Africanist activists in the US as a puppet of the South African Apartheid regime. Also see: "Social Democrats USA, 1980-84," The Bayard Rustin Papers, reel 17, frame 0497-0588. Under the folder "Trip to Lisbon," one of the major topics of the microfilm reel is that Rustin felt that "Cuba as agent of Soviet Union," which reveals his deep distrust of Communism in all its manifestations.

[36] Bayard Rustin, "A Way Out: Solutions for South Africa [1983]," *Time on Two Crosses*, 350-52.

[37] Bayard Rustin, "From Montgomery to Stonewall [1986]," *Time on Two Crosses*, 272-74.

[38] Bayard Rustin, "The New 'Niggers' Are Gays [1986]," *Time on Two Crosses*, 275-76.

people "should try to build coalitions of people for the elimination of all injustice."[39] In private letters to politicians he encouraged them to promote legislation that would enshrine equal protection of the LGBTQI community into law. For example, in a letter to New York City Councilmember Wooten he argued that by refusing to allow the proposed Gay Rights Bill to proceed to the full council for a vote on its merits, the situation was "tantamount" to the filibustering of the Civil Rights Act that Strom Thurmond exhibited in 1964.[40] He also criticized the Supreme Court's decision in *Bowers vs. Hardwick* in which the court decided that consenting homosexual adults had no right to privacy in the conduct of their sexual lives.[41]

In testimony before the General Welfare Committee of New York City, towards the passage of a Gay Rights bill, Rustin made an impassioned plea to the City Council that based on his long record of activism, "history demonstrates that no group is ultimately safe from prejudice, bigotry, or harassment so long as any group is subject to special negative treatment."[42] Though because hostile actors like J. Edgar Hoover forced Rustin to conceal his sexuality he did not view himself as a gay activist until near the end of his life. His work with the civil rights movement which culminated with the passage Civil Rights Act in 1964 and the Voting Rights Act in 1965 occurred several years before the Stonewall protest in 1969. According to Rustin,

> I was not involved in the struggle for gay rights as a youth... [as] there was no organized gay liberation movement. I did not 'come out of the closet' voluntarily—circumstances forced me out. While I have no problem being publicly identified as a homosexual, it would be

---

[39] Bayard Rustin, "Brother to Brother: An Interview with Joseph Beam," *Time on Two Crosses*, 277-80.

[40] Letter, Bayard Rustin to Council Member Priscilla Wooten, March 22, 1985, in *I Must Resist*, 448-49.

[41] Letter, Bayard Rustin to Leonard Sussman, July 10, 1986, in *I Must Resist*, 467-69.

[42] Bayard Rustin, "The Importance of Gay Rights Legislation [1987]," *Time on Two Crosses*, 295-98.

dishonest of me to present myself as one who was in the forefront of the struggle for gay rights.[43]

This ambivalence can be traced to the repressive environment Rustin was forced to navigate by the likes of J. Edgar Hoover, Strom Thurmond, and others who would attempt to exploit the fears and superstitions within American society, of the time, in order to undermine the causes Rustin devoted his activism to. In the 1980s, when gay rights were finally beginning to be recognized, Rustin used his well-earned reputation as an activist for human rights in America, Africa, and all over the world, in order to argue that the LGBT community deserved them as well. Rustin, had he lived through today, would be in solidarity with the Africans who struggle today to exist as queer in their traditional African societies.

Like Rustin, queer pan-African artist scholar-activists wrestle with the term "queer" to capture the entirety of gender- and sexual-nonconformity in Africa because the word finds its roots in the Western academy. When activists adopt the term today, decades after the continent's post-War decolonization movement, they risk disassociating themselves from the continent. So, when I see the question posed, "can writers create a universe in which characters enjoy total independence from each other,"[44] I'm immediately reminded of Zethu Matebeni and Jabulani Perreira's collaborative intellectual-activist reclamation project *Reclaiming Afrikan: Queer Perspectives on Sexual and Gender Identities*, because that's exactly what they did. "We deliberately use 'k' in Afrikan to emphasize the need to *reclaim* our existence and being in this continent," Matebeni and Perreira write in *Reclaiming Afrika*'s Preface. "As sexual and gender non-conforming or queer persons, we have been alienated in Africa. We have been stripped of our belonging and our connectedness," they continue. "For these reasons, we have created our own version of Afrika—a space that cuts across the rigid borders and boundaries

---

[43] Letter, Bayard Rustin to Joseph Beam, April 10, 1986, in *I Must Resist*, 460-61.

[44] "Living (In)Dependence" CFP.

that have for many years made us feel disconnected and fractured."[45] Queer Pan-Africanism brings sexual and gender non-conformity back into the multiple ways of being the continent has nurtured in people since the beginnings of human history.

Right now, thirty-three African states out of fifty-four punish homosexual behavior with imprisonment; that leaves only twenty-one states without laws that punish the LGBTQI community. Among the group of nations that don't punish that community, South Africa is the only nation that recognizes a right for homosexual couples to marry and to adopt children. Many of the proponents of discrimination against homosexuality argue that it is a Western/colonial import with no pre-colonial history on the continent itself, but that is a misrepresentation of the history. According to Bisi Alimi, "while many Africans say that homosexuality is un-African, African culture is no stranger to homosexual behavior and acts."[46] In the Yoruba language, *adofuro* refers to someone who has anal sex. "This is not a new word; it is as old as the Yoruba culture itself."[47] In northern Nigeria,

> *yan daudu* is a Hausa term to describe effeminate men who are considered to be wives to men. While the Yoruba word might be more about behaviour[sic] than identity, this Hausa term is more about identity. You have to look and act like a *yan daudu* to be called one. It is not an identity you can just carry. These words are neutral; they are not infused with hate or disgust.[48]

Stephen O. Murray and Will Roscoe, in *Boy-Wives and Female Husbands: Studies of African Homosexualities*, found numerous accounts of Europeans who observed homosexual or gender non-conforming

---

[45] Zethu Matebeni, ed. *Reclaiming Afrikan : Queer Perspectives on Sexual and Gender Identities* (Cape Town: Modjaji Books, 2014), 7.

[46] Bisi Alimi, "If you say being gay is not African, you don't know your history," *The Guardian*, September 9, 2015, found at:
https://www.theguardian.com/commentisfree/2015/sep/09/being-gay-african-history-homosexuality-christianity [accessed on December 27, 2017].

[47] ibid.

[48] ibid.

behaviors among African people across the continent in the early twentieth, nineteenth, or earlier centuries. Though the editors noted that these, largely, Christian observers tended to discount them because of their own sense of morality; the editors argue that these anthropologists let their prejudices influence their scientific observations of these people.[49] For example, the editors found cases of observed homosexuality or gender non-conformity dating back to 1687, in what is modern-day Angola, to 1899 in Zanzibar, to the 1910s in Zimbabwe, to 1911 in the Cameroons, and to 1925 in South West Africa.[50] In "Appendix I," they found numerous words that refer to homosexuality or gender non-conformity throughout the continent and in all of the major African Language groups: Niger-Congo, Bamu, Afro-Asiatic, Bantu, Nilo-Saharan, Khoisan, and Kordofanian.[51] In an interesting demonstration of pre-colonial gender non-conformity, the editors noted, "In the 1640s, a Dutch military attaché observed firsthand what must have struck him as the strange organization of her court. As *ngola*, Nzinga was not 'queen', but 'king', of her people. She ruled dressed as a man, surrounded by a harem of young men who dressed as women and were her 'wives.'"[52]

The recent spate of laws making homosexuality punishable by huge prison sentences or death is, largely, a result of the influence of fundamentalist Christians from the United States like Pat Robertson, Rick Warren, Scott Lively, among others, who promote homosexuality as a global plot to promote a "gay agenda." For example, Pat Robertson's *The 700 Club* is broadcast throughout the continent despite the fact that Robertson, during the struggle for African Liberation sided with the white minority governments in Rhodesia and South Africa. These anti-gay views have unfortunately found allies such as Stephen Langa of Uganda-based Family Life Network. But the influence of these American Christian fundamentalists extends beyond just African evangelical Christian

---

[49] Stephen O. Murray and Will Roscoe, ed., *Boy-wives and Female Husbands: Studies of African Homosexualities* (Palgrave, 1998), xi-xxii.

[50] ibid., "Table of Contents."

[51] ibid., 280-82.

[52] ibid., 1.

leaders into the halls of political power where politicians often promote anti-gay laws because homosexual animus is popular and sexual minorities are largely unorganized with few allies.[53] For example, in Uganda, in March 2012 President Yoweri Museveni stated, "Homosexuals in small numbers have always existed in our part of black Africa...They were never prosecuted. They were never discriminated." But facing electoral pressures from a populace unsatisfied by the high cost of living, the unemployment, and the rampant corruption demonstrated by his nearly thirty-year old regime, in 2014, "Museveni succumbed to populist pressures and condemned an otherwise law-abiding sexual minority to maximum sentences of life imprisonment."[54]

The activism of a Queer Pan-Africanist like Neo S. Musangi is important in demonstrating that while these individuals are queer, they are nonetheless African. Musangi identifies as a transgender non-conformist individual; Musangi's preferred pronouns are they and them. Musangi is a performing and visual artist, academic and researcher. There is a video on YouTube of their performance in which Musangi transitions from clothing of one gender to the other and the point being that if you were to take a snapshot it would be impossible to tell which "gender" Musangi is. Thus, the gendered binary is an artificial social construct that binds hetero-normative cis-gendered society that people like Musangi refuse to abide by.[55] According to Musangi,

> To be Trans in Kenya, like in most other parts of the world, is to exist in a space of precarity and transgression. To speak on sexuality in this country, or research—even as a 'mainstream' scholar—the sexual

---

[53] Rev. Kapya Kaoma, "The U.S. Christian Rights and the Attack on Gays in Africa," found at: https://www.huffingtonpost.com/rev-kapya-kaoma/the-us-christian-right-an_b_387642.html [accessed on December 27, 2017].

[54] Sylvia Tamale, "Homosexuality is not un-African," April 26, 2014, *Aljazeera America,* found at:
http://america.aljazeera.com/opinions/2014/4/homosexuality-africamuseveniugandanigeriaethiopia.html [accessed on December 27, 2017].

[55] Neo Musangi, "In Time and Space II," June 2013, found at: https://www.youtube.com/watch?v=ScVcSgEPV6U [accessed on December 27, 2017].

realities of non-heteronormative Kenyans is digressive and carries with it a sense of danger. These lives matter. To me, these lives are worth intellectual and political attention. They, like hetero-cisgender lives, are part of the yarn that makes up the so-called Kenyan fabric. These lives are not made-up. These lives are lived.[56]

Zethu Matebeni is a queer activist and researcher who focuses on Black Lesbian Sexualities and Identity in South Africa. Her documentary film, *Breaking Out of the Box: Stories of black lesbians*, looks at the lives of six women to demonstrate the "sheer breadth of experience in the black lesbian community."[57] Stella Nyanzi is an African feminist scholar and contributor to Zethu Matebeni's *Reclaiming Afrikan* collection.[58] Nyanzi, by working in Uganda on gay rights, has "made her a divisive figure in a country where homosexual acts are illegal."[59] Nyanzi has been critical of President Museveni and for recent remarks on social media Nyanzi has been charged with "cyber harassment." She has been detained and supporters have taken "to social media using the hashtag #FreeStellaNyanzi to demand her release."[60] Zanele Muholi is a photographer and "visual activist" whose blog *Inkanyiso* serves as a nexus for Queer activism and Queer media where LGBTI individuals can contribute to or consume its contents.[61] These activists have raised awareness of the need for Africa to recognize the rights of their LGBTQI citizens.

---

[56] Neo Musangi, "Transgender Day of Remembrance, Nairobi, Kenya," November 26, 2013, *Black | Queer | Feminist | Activist | Academic | Poet | Other*, found at: http://i-aint-a-poet.blogspot.com/2013/11/httpwwwiranti-orgcozacontentevents2013.html#more [accessed on December 27, 2017].

[57] Zethu Matebeni, et al, *Breaking Out of the Box: Stories of Black Lesbians*, 2011, found at: http://www.fortgreenefilmworks.com/projects_breaking-ouofthe-box.html [accessed on December 27, 2017].

[58] Stella Nyanzi, "Queering Queer Africa" in *Reclaiming Afrikan*, pp. 65-68

[59] Chloe Farand, "Ugandan activist detained for calling president 'a pair of buttocks,'" April 13, 2017, *Independent* found at: http://www.independent.co.uk/news/world/africa/uganda-activist-stella-nyanzi-president-pair-of-buttocks-yoweri-museveni-sanitary-pads-human-rights-a7682111.html [accessed on December 27, 2017].

[60] ibid.

[61] Zanele Muholi, *Inkanyiso*, found at: https://inkanyiso.org/about/ [accessed on December 27, 2017].

47

In conclusion, while Rustin was a Pan-Africanist interested in the liberation of the African continent from the control of European powers and the white minority regimes, it is clear that because Rustin chose to keep his sexual orientation to himself, he was not a Queer Pan-Africanist as defined by this essay. While Queer Pan-Africanists struggled to connect themselves to Africa in all their queerness—in fact, being 'out' was a requirement; well, being anything despite the limits the state placed on them—they demanded recognition, not just because they were different, but because they, too, are African. Queer Pan-Africanists would be much more interested in Rustin's Pasadena, California sex life. However, delving into it would go against the ways Rustin attempted to protect himself. Rustin explained that he never came out. Rather, his opponents outed him. While Rustin never went through the inner-turmoil of figuring out how to name his sexual orientation, he faced attacks from friend and foe as part of FBI strategies to destabilize the Civil Rights Movement. However, Rustin's activism fits within the genealogy of queer pan-Africanism, and had he survived into 2017, it is clear that Rustin would support the activism of the contemporary Queer Pan-Africanists. Finally, given the activism for gay rights in the U.S. and in the twilight of his life, Rustin would demand that African governments stop persecuting their citizens because they are queer. Both Rustin and these contemporary Queer Pan-Africanists have struggled to overcome the customs and superstitions of their societies in relation to their sexual orientation; a struggle that still continues.

Works Cited

Alimi, Bisi. "If you say being gay is not African, you don't know your history," *The Guardian*, September 9, 2015. Found at: https://www.theguardian.com/commentisfree/2015/sep/09/being-gay-african-history-homosexuality-christianity [accessed on December 27, 2017].

American Committee on Africa. "A Brief Review of Action Taken On and Around Human Rights Day, December 10, In

Connection With The Appeal For Action Against Apartheid Campaign." Records of the American Committee on Africa, Part 2-Corr. and Subject Files on South Africa, 1952-85, reel 3, 100/44-Appeal for Action Against Apartheid—Reports, Fact Sheets, Lists of Suggested Sponsors, 1963.

_____. "Americans Call for Continued Suspension of South Africa from Olympic Games," May 8, 1966. Found at: http://africanactivist.msu.edu/document_metadata.php?objecti d=32-130-FED [accessed on October 27, 2017].

_____. "Committee of Conscience Against Apartheid." Records of the American Committee on Africa, part 2-Correspondence and Subject Files on South Africa, 1952-85, reel 3, Bank Campaign, 101/10-12, frames 0896-1027.

_____. "Declaration of Conscience Campaign." Records of the American Committee on Africa, part 2-Correspondence and Subject Files on South Africa, 1952-85, reel 5, 102/22-27, frame 752-896.

Americans For South African Resistance. "AFSAR Bulletin 15," November 6, 1953. Americans for South African Resistance Collected Records, CDG-A, Swarthmore College Peace Collections, Swarthmore, Pennsylvania.

D'Emilio, John. *Lost Prophet: The Life and Times of Bayard Rustin*. 2nd edition. Chicago: University of Chicago Press, 2004.

Episcopal Churchmen for South Africa, "Missions and Movements." Number 1, November 3, 1979.

Farand, Chloe. "Ugandan activist detained for calling president 'a pair of buttocks,'" April 13, 2017, *Independent*. Found at: http://www.independent.co.uk/news/world/africa/uganda-activist-stella-nyanzi-president-pair-of-buttocks-yoweri-museveni-sanitary-pads-human-rights-a7682111.html [accessed on December 27, 2017].

"Group to Seek U.S. Curbs on Regime in South Africa," *New York Times*, December 2, 1962.

Houser, George. Interview by Zachary Peterson. Session 3, Santa Rosa, CA, May 4, 2012

Houser, George. "Interview with George Houser." By Lisa Brock. July 19, 2004, *No Easy Victories*. Found at: http://www.noeasyvictories.org/interviews/int02_houser.php. [Accessed October 11, 2018.]

_____. *No One Can Stop the Rain: Glimpses of Africa's Liberation Struggle*. New York: The Pilgrim Press, 1989.

Houser, George and Bayard Rustin. "We Challenged Jim Crow!: A Report on the Journey of Reconciliation, April 9-23, 1947." Papers of the Congress of Racial Equality, 1941-1967, Series V, Departments and Related Correspondence, reel No. 25, No. 117.

Jack, Homer. "American Committee on Africa, 1953-55." Homer Jack Papers, DG-063, Series VI: organizational work, projects travel and interests, Box 14. Swarthmore College Peace Collections, Swarthmore, Pennsylvania.

Kaoma, Rev. Kapya. "The U.S. Christian Rights and the Attack on Gays in Africa." Found at: https://www.huffingtonpost.com/rev-kapya-kaoma/the-us-christian-right-an_b_387642.html [accessed on December 27, 2017].

Luthuli, Albert John. "Appeal for Action Against Apartheid," 1962. Found at: http://africanactivist.msu.edu/document_metadata.php?objectid=32-130-B73 [accessed on October 27, 2017].

Matebeni, Zethu, et al. *Breaking Out of the Box: Stories of Black Lesbians*, 2011. Found at: http://www.fortgreenefilmworks.com/projects_breaking-ouofthe-box.html [accessed on December 27, 2017].

Matabeni, Zethu, ed. *Reclaiming Afrikan: Queer Perspectives on Sexual and Gender Indentities*. Athlone, South Africa: Modjaji Books, 2014.

Meier, August, and Elliott M. Rudwick. *Core: A Study in the Civil Rights Movement, 1942-1968*. 1st edition. New York: Oxford University Press Inc., 1973.

Irene Morgan v. Commonwealth of Virginia, 328 U.S. 373 (1946).

Muholi, Zanele. *Inkanyiso*. Found at: https://inkanyiso.org/about/ [accessed on December 27, 2017].

Murray, Stephen O. and Will Roscoe, ed., *Boy-wives and Female Husbands: Studies of African Homosexualities*. New York: Palgrave, 1998.

Musangi, Neo. "In Time and Space II," June 2013. Found at: https://www.youtube.com/watch?v=ScVcSgEPV6U [accessed on December 27, 2017].

_____. "Transgender Day of Remembrance, Nairobi, Kenya," November 26, 2013.
Black|Queer|Feminist|Activist|Academic|Poet|Other. Found at: http://i-aint-a-poet.blogspot.com/2013/11/httpwwwiranti-orgcozacontentevents2013.html#more [accessed on December 27, 2017].

Muste, A.J. "Africa Against the Bomb [1960]." *The Essays of A.J. Muste.* New York: Bobbs-Merrill Co., 1967: 394-410.

Ndi, Bill F. "Quakers, Memory & the Past in Literature." in *Outward Evil, Inward Battle: Human Memory in Literature,* edited by Benjamin Hart Fishkin, Adaku T. Ankumah, Festus Fru Ndeh & Bill F. Ndi. Bamenda, Cameroon: Langaa Research and Publishing, 2013: 3-35.

_____. "Unwavering Insubordination: Rebellion and Memory in the Letters of Elizabeth Hooton." in *Outward Evil, Inward Battle: Human Memory in Literature,* edited by Benjamin Hart Fishkin, Adaku T. Ankumah, Festus Fru Ndeh & Bill F. Ndi. Bamenda, Cameroon: Langaa Research and Publishing, 2013: 89-108.

Nyanzi, Stella. "Queering Queer Africa." in *Reclaiming Afrikan: Queer Perspectives on Sexual and Gender Indentities.* Athlone, South Africa: Modjaji Books, 2014: 65-68.

O'Reilly, Kenneth. *Black Americans: The FBI File.* Edited by David Gallen. New York: Carroll & Graf Pub, 1994.

Peck, James. *Freedom Ride.* New York: Simon and Schuster, 1962.

Reed, Merl E. "The FBI, MOWM, and CORE, 1941-1946." *Journal of Black Studies* 21, no. 4 (1991): 465–79.

Rustin, Bayard. *I Must Resist: Bayard Rustin's Life in Letters.* Edited by Michael G. Long. San Francisco: City Lights Publishers, 2012.

Rustin, Bayard. "African Affairs—Sahara Protest Team, 1959." The Bayard Rustin Papers, reel 1, African Affairs—Sahara Protest Team, 1959, frames 0001-0049.

_____. "African Revolution [1958]." *Time on Two Crosses: The Collected Writings of Bayard Rustin*. Edited by Devon W. Carbado, and Donald Weise. 1st edition. San Francisco: Cleis Press, 2003: 306-13.

_____. "A Way Out: Solutions for South Africa [1983]." *Time on Two Crosses: The Collected Writings of Bayard Rustin*. Edited by Devon W. Carbado, and Donald Weise. 1st edition. San Francisco: Cleis Press, 2003: 350-52.

_____. "Brother to Brother: An Interview with Joseph Beam." *Time on Two Crosses: The Collected Writings of Bayard Rustin*. Edited by Devon W. Carbado, and Donald Weise. 1st edition. San Francisco: Cleis Press, 2003: 277-80.

_____. "From Montgomery to Stonewall [1986]." *Time on Two Crosses: The Collected Writings of Bayard Rustin*. Edited by Devon W. Carbado, and Donald Weise. 1st edition. San Francisco: Cleis Press, 2003: 272-74.

_____. "Letter to the Draft Board [1943]." *Time on Two Crosses: The Collected Writings of Bayard Rustin*. Edited by Devon W. Carbado, and Donald Weise. 1st edition. San Francisco: Cleis Press, 2003: 11-13.

_____. "Log of Journey of Reconciliation." Fellowship of Reconciliation Records, DG-013, Section II, Sub-Section D-Program Staff, Bayard Rustin, Box 51: Journey of Reconciliation, Swarthmore College Peace Collections, Swarthmore, Pennsylvania.

_____. "Montgomery Diary [1956]." *Time on Two Crosses: The Collected Writings of Bayard Rustin*. Edited by Devon W. Carbado, and Donald Weise. 1st edition. San Francisco: Cleis Press, 2003: 58-65.

_____. "Preamble to March on Washington [1963]," *Time on Two Crosses: The Collected Writings of Bayard Rustin*. Edited by Devon W. Carbado, and Donald Weise. 1st edition. San Francisco: Cleis Press, 2003: 112-15.

Rustin, Bayard. "Press Release, June 27, 1960." Bayard Rustin Papers, CDG-A, Bio Material, 1943-79. Swarthmore College Peace Collections, Swarthmore, Pennsylvania.

_____. "Social Democrats USA, 1980-84," The Bayard Rustin Papers, reel 17, frames 0497-0588.

_____. "The Failure of Black Separatism [1970]." *Time on Two Crosses: The Collected Writings of Bayard Rustin.* Edited by Devon W. Carbado, and Donald Weise. 1st edition. San Francisco: Cleis Press, 2003: 217-36.

_____. "The Importance of Gay Rights Legislation [1987]." *Time on Two Crosses: The Collected Writings of Bayard Rustin.* Edited by Devon W. Carbado, and Donald Weise. 1st edition. San Francisco: Cleis Press, 2003: 295-98.

_____. "The New 'Niggers' Are Gays [1986]." *Time on Two Crosses: The Collected Writings of Bayard Rustin.* Edited by Devon W. Carbado, and Donald Weise. 1st edition. San Francisco: Cleis Press, 2003: 275-76.

_____. "Trip to Africa (Gold Coast/Ghana), 1952." Fellowship of Reconciliation Papers DG-013, Section II, Series D-Program Staff, 1941-1984, Box 52. Swarthmore College Peace Collections, Swarthmore, Pennsylvania.

_____. "Twenty-Two Days on a Chain Gang [1949]." *Time on Two Crosses: The Collected Writings of Bayard Rustin.* Edited by Devon W. Carbado, and Donald Weise. 1st edition. San Francisco: Cleis Press, 2003: 31-57.

Sutherland, Bill. "Biographical Sketch, Southern Africa Representative, American Friends Service Committee." Found at: http://africanactivist.msu.edu/document_metadata.php?objecti d=32-130-16BA [Accessed on December 11, 2017].

_____. "Interview with Bill Sutherland." By Prexy Nesbitt and Mimi Edmunds, July 19, 2003. Found at: http://www.noeasyvictories.org/interviews/int01_sutherland.p hp. [Accessed December 11, 2017].

Tamale, Sylvia. "Homosexuality is not un-African," April 26, 2014, *Aljazeera America.* Found at:

http://america.aljazeera.com/opinions/2014/4/homosexuality-africamuseveniugandanigeriaethiopia.html   [accessed   on December 27, 2017].

Chapter 3

Women, Dependence, Independence, and Land Usage in The Cameroons: An Ecofeminist Reading of Bole Butake's *Lake God* and *And Palm Wine Will Flow*

Elisabeth N.M Ayuk-Etang
University of Buea

Introduction

FAO 2014; UN Women Watch 2009; GGCA 2009; and Warren 1997 have identified women from developing countries as the backbone of their economy and key players of household sustainability. Globally, the women provide up to 90 % of food and produce 60-80% of the food in their societies for the sustainability of their economy (JOTO Africa 1, Warren 8). Women from the Cameroons constitute part of this category of women who are active in subsistence farming, and their contribution to agriculture (ploughing, planting, and caring for livestock, harvesting, weeding, processing and the storing of crops) has been remarked by the First World Development Policies and Practices (FWDPP) (Warren 8). The women's engagement in farming is, first and foremost, to fulfill their distinct and independent reproductive roles as mothers, nurturers, caregivers and food providers. Their dependence on land, plants, and forest and field products is inextricably connected to independent rural and household economies, which fall within the scope of household gender division of labor i.e. cooking, cleaning, and gardening. To manage and exercise these responsibilities fully and with a sense of independence, owning land is paramount.

Women's dependence on and/or access to land, to land rights, and to land ownership is essential for a freedom society. This topical process for attaining autonomy has raised a lot of concerns in and around the world in general and in the Cameroons in particular; to be precise in the Southern Cameroons (Fonjong 25, Ngassa 43, Njoh et al, 72). From a purely Afrocentric cultural perspective, land belongs to the forebears (ancestors), the living and the unborn. Associating land to these categories of persons, assumes that it is a cultural asset that should be managed by the custodians. Thus, men and women are both custodians of the land in The Cameroons but there is a gender disparity in land allocation (Njoh et al 117) and with such disparity, researchers face challenges as to "how to cope with fragmentary information (Kilson qtd. In *Journal of Religion in Africa* 133). However, the rural woman's interest is not on economic valued land, but on used value. This is in relation to her reproductive role that compels her as nurturer and sustainer of humanity. In most Cameroonian communities there are gender divisions of roles on land usage. Women use land for subsistence farming which is considered "female crop' for immediate family consumption" while cash crops are considered 'male crop' (Fonjong 26). Men and women also "perform different gender roles which are socially/culturally determined" (Ibid 25). Also, men do the clearing of farmlands while women do the tilling, planting, and weeding. During this process, there is an interconnection between the woman and nature whereby the notion of fertility is transferred from the woman to the land. This connection that a woman has with the land is interpreted in ecofeminist discourse as a spiritual connection. Ecofeminists argue that a woman is physically and spiritually linked, and closer to nature than men (Warren 30). This is substantiated by her attachment to land and other elements of nature. Annette Kolodny, and other critics associate the woman's closeness to nature as inferior and non-assertive (1968). However, Cameroonian rural women are farming people. A position that is inferior to none because it keeps their community alive as exhibited in *Lake God* and *And Palm Wine will Flow*. So, whether closer to nature or not, as custodians of the land, women should be given equal access to land usage as men in the Cameroons. Equality in land rights is a critical element in women's economic empowerment, but women most often only have use rights (Fonjong 23 – 24); which have been denied in the world of Butake's plays. The aim of this study is to demonstrate that the Cameroonian rural woman depends on the land for a sustainable livelihood for her family and her community. Land is a source of sustainable livelihood through the woman/nature connection. So "endowing women with land will empower them economically as well as strengthen their ability to challenge social and political gender inequalities (Fonjong 24) Nevertheless, the man has always undermined the woman in land policies and practices. Power dynamics puts the man at the center of woman and nature's marginalization/destruction. Bole Butake articulates the discontented voice of the women on land discrimination in *Lake God* and *And Palm Wine will Flow*.

These plays are a mimicry of the Cameroonian society from which he emanates. The Cameroons constitute a bilingual country with two official languages, as a result of its colonial heritage of the British and the French. After the Second World War, with the defeat of Germany, the country was partitioned into The Northern and Southern Cameroons. The Northern part was governed by the French and the Southern part governed by the British. In the wake of their departure, a plebiscite was organized that brought the two Cameroons together. Since then, there have been many schools of thought that condemn this reunion as a marriage of convenience. This is because the former Southern Cameroonians feel that they are not fairly treated in this reunion, due to their minority status. As a result, Cameroonians of English expression started expressing their grievances through their writings. Examples of such writings include: "If an Anglophone Must Die", *The Dance of the Vampires, Beast of No Nation, The Most Cruel Death of the Talkative Zombie, Across the Mongolo, Death Certificate* and more. So, many Cameroonian writers, such as Bate Bissong, Bole Butake, Victor Elame Musinga, Ba'Bila Mutia, Fale Wache, Asong Linus, Nol Alembong, Francis B. Nyamnjoh Peter W. Vakunta, Bungashu Tanla Kishani, Bill F. Ndi, Tatah Mentan, Victor Epie Ngome, Joyce Ashutantang, John Nkemgong Nkengasong, and Emmanuel Fru Doh, have written extensively to address the Southern Cameroons problem in the Cameroons.

However, some critics like Emmanuel Fru Doh, Shadrack Ambanasom, Nol Alembong, Fai Donatus, Mbu Tennu Mbuh,

Victor Ngomia, have interpreted Butake's plays from the context of Anglophone Cameroon Literature. Even though Emmanuel Fru Doh in his critique cursorily mentions, "...the traditional earth goddess from Butake's Noni traditional pantheon," (34) none of these critics, to my knowledge, has addressed the woman's connectivity to land and her denial in decision making on her right to land usage. From an ecofeminist lens, this paper focuses on women's access to farming land, their physical and spiritual connection to nature and their invocation of the goddess of the land and sea when denied access to farming land in the governance of their community. These women's spiritual connection to the land and their environment is better understood from Starhawk's earth-based spirituality. Earth-based spirituality, otherwise known as eco-spirituality, sees the Earth/Nature as sacred, where immanence replaces transcendence to reiterate Judith Plant (Healing the Wounds 113). Earth-based spirituality, Starhawk contends, "is rooted in three basic concepts [...] immanence, interconnection, and community (113). To her, "immanence – names our primary understanding that the Earth is alive, part of a living cosmos" (113). She explains that spirits, sacred goddesses and gods are embodiments of the world. They are the world. They are in us. She further reiterates that "Our deepest experiences are experiences of connection with the Earth and with the world" (113). The woman's connection to nature is seemingly the strength of the Ewawa women in reclaiming their space. The study therefore respects the different strands of Ecofeminism, which Karren Warren in her 1997 *Women, Culture and Nature* considers an umbrella term for a wide variety of perspectives.

In *Lake God* and *And Palm Wine Will Flow* Butake laments the deviation of such villages as Ewawa community from the positive cultural norms that used to inform its people. Emmanuel Fru Doh, in his *Anglophone Cameroon Literature: An Introduction*, highlights Butake's leitmotif in writing these plays. Writing especially about *And Palm Wine Will Flow*, he says, "it becomes obvious that by the time Bole Butake wrote *And Palm Wine Will Flow*, he was already disgusted with sham of a system in which he found himself" (87). Ewawa is a community in which gender role stereotypes have inhibited the voice of the female gender. These women are filled with words and voices; they do not despise men but complement each other. It is, as Emmanuel Fru Doh would have it, a society which no longer "has a system nor a vision as chaos reigns supreme instead" (88). Several calamities befall the land as the rulers succumb to greed and avarice while eroding the culture and devastating the land. Those who benefit from these malpractices sing the praises of the monarch while others stay quiet for fear of being chastised. "Corruption, in a nutshell, the norm in Ewawa. The fon rule by decrees instead of consulting with the council of elders and has consequently succeeded in flinging the citizens at each other's throats. This is the case when he seizes the farmland of one family and presents it to another" (Emmanuel Fru Doh 88). In the plays under study, women, who have been hitherto isolated from land governance have to take the lead role in uprooting the evil that is consuming the land restore harmony. This "saving power of the women" is what has encouraged an eco-feminist reading of the plays.

Lake God and *And Palm wine will Flow* capture the rise of a patriarchal religion and gender hierarchies that project immanent divinity. These conundrums have adverse effects on both women and the environment as elucidated in the plays. The chapter is articulated into three sections. The first looks at the ecosystem and culture of the different communities in the plays, the second section focuses on the woman in the eco-cultural space, and the third dwells on the woman as revolutionary transformer.

The Ecosystems and Culture

The relationship between the environment and culture constitutes an integral part of Butake's plays. "The ecosystem is based on the interaction between the living community and its environment" (Gerhard Helmut Schwabe Plön 213). The environment of the living communities in Butake's plays are characterized by mountainous landscape, the lake or inland waters, the groves and palm bushes. The cold and mountainous landscape of the grassland setting of the communities in *Lake God* and *And Palm*

Wine Will Flow influences the farming and grazing culture of the people.

This environment is structured into natural gender order, with the women engagement in subsistence farming while the men own the palm bushes. The palm bushes are seemingly a more superior space owned by the men because of their gender roles. From this bush come produce such as palm wine, palm nuts, coconuts, palm oil and more. These produce are cash crops (male crops) which can also be exported to enrich the man. Besides, palm wine is a symbolic drink that is shared in cultural ceremonies as well as a drink that men use during their evening gatherings. Palm wine, here, represents communality. In *And Palm Wine Will Flow*, Lagham and his friends comfort their hungry stomachs (when starved by their wives) with palm wine while they discuss solutions to significant problems in the land. The source of the palm wine (palm bushes) and the sacred grooves belong to the men and the fondom, and can never be a site of dispute with grazers.

The lake and inland waters in limnology, "is well suited as models of ecosystems" (Schwabe 214). In "The Lake as Ecosystem", Schwabe holds that the lake has its own "peculiar living community depending on physical and chemical conditions, and yet exhibiting change, diversity…and a highly complex domain of interaction" (215). The lake harbors both living and nonliving objects. From the religious background of Butake's plays, the lake is an abode for the sea goddesses known, in some circles, as Mammy Wata. "Mammy Wata is acknowledged and worshiped in myriad ways from Liberia, Nigeria, Cameroon and Congo extending to the former slave trade destinations of Cuba, Brazil and Suriname" (Friedli 84). The role of the lake gods/goddesses cannot be underestimated in Butake's *Lake God*. These 'water harbor spirits,' strengthen the woman's spiritual connection with nature. They are an embodiment of fertility to both the woman and the land as evident in Flora Nwapa's *Efuru* and Buchi Emecheta's *The Joys of Motherhood*. Butake employs the role of the sea goddess to resolve the infertility problem of both the queen and the land in the world of his play, *Lake God*. Rituals to pacify the lake goddess, and purify the land from infertility are expected by the women for a better harvest. The Fon i.e. the King, entrenched in his new religion, ignores the women's call. The resulting effect is outrageous. The intrigue arises when the fon and his cohort shift` away from the status quo and imbibe foreign traditions to the detriment of their people.

Again, in *Lake God*, the Fon admires foreign cultural practices to the detriment of his traditional beliefs. He tells Father Leo 'We will never catch-up with Europe, Father. We will never catch-up. Thank God you came. Praise be to Jesus who sent out his disciples to convert the heathen' (10). He believes his people are still backward. When they confront him for not offering sacrifices to the Lake God, he tells them 'Enough! Are you accusing me? Your Fon? Did you expect me, a Christian Fon, to sit back and watch a handful of senile fanatics perpetuating the barbaric and heathen customs of human sacrifice?' (16). He goes as far as imprisoning the 'Kwifon', the people's most dreaded masquerade. This is ironic because, as the Fon of the land, it is his duty to uphold traditional values. He is rather a puppet of the white priest Father Leo, and this creates confusion and upheaval which later lead to his demise. Father Leo's view on Ewawa traditional practices and religion is fetish and polytheist. In the early scenes of the play, the Fon in line with Father Leo's teachings considers this veneration as idol worship. He reprimands the women who ululate in front of him:

> How many times must I tell you that this is a Christian kingdom? How often must I drive it into your heads that the heathen era of idol worship is history? How many times must I decree that the age of savagery and jungle law is over and done with in this land? How many? How many? How many? (To guards) Release that man at once! Undo those shackles of my disgrace right now. (14)

It is ironical that the Fon, a traditional leader, is ignorant about his traditional values, and rejects them as idol worship. African traditional religion, though considered fetish by worldview, does not reject God. This is evident in the Ashanti culture of Ghana, the Bamileke culture of The Cameroons, the Yoruba and Ibo cultures of

Nigeria. Also, the women's grazer conflict is considered savagery by the "modern" Fon. The women use the land for subsistence farming to fulfil their primary role as life/care givers. In *Ecofeminism Women and Culture*, Karen Warren sees African women as very energetic in the socio-cultural and economic development of their community through subsistence farming (8). Maria Mies and Vandana Shiva consider the woman-land relationship through subsistence farming as a major tool for sustainable development (6). In "The Need for a New Vision: The Subsistence Perspective," Mies believes in a "new life for present and future generations, and for our fellow creatures on earth" (297). This new vision has to do with reaping the fruit of development, the need for ecological awareness, non-exploitative tendencies of the environment, self-sustaining society and non-patriarchal propensity. Mies considers this vision to be a subsistence perspective or the survival perspective (297).

The Ewawa women's farming vision is authentic, according to Mies. Emmanuel Fru Doh shares a similar opinion when he writes that, "Butake's characters are true to life and succeed in exposing the ideas and conflicts the playwright sets out to highlight and criticize" (89). Their complaint of Dewa's encroachment on their farmlands is simply to reclaim their space. Nkfusai, one of the women leaders tells the Fon 'All the women who have farms in Ngangba will starve this year. Dewa's cattle have ruined all the corn' (15). The women lament so much because these lands are what they depend on to grow crops for family/community sustenance. Looking at the role of women in the *Lake God* and *And Palm Wine Will Flow*, Emmanuel Fru Doh emphasizes the aggressive nature of the women, showing how "even before the Kibaranko executes the final and highest penalty on the fon… the women had already tried and condemned the fon" (89).

The Woman Land Relationship

Eco-feminists reiterate that capitalism, and its intrinsic need for exploitation and devastation in the wealth creation process, is the cause of problems that affect both humanity and the natural environment. Worthy of note is the fact that the man is at the center of the woman and nature connection. Though the man exhibits a patriarchal strength, the Cameroonian woman does not seek equality here but she asks to be given an opportunity to achieve her desires. Charles Fonchingong in "Negotiating Livelihood Beyond Beijing," using The Cameroons as a point of reference, confirms that "women running households complained of lack of access to productive resources, especially land, which is vital for the acquisition of credit for start-up capital and expansion" (251). Fonchingong's observation is very pertinent in black communities where the woman's role in sustainable development is relevant, but her access to productive resources is limited. If given the opportunity to own land and her own seeds, her sustainability project will flourish in leaps and bounds. In *Lake God* and *And Palm Wine will Flow*, there are clear demarcations of the land for different purposes. There is the sacred groove where the chief priest goes to venerate and appease the gods, the palm wine grooves where they get wine for entertainment, the farmlands where they harvest crops, and the grazing lands on which the cattle feed. The communities flourish because all parties respect these natural arrangements. Unfortunately, Butake's dramatic world "is a society with only a few sane people..." (Doh 88). The leaders are avaricious, the grazers are reckless and allow their cattle to destroy farmlands while the Fon, "custodian of the village's culture," remains taciturn being a cattle owner himself. Also, the attempt to unseat the chief priest and take over the sacred grooves brings the calamity on the ruler. This calamity is brought upon the ruler because women are, according to Ngugi in *Something Torn and New: An African Renaissance*, "Dismembered from the land, from labor, from power, and from memory, the result is destruction of the base from which people [women] launch themselves into the world" (wa Thiong'o 28). Also, to Vandana Shiva, the fact that women are capable of producing wealth through a partnership with nature gives them an upper hand in deciding what is good for the environment. However, it is important to find out what the connection between woman and nature is. Ecofeminists have identified eight connections: the first is the historical. Karen Warren and a host of other ecofeminists assume that the earth and woman share the same history of oppression and maternity. That is why the earth is referred to as mother earth. Thus, the domination of the earth has links with the domination of woman. The symbolic connection is linked to earth-based spirituality as stated by Wohlpart who asserts that there is a connection between the spiritual and the physical landscapes (172). This connection seems to be explored in Butake's women who delve into spiritual landscapes to save the physical landscapes with which the women connect. It is in line with this connection that Charlene Spretnak has explored the symbolic association and devaluation of women and nature that appears in religion, theology, art, and literature. Documenting such connections and making them integral to the project of ecofeminism is often heralded as ecofeminism's most promising contribution to the creation of liberating, life-affirming, and post patriarchal worldviews and earth-based spiritualities or theologies. Ecofeminism is then presented as offering alternative spiritual symbols. These spiritual symbols are those of the goddess that Butake employs to show the strength of the Ewawa women in particular and that of the African woman in general. Emmanuel Fru Doh must have had this in mind when he asserts this instance to be "Butake's subtle assertion about African women in African society [which] seems to deny a long standing opinion of African women as passive" (89).

Ecofeminists blame binaries of opposition as the reason for the marginalization of women and the environment which is evident in Butake's *And Palm Wine Will Flow*. Like Shiva, Butake insists that women should have a voice in deciding what happens to the land. This explains why Kwengong, Shey Ngong's wife, joins him in the mission to salvage the land. They would get rid of the Fon who has desecrated the land. She tells the Fon;

> ...Die and deliver the land from the
> Abominations of drunkenness and gluttony!
> (The Fon begins to reel until he collapses.)
> Die! Chila Kitansi, die!
> And save the land from merry-making!
> Die, Fon! So that we may think!
> The people need your death to think!

Die! Die! Die! (110)

Kwengong and the other women come together at the twin-streams, stark naked and perform rituals which culminate to the liberation of the land. Once the Fon and his collaborators have been ousted, the people can get their lands back. The women have a particular attachment to the land because it is their source of nourishment. They have a right to resist negative phallocentric actions such as uncontrolled grazing devastates the land. To the Fon, the women ought to be pleased that the cattle are in the land because cattle rearing constitutes an economic sustainability and development scheme. However, the fact that this grazing is unchecked, with cattle wandering into farmlands and destroying crops creates a polemic. In an agrarian community, where people depend solely on subsistence agriculture, grazing practices must be checked. The abuses of the land come from a disregard to cultural values which for the women must be restored. Ma Kusham lays emphasis on this as she avers that:

> These are things of the land. Things of our gods and our ancestors which the white man has fooled us to abandon. Things of the white man have brought suffering to the land. (She dips her hand into the pot and takes out broom-sticks of equal length which she proceeds to distribute to all the women). These broom-sticks have been cooked in the most potent medicines and herbs in the land. However, the most important ingredient as far as our oath is concerned comes from the sacred pot of the lake god which Shey Bo-Nyo guards jealously. The link is simple. There is no Queen in the palace and the Fon has refused to lead the people in sacrifice to the god of fertility. (25)

Rites of fortification are performed to rid the land off the suffering and taboo brought about by the western ways of the fon. These rituals transmit some spiritual transformation which Reine Eisler in "The Gaia Tradition and Partnership Future: An Ecofeminist Manifesto" considers as the woman's spiritual connection to the goddesses. The women's connectivity to the land/nature remains an asset. Their spiritual and physical connectivity to the goddesses, ancestors and the land is strength in reclaiming their space. These women have proven as Emmanuel Fru Doh asserts that "these women are not unnecessarily vociferous but would come out if need be" (89). Their action culminated to an inexplicable destruction that even Shey Bo Nyo, the Chief Priest could not reverse. The women's application of the above rites works well for the reclamation and sustainability of their land. An action which Vandana Shiva in "Development and Western Patriarchy" considers to be a liberation from 'development' and the grip of colonialism. Maria Mies, on her part, sees the women's resistance to the men as a vision of "survival perspectives" (6) It is the result of "power drunkenness, corruption, near total debauchery... [that] amount to the trouble with Ewawa..." (Doh 34).

The Woman as Revolutionist and Transformist

For their liberation and survival, the Ewawa women in Butake's plays are resilient to tyranny through pacifist means that undermine the status quo. In *Lake God*, and *And Palm Wine Will Flow*, the women envisage the fall of the clan because of the fon is infatuated with western Christian values and power. Father Leo in *Lake God* is essentially the de facto ruler because of the way in which the Fon fawns over him. Emmanuel Fru Doh examining the setting of both plays draws attention to the fact Father Leo is "around to cause confusion" (89) and further suggests the possibility of Butake "preaching the total return of our mores" (89).

The women insist that there is no Queen in the palace because Angela, the Fon's wife, is not a daughter of the soil and is also unable to bare children, as a result, she cannot perform the expected rituals. It is assumed that, without a queen, fertility rites cannot be performed to bring bounty to the land. The people beseech the Fon to lead them in sacrifice to the Lake God and consummate their "love and kinship by sharing the royal bed with the Queen. And we shall have more children and a good harvest" (17).

The women therefore not only stand up to tyranny by refusing to feed their men and satisfy their sexual urges, they also refuse to sell to Angela, the Fon's wife who is miffed by the insult and takes it out on her husband. Ironically, she is the one that exposes the incompetence of her husband through their private conversations. She mocks his impotence and even suggests that he take another wife. Angela is astute and knows that the women have a right. She tells her husband that the villagers do not need an enlightened ruler. To her, no "graffi man ever had only one wife" (35). It is therefore Father Leo who has caused the Fon to refrain from taking other wives. Coming from the Fon's own wife, this is biting criticism because, although she is the one who is privileged by the Fon, she actually believes that some of their problems could be resolved if he conforms to the wishes of the people. She tells him 'They want you to marry one of their kind and make heirs to the throne. I have told you to go ahead and marry as many as you want... I know you want children. I know you want to marry another woman, their queen' (35). She is also critical of Father Leo, before whom her husband grovels. All this goes to show that women have foresight and, even at their worst, they can better understand issues than men. She believes her husband should do what is right, to make the people happy.

The women's revolution takes the men by surprised because the men had become complacent about the machinations of the Fon. Their attempt to stand up to tyranny is effectual because it is a unified action. They refuse to cook for their men, refuse to sleep with them and stand up to the men when they attempt to beat them into submission. Father Leo, in his arrogant fashion, waves off the Fon's concerns about the women's uprising. In his chauvinist fashion, the priest delivers a sermon which he thinks will intimidate the women:

> Dear sisters and daughters in Christ, I want to talk to you this morning about the recent events of the last few days in this village. The Fon, your Fon, has told me that there is a group of five rebellious women in this village who are leading the rest of you astray. They are pulling you away from the steep and narrow road that leads directly to hell, where Satan reigns supreme, and where you will burn in everlasting fire. Yensi, Kimaa and the other devils; yes, they must be called by the

names they deserve... you are not ashamed that you went to soil the Virgin Mother's name in Satan's play? You were in Fibuen, participating in Satan's play and eating of his food and taking oaths... I received a little money from my country, I give it to your Fon who invests it in the purchase of cattle. That is how we have been able to move mountains. (32)

The intimidation tactic is obvious and the demonizing of the strike leaders is an attempt to scare the Christian women into submission. Finally, the agenda of the priest as an entrepreneur is made manifest. He is the one who actually owns all the cattle that wreaks havoc in the land. Innovation is good, but not when it comes at the detriment of the land a starving cross section of the population. The uprising comes about because the cattle grazers allow the animals to plunder the crops that sustain the people. As a capitalist, Father Leo is only interested in the profit he makes from the sale of the cows, and not in the welfare of the people as he pretends to. The Fon is just a tool that he uses to accomplish his mission but the women are there "to deal a final blow to the Fon's authority" (Doh 89).

In *Lake God*, the women make a valiant effort to defend the land against tyranny. They use the most potent potion women can use traditionally for a curse. Butake spells this out in no uncertain terms: "the savory juice from their vaginas of those upon whom you wield power" (48). Unfortunately, things had gone out of hand and their attempt seems a little late. The land is annihilated. The only survivors include Shey Bo-Nyo, a boy and a girl, a woman and a man, who had slept out of the village on the fateful night. There is hope in a new beginning as there seems to be room for mentorship and cultural sustainability indicated by the different generations. *And Palm-Wine Will Flow* showcases a society in which the efforts of the women are met with success and that leads to a restoration of the values of the land. The ruler of Ewawa is corrupt and greedy and sells titles and favors for food and palm wine. At the opening of the play, Shey Ngong, the Chief Priest of Nyombom is the only one who seems concerned about the state of affairs. As people hurry to the palace because palm wine is flowing, he seeks refuge in the sacred groove where he prays to the ancestors. This is seen as dissention especially as warned by a messenger, the chief priest avers that "a gorilla can do nothing to the iroko tree" (88). The king's messenger sees this as open rebellion and Shey Ngong later loses his farmlands to Kibanya as punishment for his insubordination to the Lion of Ewawa.

In *Lake God* the Fon's and his cohorts' decision to not redress the land issue leaves the women disappointed and discontented. Consequently, like the peculiarly resistant oppressed would do when once pushed to the wall (Cheo 27) the 'Fibeun' - their secret society is invoked. At the women's gathering, Yensi declares the revolution in the following words:

> I lack the words with which to express my joy. The happiness that is in my heart cannot be shown on my face. The happenings of today have shown that, in spite of what some people say, the ways of the land are alive. We must be one person to succeed in our present undertaking. We must be one woman. Some here have only recently been given into marriage. Their bellies are hot. There are others who cannot control their emotions of love and sympathy. There are still others who will easily succumb to threats and the fear of being beaten. You all know where we have built the sanctuary of the Fibeun. We have taken it away from that place which I don't want to call by name. The sanctuary is the refuge for those without a heart. Go there if you cannot look your man in the face and tell him to go and eat shit. (24)

The above excerpt is a declaration of war by the women in the community who feel it is time for them to take action and reclaim the land. Yensi is the designated leader who expresses joy that the women have responded quickly to the summons. The message is simple; it is time to reinstate the values of the land. This will only be achieved through sexual deprivation of the men as other subtler methods seem to have proven ineffective. At this point, it is evident that, what the women seek to utilize is what Chiwezie refers to as the power of the anatomy. Here, there is an echo of Aristophanes' *Lysistrata* in which women have to starve men of their needs in order to achieve peace in the land.

Butake's women, in both plays, are revolutionists and transformists of the society. These women are reliable and troubleshooters in times of crises for the stability and sustainability of their family/community. In *And Palm Wine will Flow*, the women, led by Kwengong, dethrone the chief and restore stability to the land. Kwengong is the channel through whom the Earth goddess incarnates and issues a warning of the calamities that befall the land. Although the Fon escapes the devastation of Kibaranko, the dreaded masquerade, he is ruined by "the wrath of the women" (108). After reincarnating earth goddess, Kwengong has an aura that is recognized by the women leaders who delegate her to carry the curse to the palace. This curse is uniquely feminine:

> When I got to the twin-streams, there was a large gathering of women, mostly the elderly ones. They were all naked, stark naked. It seemed that they had been performing some rites. Upon my arrival, they raised a great shout and one of them placed a pot full of some potion on my head. Go to the Fon! Go to the palace! They shouted. And make him drink. (109)

In most African cultures, the curse of a woman is potent. The nakedness of an elderly woman is a curse and for these women to come together to mete this jinx on anybody, he must really be reprehensible. The Fon, because of avarice has brought ruin to the land and himself. Kwengong is the emissary empowered spiritually with the task of delivering the curse. The women's spiritual connection with the goddess is hereby demonstrated

In *And Palm Wine Will Flow*, Shey Ngong, the seer is the only person who understands the power of the goddesses. This is seen through Ngong's reincarnation of the earth goddess when things go awry in the community while the ruler and his allies denigrate the gods and abuse the chief priest. This reincarnation sends a surge of power throughout the land, first with the empowerment of Kibaranko, the dreaded masquerade and then, the women's cult that

70

finally curses the ruler. An investigation of the self and other dualisms along with the innate power and domination ethics is seen as another framework of eco-feminism which Butake invokes with the incarnation of the earth goddess. Thus, ecofeminism is then presented as offering alternative spiritual symbols. These spiritual symbols are those of the goddess that Butake employs to show the strength of the Ewawa women.

Butake uses his artistic muse in his plays to fictionalize an historical event in the North West Regions of The Cameroons where the women's cult was established during the farmer's/grazer's conflict. Again, the critic, Emmanuel Fru Doh suggests, "the influence of Bamenda grassfield culture here is paramount" (89). Indigenous female institutions were common in the Bamenda Grassfields as part and parcel of traditional administration. The *Ndugumfumbui* of Wum, *Anlu* of Kom, *Takumbeng* of the Ngemba chiefdoms, *Ufarp* of Esu and *Fumbuen* of Kedjom Keku (Big Babanki) were some examples (qtd. in Susan Diduk 340). In these areas, they used women power and coercive measures in resolving farmer-grazer and other conflicts. Through public singing, verbal insults, dancing, demonstrations, physical confrontations and sit down strikes, they attempted to get the offending parties to change. They refused to tolerate any attempts that destroyed their farmland and endangered the livelihood of their families. This is very similar to the struggles of women in other parts of Africa who fought against exclusion from state resources, inequality of access, neglect and outright oppression. To further attract attention to their plight, the women took three draconian measures, namely that they would not sell food in the market again; that they would not go to church any longer, and that they would stage a match to Bamenda. They took upon themselves to enforce the boycotts by stopping any person who was going to sell food in the market.

Women's cults are extremely potent and feared in the grasslands of The Cameroons and most African cultures. Such cults only come out occasionally especially when there is dire need to protect the land or a notable. Emmanuel Fru Doh brings to mind, through his critic, that "Fibuen in *Lake God* had been dormant for 8 years, the

Takenbeng in the Grassfields had been quiet for generations or decades at least as only oral history could justify the existence and potency of such a lodge" (89). Whenever this women's cult plans a public appearance, men run and hide least they are cursed accidentally. Kwengong becomes fearless when she is given this mission, she recounts:

> I walked straight into the inner court. Of course, the whole place was deserted. Not a single body around. When I opened my mouth to speak, I could not recognize [sic] my own voice... ChilaKintasi! ChilaKintasi! Come out and receive the wares the women over whom you wield great power have sent you! Come out, I say, and receive the goods sent by those you dishonor [sic] so... Earth-goddess needs no one's leave to walk where her feet will, ChilaKintasi. (109).

From the moment the women got naked to prepare the spell in the stream, it becomes evident that the Fon is doomed. This realization is emphatically made when Kwengong calls the Fon by his name. This is the singular slur the Fon receives because he should be addressed by his office, thus, dishonor and defiance to his person and office. To execute the earth-goddess' instructions, Kwengong is transformed spiritually into an extraordinary human being with a sense of boldness. She confronted the palace with dexterity and a revolution is ascertained. "...the earth-goddess needs no one's leave to walk where her feet will (109).

In *And Palm-Wine Will Flow*, the women kill the Fon without mercy to substantiate the irreparability of the Fon's nefarious acts and insidious nature. Unlike in *Lake God* where deprivation from sex is meant to force the complacent men into action, in *And Palm Wine Will Flow*, this same craved for organ, is the source of the worst curse possible. *The* jinx used on the Fon is "the savoury [sic] juice from [their] vaginas" (110). Evidence of the women's cult is also present in *Shoes and Four Men in Arms* to end the excesses of the military. This is because they are tired with the atmosphere of brutality, looting and rape that the troops bring to their community.

The Fon in *And Palm Wine Will Flow* fails to realize the potency of the curse and challenges the women when he says "I will rather die"/ I will die first (110). He is told that "your own mouth pronounced judgment. Die and deliver the land from the abomination of drunkenness and gluttony" (110). This Fon's dilemma can be likened to that of the Fon of Nso. Nso women mobilized themselves and took siege of their fon's palace in 1979. According to Miriam Goheen—quoted in Susan Diduk—who witnessed it:

> … during my first week or two in Nso, I was startled in my trek down the steep hill to the Fon's Palace by a group of about twenty women running down the main road to the palace. Naked to the waist, faces painted white, with long sticks in one hand and hoes in the other and leaves tied around their necks draped down their chests… (341).

The appearance of semi-nude women painted white suggests ritual activity, and the presence of long sticks, hoes and other leaves shows their concern to be agricultural. This eyewitness report, as far back as 1979, evinces that women intervention in traditional politics in land usage as well as farmers-grazers' conflict is a long standing tradition, which could have served as inspiration to Butake. He is not alone in these observations as Lena A. Ampadu sees women as courageous freedom fighters dressed in fatigues with runny-nosed babies on their backs, and yet with a determination of their own (5). The women's determination in *Lake God* and *And Palm Wine Will Flow* brings in a complete revolution and transformation in the world of the plays; the Fon is ousted from power.

After getting rid of the Fon and his covetous cohorts, Kwengong as the spokesperson of the new custodians attack the very source of their difficulties by making sure that dictatorship never recurs. "No more Fons in the land!" (113). The fact that her husband, Shey Ngong was the candidate to take up the position does not sway her. What the women want is a council that rules with the consent of the people. Important issues must be decided in the marketplace by the people with Shey Ngong as the leader of the council of elders. This is baffling even to Shey Ngong. He has to go with the will of the people. Butake's women are known to be transformist. This is also reminiscent to *The Survivors* and *Shoes and Four Men in Arms*, in which the women bring revolution and transformation. Mboysi is fed-up with the cat and mouse games the Officer plays on the survivors. She attempts to get the others to resist the tyranny to no avail. Then she takes matters into her hands at the end of the day by seducing him, getting his gun, and ultimately killing him. Although she pays with her life she does so happily because "the elephant has fallen" (84) and the people can celebrate their liberation.

Conclusion

This chapter set out to examine the role of women in nature conservation and sustenance vis-a-vis land ownership and usage in a bid to advocate more rights to land ownership. Using the ecofeminist perspective from an Afrocentric standpoint, it shows the proximity between the woman, on the one hand and land /nature on the other hand. From the contentions raised in the plays under study, it is clear that women have a closer connection to nature than other members of the community. This seems to account for their obdurate stance when it comes to keeping their lands marking their dependence on land for their total independence, thus living (in)dependence. If women can go to all lengths including, but not limited to, using the power of anatomy to preserve the traditional and cultural norms, so as to cater for their families and society, it stands to reason that they are the custodians of lands and should be associated with land governance, in order to fulfil their reproductive role. In *Lake God* and *And Palm Wine will flow*, the women's interest is not on value land for building houses or more, but for economic land (farming land). The women's dependency on the land makes them independent in household sustainability. As farming people, they are physically and spiritually linked to the land in ways that men are not. Physically, through their fecundity, and spiritually through the goddesses as exhibited in the plays. Even if the man is always at the center of the woman/nature relationship, and the Fon and his regiment in both plays try to pull women down. This underestimates the wrath of an angry woman and brings doom to the leaders of the land. Thus, only a woman's dependence on land and her independence to produce and reproduce can rescue the land and render it fertile.

Work Cited

Aguilar, Lorena. *Training Manual on Gender and Climate Change*. GGCa, 2009.

Alobwed'Epie. *The Death Certificate*. Editions CLE, 2004.

Ampadu, Lena M. "Black Women as Dynamic Agents of Change: Empowering Women FromAfrica to America." *Forum on Public Policy*, 2006. Pp 1-14

Besong, Bate. *Beasts of No Nation*. Nooremac, 1991.

___. *The Most Cruel Death of the Talkative Zombie*. Nooremac, 1986.

Butake, Bole. *Lake God and Other Plays*. Editions CLE, 1999.

Cheo, Francis T. "A Mirror of Convergence: Association and Racism in Anglophone Cameroon Literature". *African Cultures and Literatures,* edited by Gordon Collier, Brill Books, 2012, pp. 20-34.

Diduk, Susan. "Women's Agricultural Production and Political Action in Cameroon Grassfields." *Journal of the International African Institute*, vol. 59, no. 3, 1989, p. 341.

Doh, Emmanuel Fru. *Anglophone Cameroon Literature: An Introduction*. Lexington, 2015.

Food and Agricultural Organisations. "The State of Food and Agriculture: Innovation in Family Farming" *FAO* Rome, *2014*.

Fonjong, L. Lawrence, and Irene Sama-Lang. "The Paradox of Gender Discrimination in Land Ownership and Women's Contribution to Poverty Reduction in Anglophone Cameroon." *Geo Journal* vol. 78, no. 3, 2013, pp 575 - 589

Fonjong, Lotsmart. "Women's Land Rights and Working Conditions in Large-scale Plantations in Sub-Saharan Africa" *Africa Development*. XLI. 3, 2016. 49-69.

Forchingong, Charles. "Negotiating Livelihoods beyong Beijing: The Burden of Women, Food Vendors in the Economy of Limbe." *Cameroon International Science Journal,* vol. 57, no. 84, 2005, pp. 243-253.

Friedli-clapié, Lisa. "Undercurrents of Mammy Wata Symbolism in Buchi Emecheta's *The Joys of Motherhood."* West Virginia Philological Papers, Vol. 51, 2005. 115 – 128, U. of Washington

Kilson, Marion. "Women in African Traditional Religions." *Journal of Religion in Africa,* vol.8, 1976 pp. 133-143. Accessed 25 Sept.2018.

Mungai Catherine and Fiona Percy. "Adaptation to Climate Change and Achieving Resilience in East and South African Drylands." Joto Afrika, Special issue 15. December 2014.

Njoh, Ambe et al. "Institutional, Economic and Social Factors Accounting for Gender-based Inequalities in land Title Procurement in Cameroon." *Journal of Land Use Policy,* vol. 78., 2018, pp. 116 – 125.

Njoh, Ambe et al. "Africa's Triple Heritage, Land Commodification and Women's Access to Land: Lessons from Cameroon, Kenya and Sierra Leone." *Journal of Asian and African Studies,* vol. 1, no. 14, 2016, pp. 118 -135.

Nkengasong John Nkemngong. *Across the Mongolo.* Anucam*,* 2014.

Schwabe, Gerhard Helmut. *The Lake as Ecosystem.* G.H Universitas, 2010.

Shiva, Vandana and Maria Mies. *Ecofeminism.* Zed Books, 1993.

Starhawk. *Truth or Dare: Encounters with Power, Authority and Mystery.* Haper Sanfrancisco, 1987.

Tagem, Dunatus Fai "Youth, Ageing Persons and Intergenerational Interdependence: A study of Selected Works by Bole Butake." *Panel: Old Age Community Dialogue in African Literatures and Cultures: Constructing the Future Beyond Dichotomies.* VAD Congress, 2014.

UN Women Watch. "Women, Gender Equality and Climate Change" *Prezi* 2009.

Wohlpart, James A. *'Walking in the Land of Many Gods: Remembering Sacred Reason in Contemporary Environmental Literature.* U.of Georgia P. 2013.

wa Thiong'o, Ngugi. *Something Torn and New: An African Renaissance,* Civitas, 2009.

Warren, Karen. *Women, Culture and Nature.* Indiana UP. 1997.

Warren, Steven T. "Emerging Model of Communication and language Intervention". *Mental Retardation and developmental Disabilities Research Reviews,* vol.3, no. 4, 1997.

Chapter 4

The Strangers' Indifference or Powerlessness in an Unprotected Market Economy? A Critical Reading of Emmanuel Fru Doh's *The Fire Within.*

Benjamin Hart Fishkin
Tuskegee University

At first glance, it would seem that the problems of a young, pregnant Cameroonian are not worth a hill of beans in comparison to the inner workings of a complex financial system that moves around the world at the speed of light. The hidden narrative of *The Fire Within*, one that lies just beneath the surface and is rarely mentioned at all, is that cross border trade is not a new trend that is there to accent the main character. It is the main character. Imported colonial languages, educational systems, traits, currencies, goods, services, and administration dominate the life of Mungeu', the heroine of Emmanuel Fru Doh's novel, *The Fire Within*. What's more, she does not understand these entities, nor does she know that she is ensnared within them and dependent upon them. The purpose of this essay is to add texture and background to this often-opaque relationship.

When people begin to examine this fantastic novel, it feels as if they are eavesdropping into a bad dream that is being experienced by someone else. Mungeu' thinks of herself as an independent person who wants to succeed, but that is an impossibility that could never happen. In a sweeping take on the classic coming of age story, Emmanuel Fru Doh's *The Fire Within* is a novel of psychological depth. It marks the evolution from the largely male journey of self-discovery and self-realization narratives of authors like Johann von Wolfgang von Goethe, Henry Fielding, and Charles Dickens to the education, development and maturing of young women such as Jane

Austen's Elizabeth Bennett, Charlotte Bronte's Jane Eyre and George Eliot's Dorthea Brooke to the (finally) modern emergence of the moral, political, and financial growth of the African female (Kuehn 27). It is not a common occurrence that a text set in sub-Saharan Africa, in the twenty-first century, and one written by a male novelist, takes such an approach. In her search for what Julia Kuehn refers to as a middle-class professional, working life Mungeu' is slowly forced to have a reckoning, count or computation of what she does not have. She does not have a mother because she died giving birth to our so called heroine; she does not have a husband or partner because she is knocked up at age sixteen by her economics teacher who then quickly disappears and abandons her; she does not have a father because her biological father is poisoned against her by his first of four wives; she does not have her half-sister, Mabel, who is involved in a car accident when a truck skidded in the mud; and she does not have any knowledge of the free-market economy that will determine the prices of all the goods produced at her nascent clothing business (Kuehn 32).

Let's take the last of these independence erasing misfortunes, disasters, and afflictions first. Globalization removes controls on prices. The theory is that this action will allegedly raise the standard of living for everyone who participates in the market economy. What it will do, and Mungeu' is too young to realize this, is cut her off from her past, erase her living family tradition, and make it demonstrably harder for her to her to feed her daughter, Ndolo-Mabel, as a single mother. Western intervention from the World Bank and the International Monetary Fund (IMF) will make her life harder and not easier. Africa forced to compete without any form of trade protection would see its growth hindered by having to compete with China, Indonesia, Malaysia, Singapore and Thailand. Mungeu' is upbeat, but not because the facts that surround her are positive—she is upbeat because no one has sat her down and told her about the reality of living in a wholly integrated world.

When Mungeu' states that she is looking for peace of mind, the great surprise is that she pursues it by running away from her family rather than by running towards it (Doh 52). "There is always something wrong with my people" is her heartbreaking appraisal and once the reader realizes the universality of such a statement he or she is ready for Emmanuel Fru Doh's *The Fire Within* (Doh 43). Instead of an upbeat and entrepreneurial story involving business, vitality, independence and wealth we get a text that says that nobody, especially a woman, can escape the difficulties, the demands, the pressures and the psychological tensions that emanate from her family. It is impossible for a girl in her teens who is born with a father, a mother who dies giving birth to her and three stepmothers to be an orphan without tether even though she believes this would be a decided advantage. A family is undercut by discord and, while Mungeu' recognizes this, she cannot escape it.

When someone looks for help and does not get it they are extremely disappointed. If such a scenario is a standard Mungeu' rebels from the rebellion. She asks for nothing, receives nothing and relies on no one other than herself. She builds fortitude because her people are unable to set a good example and she does not look back, expecting that the strength of her secure and solidly fixed personality will be enough to power her through. In her mind there would be no reason why a woman could not start a business, raise a daughter and move to a coastal city in The Cameroons all by herself. But these prove to be childish and naïve thoughts, just like her lack of knowledge and training in terms of sexual reproduction. Our heroine thinks she is in control, but she is the epitome of non-control. She thinks of herself as being independent only to be sadly, and some would say predictably, mistaken, fooled, tricked and self-deceived. The text is saying that in a continent brimming with chaos, destinations and intentions mean nothing. It is what Robert Burns said in "To a Mouse" more than two hundred years ago; you cannot count on anything. Mungeu's initial optimism yields bitterness, grief, and pain. Everything, at least, at one early point in time, "…was so simple and natural…" that the reader is teased and tantalized with the hope of a happy ending (84). Doh instead tells us how things go askew. Things are not so simple or are no longer so simple. Africa is not the same.

The African is not the architect, pilot, or master in control of his or her own destiny. The continent and the character, so hopelessly intertwined with one another, are caught in a deceptive and tangled web that no one is able to completely see. Even though Mungeu' has no attendants at her graduation, and is consequently sad and lonely, this is a good thing and maybe the best thing in a world where life's markings, guides, and signposts have been hopelessly rearranged. At age sixteen at the Holy Rosary Home Craft Centre in Bari Mangeu' "…wondered where she was to go now that she was sure she meant so little, if not nothing, to her family…" (7). Her mother has died giving birth to her. Her father has been married four times and is a surly, ill-tempered sourpuss. The first of his wives who cannot stand her is the source of his torment and continual persecution. It would seem that Munny is free to choose her own designation, her own individuality, and her own identity. Undeservingly our girl, and at this point she is only a girl, can only whistle as it is slowly revealed to her that she is not in control of her nature or her surroundings. Her heredity and social environment, and not her independence, are going to ultimately make it abundantly clear that no matter how carefully a project is planned, something may still go wrong with it.

This issue of not being able to chart one's own course goes back a long way. Mungeu' reaches back into her own memory to imagine "…her late grandparents sitting on a bamboo bed in their smoke-filled kitchen, with the red hot coal smouldering in the hearth, complaining about what the coming of the white man had done to our people" (98). The words "smouldering in the hearth" surely have more than one meaning. In addition to there being an actual fire for cooking Emmanuel Fru Doh is making a declarative statement about what the white man has done to the black family. Yes, Mungeu' has been through a great deal in life, but her unpredictable twists and turns are a microcosm of a much larger source of heat and contention; the fact that a culture has been blown off course, separated from its past and seen its day to day habits and characteristics overthrown.

In this case globalization, integration, and cultural exchange are not positives. Such economic encroachment on a previously unscathed landscape yields chaos, disharmony and distemper. Mungeu's story is as much a primer about business and finance as it is about psychology and psychiatry. It should be wasted on no one that when Sister Mungeu' leaves the Cameroons and goes to a foreign nation to buy supplies and materials that she comes back with her left arm amputated from her elbow down. I call this a tariff—a customs duty levied on the import or export of goods, although it is paid in human flesh instead of the Nigerian naira. Mungeu' is juxtaposed multi-directionally between the state and the people or, more to the point, between a large social institution and her desire to use her individual talent as a businesswoman to circumvent it. There is tension between whether or not her sense of belonging belongs to herself or to her nation.

As certainly one of the first generation of women to work for herself in this part of the world Mungeu' is indeed developing, but are her eyes too big for her plate? One of Doh's points is that she may believe that she is on her own, but that is because she cannot see the constraints that she is free of by any means. The old world wants her in the compound; the new world wants her to bend to the world of trade and economic activity. Notice the checks and restrictions she has as she shuttles back and forth between Batemba and Nju'nki. One city envelops her personal relationships and her romantic life with Adey while the other is where she runs her expanding business empire. Regardless of what pathway she decides to take there is going to be irreparable trouble. Moreover, as if that is not enough to get by, evade, or find a way around, there is her daughter by another father. The survival of a family is by no means guaranteed even with two parents. Mungeu' has more constraints then an actuary can count.

At one point in Chapter 14 of *The Fire Within*, Munny turns to her boyfriend Adey and states "How can I plunge you and me into such a situation, being completely aware of myself" (Doh 159)? I would rearrange this sentence so that it reads; "Only someone that is not aware of herself can be in such an unenviable situation". Mungeu' has no freedom, her life being a series of outright refusals. Yet she engages in magical thinking, finding herself pregnant twice in an era where this could be easily avoided and should by no means be the case. Her independence is little more than a shitty pipe dream and her suffering has more than one dimension. She is motherless, she is female, she is an amputee and she must fend for herself in a cosmopolitan world that is so very different from the Africa that existed before "...French-speaking Caramenjuans flooded the West ..." (83). This point in time is a line of demarcation. The Cameroons is changing and the language issue steps in to form a political and cultural tsunami that no one can control. This subsumes Mungeu's attempt to be a female Horatio Alger figure—an impoverished hero who pulls himself up after horrible beginnings via perseverance, preparation and hard work. Munny cannot win, it is an impossibility that can never happen, and yet she does not know it.

Now the question is why are her plans denied the realistic goals she yearns for? Why has Africa changed, when was this transformation and what does the rest of the world have to do with it? It may not seem like it at first, but *The Fire Within* is more than just the chronicling of a love affair. It is a look at colonialism and the disadvantages that the female has, not having either international experience or an involved and supportive family. Into this two-front war is sent a sixteen-year-old girl with virtually no one "...who cared genuinely about her..." (5). Mungeu' grows up all by herself and that is when we know she is truly alone in the world. The economics of globalism imply connection, but the term is an oxymoron. One gets competition without collaboration. One gets transaction without camaraderie. One gets an awareness of the alleged opportunities of the marketplace without a genuine and penetrating look at the sharp elbows of the market. Africa is no longer a lonely, isolated and separate continent and the economic health and culture of the African has suffered because of this occurrence. Alhaji Ahmadu Ibrahim refers to this as "...power erosion..." in "The Impact of Globalization on Africa" (89). The Nigerian sociologist argues that interdependence has been far from a blessing. Money is the least part of the bargain as world bodies have eroded the confidence, legitimacy and spirit of those they publicly profess to help.

Many years ago, in the 1932 film *Grand Hotel*, the famous actress Greta Garbo stated, "I want to be alone." If only Africa could have followed this advice think of the pain it could have avoided. Predatory transformation has taken this portion of the world and weakened it socially, psychologically, and personally. The term economically has been purposely left out because that topic belongs in another category. Money can be replaced. Buildings can be rebuilt. Stocks and securities can be revitalized. Emotional damage and cultural dilution cannot be fixed so easily. Once gone, like a once thriving language now spoken by only a handful, stability and control are gone forever. Free and open trade among nations does not benefit everybody and it is in this manner that independence is to be prized. While globalization is good for business it is not necessarily good for people. No one wants to live with constraints and it is the locals who suffer by integration and interconnectedness.

International competition is the very opposite of independence. As goods and services move effortlessly across international borders the inevitable problem is debt and namely who has it, who services it and can it ever be repaid? Africa, once in a position to adequately handle its own problems, is now thrust into an arena where it cannot easily compete. Isn't this similar to what happened to Greece in 2010? While officials debate policy Greece could not have full control over its finances and simultaneously be intertwined with Austria, France, Germany, Italy and the other nations of Europe. Africa, although not part of this geographic, is no different. There is no way a nation can import, consolidate, tax and trade without being beholden to people far, far away.

Literary theorists are often interested in power and control. I am interested in how these elements are implemented by using, and misusing, fiscal policy. The famous British Prime Minister Benjamin Disraeli once said, "Colonies do not cease to be colonies simply because they are independent" (Ahluwalia 52). Unfortunately, this nineteenth century sentiment yields more than a bit of twentieth century resonance. Mungeu', although she may not be fully aware of her predicament, suffers twice; first as a victim who must navigate the oceanographic swells and breakers that create irrevocable instability in her family and second as a businesswoman who must battle, compete and produce in a global economy that cares not a farthing for her or any other African.

When the Cameroonian gives an account of himself or herself and the role that he or she now occupies in the postcolonial world, the debate, sooner rather than later, comes to money. No one can live without it, and no one can be independent without it. Imagine how the almost insurmountable odds multiply for a girl who must raise an infant daughter all by herself. She has no autonomy and neither does Africa. When a nation in Sub-Saharan African has a foreign debt that is larger than it can ever repay, just like the crisis that engulfed Greece almost a decade ago, it stands to reason that its young feel this deficit on a personal and individual level even though they have no idea that they are professional victims of swindles that ricochet, rebound, and simultaneously move in rapid succession between regional, national, and global economies. *The Fire Within*, although it may not seem like it, is a story of about how money crosses boarders. Emmanuel Fru Doh is telling the reader about integral market behavior; and how this behavior affects a part of the world that never wanted this connection in the first place.

Great economic figures such as Robert M. Solow, Robert J. Shiller, and Joseph E. Stiglitz are often asked why some economies grow faster than others. Answering questions like this involves more than mathematics, numbers, ratios, and percentages. Life cannot be lived on a balance sheet. Such figures are so easy to hide behind, manipulate, and misinterpret. The key to finding macroeconomic solutions—the key to understanding international economy-wide events—requires curiosity, social awareness and a real knowledge of the benefits, and abuses, of free-market capitalism.

On June 26, 2005 Nicholas D. Kristof wrote in *The New York Times* about how, at birth, that every newborn baby owes a tax to offset its nation's national debt. The United States, according to the author, "will leave every American child facing a 'birth tax' of about $150,000" (Kristof). And this data is for the most powerful and wealthiest nation in the entire world. Such a figure had David Walker, the comptroller general of the United States, "...running around with his hair on fire, shrieking about America's finances" (Kristof). If this is the plight and circumstance of the nation that has it "going on" where does that leave the economies of the nations that have traditionally lagged behind? What is the comparable "birth tax" or "baby debt" or "ovarian penalty" figure for Ghana, Uganda, Cameroon, and or Liberia? The scary part of Africa, the conundrum that I would argue is even more important than Mungeu's romance, is its debt. No wonder babies cry, and no wonder it is the baby her boyfriend, Adey, has impregnated her with that causes both of their lives to spin out of control.

The problem with the love match in Emmanuel Fru Doh's *The Fire Within* is not comprised of the classic themes that can be found in William Shakespeare's *Romeo and Juliet*, F. Scott Fitzgerald's *The Great Gatsby*, and Thomas Hardy's *Far From The Madding Crowd*. The problem here is the power of markets. The problems of human life, attraction, affection, sex, having a profitable career, running a household, and raising kids are exacerbated by the fact that there are no constraints to sending money abroad. Caleb Crain, in the May 14, 2018 issue of *The New Yorker* tells us that, "Starting in the eighties, developing nations found the free-market doctrine written into their loan agreements: bankers refused to extend credit unless the nations promised to lift capital controls, balance their budgets, limit taxes and social spending and aim to spend more goods abroad..." (90 – 95). A plethora of African nations, starting with Ghana in 1957 and others fell into an international monetary system that has caused more problems than it has solved. Free trade has not necessarily benefited the Cameroonian and this is the kernel of Doh's novel.

Things could have been different. The character of society has changed. The need to enjoy things and to buy things right now has harmed and hampered the African economy. This philosophy, if that is the correct word, has made people individuals rather than part of the community. Furthermore, it has robbed them of their past so that they are unaware that they are struggling in a way that no one has struggled before. Mungeu', Adey, and their friends are losing their (collective) memory and in so doing they are encountering a form of globalization that takes them farther and farther away from their home. Nowhere is this more apparent than when Emmanuel Fru

Doh focuses upon the grandparents. The world of the past, in many ways, is far better than the present but our protagonists are so wrapped up in the moment that their identity, their history, and their culture are lost in the bargain.

That evening as Adey prepared to go out, he heard those sounds on the roof once more—tac! Tac! Tac!... He walked into the parlour where he found his parents relaxing over a bottle of Gordon's Dry Gin and two other tonic bottles with their contents halfway gone.

The sight of the gin bottle brought to mind Adey's grandmother's voice as she sat some years ago in a smoke-clouded kitchen, telling him stories of the days before the white man came when all was good. "In those days that were long gone by," Mapah would begin, "long, long, ago, even before those people with their shoes reaching their knees, the *Dzamans* came, when I was still like your second follower, life was good, beautiful. There was order, and whatever happened, be it farming, hunting, or fishing was done by the villagers and for the good of the village and the citizens. But when I attained your present age... [things began to change] ... This village, which until then had been one, was torn apart because of the arrival of these uninvited guests with large appetites [...]

Yes, that has been the meaning of the coming of *acara* to us—the death of that true society of ours. Today our men are no longer themselves. Because of the white man and his strange ways, our men no longer have dignity and respect for themselves and their own people. They now tell lies even to their own sons. The market, the stream, and the forest are no longer the same (Doh 106 – 107).

This is not an innocent and charming smoky meeting by the fireside. It is about just how fragile life has become in the Cameroons and why it has become that way. Mapah's tale is one of grim times and how in three generations, Mungeu's graduation from the Holy Rosary Home Craft Centre in Bari at age sixteen is on June 30, 1975 making her birth date tellingly nearly exactly the same as the date of the Cameroons' independence, things have irrevocably changed (Doh 7). From roughly 1929 to 1989 the collective family in this portion of Africa, and perhaps in all of Africa, has been destabilized and made a facsimile reproduction of what it once was and Doh gives us clues as to whom has wrought such a change. The author, who taught at the University of Yaoundé from 1990 to 1997, would be perfectly positioned both geographically and chronologically to tell this tale. It is a (Greek) tragedy about a woman trying to be independent in a world where international financial markets, of which she knows nothing about, would not see fit to lend her a farthing.

While the World Bank and the International Monetary Fund would not lend money to Africa unless the terms were quite favorable, the nations that helped give rise to these bodies would have no problem selling things. The New Hampshire Conference that established both of these organizations, often referred to as the Bretton Woods Conference, was powered by Great Britain and the United States and took place in July of 1944. The idea was open markets. Seventy-five years later this term has morphed, metamorphosed, and metastasized into globalization. Why else does Doh have Cameroonians who are old enough to have children in their twenties drinking highball cocktails whose chief ingredients are Gordon's Dry Gin, tonic water, ice, and lime? Is anything more British then Gordon's Gin? Founded in 1769 its headquarters in Southwark, London was not far from the plot of land where Shakespeare's Globe Theater had been originally built in 1599 (Web.). The very fact that this company has now earned "…the status of the World's Favourite [sic] Gin…" says more about globalization then it does about alcohol (Web.). Yes, Adey's parents are relaxed, but at what cost? The phrase "halfway gone" resonates, but for all sorts of reasons among them the money it costs to purchase such an expensive liqueur, the cultural cost of not drinking calabashes of palm wine, and, of course, drunkenness. The interdependence of a unified and cosmopolitan world has caused these three problems and remember that England has more products to sell, all of them appearing on the streets without an invitation.

If alcohol is the symptom, colonialism is the pathogen. Things were good, better than good, before the causative and corrosive agent arrived to eclipse, obscure, and take the place of the old and independent rural African village where everyone felt like part of the population. Globalism is not necessarily based on good economic planning. Bill Easterly, senior fellow at the Center for Global Development and an economist at the World Bank, states in *The White Man's Burden: Why the West's Efforts to Aid the Rest Have Done So Much Ill and So Little Good* that "When a high willingness to pay for a thing coincides with low costs for that thing, Searchers will find a way to get it to the customer" (7). A famous ad for Gordon's features Humphrey Bogart unloading two cases of the spirit with the brand name written boldly in red letters upon the wooden boxes, all of this from the film *The African Queen*. The 1951 film, based on the British novel by C.S. Forester, is set in present-day Tanzania and emphasizes a gin addled Cockney riverboat captain and the sister of an Anglican missionary who fall in love while battling Germany, who also wants a presence in Africa to further its own gunboat diplomacy. The dynamic is clear; two nations (at minimum) wanting a measure of control over a land with unquantifiable wealth. In telling this and other tales about the Royal Navy, for example the *Horatio Hornblower* series, Forester is telling us why there is a need for such an amphibious fighting force consisting of frigates, warships, submarines and aircraft; all of this exists to protect markets, to keep supply lines open, and to make sure that the names of brands of British companies are known outside Britain. Doh is making a point, in Adey's reminiscences of his grandmother, of the word "gin", which also can be defined as a snare or trap for game. It is clearly the citizen of Douala, the Cameroons' largest city and economic capital, who needs the distiller and not the other way around.

Mapah's beef is that daily life is depreciating and disintegrating. The familiar refrain "...when I attained your present age..." could, if one changed the context, be a sentiment expressed in a William Faulkner novel. What is important here is not the bottle that tastes like juniper berries, but what it represents. Products from Europe are so ubiquitous, so easy and so immediate that the danger here is not a harmless drink but the perpetuation of a circumstance based on debt and dependence. The fright here is an influx of cultural influences that can erode, distract, disorient, and separate the African from his or her past. Doh's text, told brilliantly in flashback in the quotation, is revelatory. The sound is fading. Ghosts of the past know that this—this loss of identity—is their worst fear realized.

America's side of the ledger is no better and statistics bear this out. According to the International Trade Administration of the United States of America's Department of Commerce "U.S. exports to sub-Saharan Africa now top $ 21 billion a year. We want to help you tap into those markets" (Web.). Nowhere does it mention whether or not what is sold is of genuine benefit to individuals like Mungeu', Adey, Pa Anye, Loretta, Ndomnjie, and Yefon. The second sentence tells all, and we are not just talking about trivialities. What about healthcare, what about diet, what about obesity, what about diabetes? I realize that these are medical and health concerns rather than cultural ones as depicted in in the quotation where a dead character states, "The market, the stream, and the forest are no longer the same.", but they are no less essential. To be blunt, who truly benefits from this level of export and is Africa's young and dynamic population aware of the Faustian bargain they have taken?

Clearly Mungeu' knows none of these as she tries to climb out of life's penalty box and establish a clothing, tailoring, and knitting business in Nju'nki. "She now had twenty girls looking to sew from her" (Doh 60). This is the positive and energetic business story that all readers are hoping for, but *The Fire Within* does not stay there. Prison is no fairytale world and, make no mistake, an unmarried woman with a five-year-old child in The Cameroons at this time is trapped securely within one. Mungeu' suffers like Thomas Hardy's *Tess of the d'Urbervilles: A Pure Woman Faithfully Presented*: both are economic, sociological and emotional victims who would not be suffering if things operated correctly. These two heroines do their best to adapt to new circumstances, but ultimately cannot overcome them. They labor and toil, but the character of Tess, written in 1891, does not have to deal with the international trade issues of the modern economy. There is no longer such a thing as a self-contained national or local economy. If there were Mungeu's youth of the 1980's would look a lot more like Tess' youth of the 1870's (with all the important events taking place in England). Fred Halliday, an Irish academic who taught at the London School of Economics for more than 20 years, comments that,

> ... we should not assume that the content, the political programme [sic], of national relations remains the same. While the 1980's and 1990's have seen a flowering of nationalisms...there is one respect in which the nationalist agenda has changed... [the old system has been] ... replaced by another, almost national idea, that separate statehood can provide the best means of negotiating a favorable position in the international market-place" (Fred Halliday, Qtd. in John Baylis and Steve Smith 534).

Globalism, if you agree with people like Halliday and the historian Eric J. Hobsbawm whom he refers to often, has the potential to be remembered historically as something horrible. No one is independent. The social, economic, and political reality of the twentieth century, roughly the dates between Hardy's *Tess* and Doh's *The Fire Within*, is that we can't get away from each other. In Disraeli's colonies, the ones England no longer has any official claim to, globalization is accelerating. This is why Mungeu' must go to Nigeria by powered canoes to get all of the materials she needs to run her business. The international trip is not a minor detail. It leads to all sorts of problems. In essence, the market and the need of the proprietor to satisfy that market, ushers in and opens up the floodgates to all sorts of problems. Hobsbawm states, in *The Age of Extremes: A History of the World, 1914 -1991*, that an attempt (especially for a woman) to be independent comes at an unspoken price.

> Capitalism was a permanent and continuously revolutionizing force. Logically, it would end by disintegrating even those parts of the pre-capitalist past which it had found convenient, nay perhaps essential, for its own development. It would end by sawing off at least one of the branches on which it sat. Since the middle of the century this has been happening. Under the impact of the extraordinary explosion of the Golden Age and after, with its consequent social and cultural changes,

the most profound revolution in society since the Stone Age, the branch began to crack and break. At the end of this century it has for the first time become possible to see what a world may be like in which the past, including the past in the present, has lost its role, in which the old map and charts which guided human beings, singly and collectively, through life no longer represent the landscape through which we move, the sea on which we sail. In which we do not know where our journey is taking us, or even ought to take us" (Hobsbawm 16).

This is a compelling argument of a world in retreat. Emmanuel Fru Doh knows this problem is a universal one and sees how it leaves Munny rudderless. She cannot step back or lean upon the receding past as a model and she is ill equipped and does not have the ballast to survive in an unstable global economy. She is forced to go to Nigeria by market forces and once there, she is completely vulnerable to devastation, destruction and ruin. This is not a move forward or a glimpse at progress. This is an ambush. She cannot be independent if the West is dead set on imposing its values, interests, tastes, and desires upon her. As a single mom she needs money; to get it she must look overseas to the only consumers who can easily buy the clothing she produces piecemeal in Nju'nki.

Look at the fifth line of the indented quotation. It throws up the metaphor of "...sawing off at least one of the branches...". Eric J. Hobsbawm is saying that a completely unrestricted economic system, the kind of setup that has now appeared in the form of globalism, has sharp edges. Without some type of protection, some mechanism to contain, regulate and order, the merchant in any one of Africa's 54 countries has no power. Mungeu' is forced to compete with clothing manufacturers in China, Japan, Singapore and other parts of Europe with each player cutting prices and cutting costs to obtain an even better deal. It is in the pursuit of cost savings that she leaves her home only to be "...attacked by armed robbers..." in a foreign land (Doh 63). The fact that her left arm is amputated in an offshore hospital belonging to Schlumberger "...one of the oil prospecting companies along our coastal waters..." pursues the complex theme of international business and how it operates (Doh 73). The French company spelled "Schlumberger Limited", was founded in the Alsace region of France. It is the world's largest oilfield Services Company with headquarters located in Paris, London, Houston, London, The Hague and Curacao. An investment in this company with, a Ticker Symbol (SLB), that had been made 30 years ago today would have realized more than an eight-fold return. When it comes to driving a hard bargain in the international marketplace how many of these dollars flow back to The Cameroons? This question is consistent with Fred Halliday's idea as quoted in John Baylis and Steve Smith (534). It is impossible to live independently, or even fairly, with a Fortune 500 company at your doorstep. The shareholders of Schlumberger, many of whom have never been to Africa, have only a passing knowledge of where it does business, caring only that the quarterly dividend checks keep coming and they continue to profit while others clean up the mess.

The official website of the World Bank, in its very first line, uses the words "financial inclusion" (Web). Each letter of this phrase is capitalized and, while this may be a pleasant-sounding message, one could not fault someone in Sub-Saharan Africa from being a little bit hesitant. This is not to say that the people who work for institutional financial institutions like this one do not mean well in their attempt to further foreign investment and international trade, but rather what good does this fine flight do to the actual individual on the ground? For example, of the World Bank's 143 Projects and Operations currently slated for The Cameroons would any of them keep Mungeu' in school beyond age sixteen, keep her from becoming pregnant, and prevent her from having her left arm amputated at the elbow? After all, she is impregnated by her Economics teacher at the Holy Rose Home Craft Centre. This should say a lot about what the author thinks of financial experts. They create problems when they should be solving them. They engage in hypocrisy, promising the stars only to fail to deliver (just like the arc of Mungeu's life from neglect, to remarkable business success to tragedy). They inflict suffering and present what Doh calls "…the wicked poisonous nature of humankind as people pried into the affairs of others… (25). When in July of 1995 James Wolfensohn became the president of the

World Bank Group, the board "…reacted in disbelief at Wolfensohn 's request that a private jet be put at his disposal: Many of the board members represented countries where the prime minister himself did not have standing access to an aircraft (Mallaby 86)". No one could blame someone from this part of the world for keeping his or her hand on their wallet, turning around and running in the other direction.

There are financial institutions that are suspect just as there are medical doctors who are suspect. If Mungeu' had not been directed to a quack to obtain an abortion and instead consulted someone else at the "…General Hospital on the edge of the centre [sic] of town…" then *The Fire Within* would have been a very different novel (Doh 165). The problem is not the bank but the banker and, even more to the point, we are here dealing with an *international* banker. There is nothing wrong, and a hell of a lot right, with careful financial stratagem. No one objects to conscientious planning, saving, and allocating capital but is this feasible for people who live far away, who know little about local customs, who have white skin, and whose paycheck does not fluctuate with their performance? It is no accident that when Doh begins his narrative, Mungeu's older stepsister, Mabel, is attending the training school for the African Progressive Bank. This is a bank that operates within the boundaries of the nation, whose workers live beside the bank's customers in the community, who have black skin, and have a knowledge of the culture that includes a respect for their elders and society as a whole (Doh 98). International agreements and global extension work against such a model. They encroach upon existing order at behavioral patterns that had worked for centuries. At one point in its history, The World Bank changed and shifted to include "…a new and narrow focus on exchange rate policies, budget balances, and other macroeconomic challenges" (Mallaby 37). Mabel and her work at what she terms "our" bank instead presents solutions to microeconomic ones. Such funds furnish Mabel's home and whatever proceeds remain are plowed back into the businesses, mortgages and debt consolidation loans of her neighbors. Mabel says, when explaining her own individual success to Mungeu', "I agree, but it's all a matter of how one plans one's life" (Doh 13). What is unsaid here is that to plan one must be left alone so that they may be left alone to hear the ticking of their own heart.

Emmanuel Fru Doh, thus creates a Mungeu' who thinks that she is in control, independent, and self-sufficient when modern Africa, at the beginning of the twenty-first century, is none of those things. She is unaware that people follow fortune and that most people are not as decent as she is. Her ultimate success would be an impossibility, a Hollywood ending, which could never happen. That never will happen. She suffers on more than one level, first as a girl who does not get the emotional protection she needs from her biological family and second as a woman, more specifically a citizen, who does not get the financial protection she needs from her own government. In a complex tangle of complicated details and painful reasons the reader is confronted with a personal tragedy that is a microcosm of public treason. Furthermore, it exposes a terrible truth that a unified world, when it comes to trade, does not deliver for everybody. *The Fire Within* is less about a woman trying to break through a translucent glass ceiling than about a culture that cannot prevent weights from being tied to its feet.

Works Cited

Ahluwalia, Pal. *Politics and Post-Colonial Theory: African Inflections*. Routledge, 2000.

Baylis, John and Steve Smith, *The Globalization of World Politics: An Introduction to International Relations*. Oxford UP. 2005.

Crain, Caleb "Merchants of Doom: Is Capitalism a Threat to Democracy." *The New Yorker* May 14, 2018, pp. 90 – 95.

Doh, Emmanuel Fru, *The Fire Within*, Langaa Research & Publishing, 2008.

Easterly, William. *The White Man's Burden: Why the West's Efforts to Aid the Rest Have Done So Much Ill and So Little Good* Penguin, 2006.

Halliday, Fred, "Nationalism" in John Baylis and Steve Smith. *The Globalization of World Politics: An Introduction to International Relations.* Oxford UP, 2005.

Hobsbawm, Eric. *The Age of Extremes: A History of the World, 1914 - 1991.* Vintage Books, 1994.

Ibrahim, Alhaji Ahmadu "The Impact of Globalization on Africa." *International Journal of Humanities and Social Science* vol. 3, no.15, 2013, p. 89.

Kristof, Nicholas D., "A Glide Path to Ruin." *The New York Times,* 26 June 2005, www.nytimes.com/2005/06/26/opinion/a-glide-path-to-ruin.html Accessed, 10/23/2018

Kuehn, Julia. "David Copperfield and the Tradition of the Bildungsroman." *Dickens Quarterly*, vol 35, no. 1, March 2018, pp. 25-46.

Mallaby, Sebastian. *The World's Banker: A Story of Failed States, Financial Crises, and the Wealth and Poverty of Nations.* Penguin, 2004.

The Grand Hotel Director: Edmund Golding Screenplay: William Absalom Drake 1932.

The African Queen Director: John Huston Screenplay: James Agee 1951

Chapter 5

Formalizing Freedom:
Land Tenure Arrangements from the Perspective of
Social Modes of Production

Andrew Bonanno
University of Georgia

Introduction

In the classic movie, *It's a Wonderful Life*, George Bailey is a fictional building and loan agent in 1920s to 1940s small town America. Throughout his life and career, George sacrifices commercial success to build personal relationships and help people meet their basic material needs. This puts him at odds with Mr. Potter, "the richest and meanest man in the county." At one point during an argument with Mr. Potter over financial strategy, George sums up their opposing positions by asserting that he views people as human beings while Potter views them as cattle. Eventually, Mr. Potter connives to have George arrested for financial mismanagement. However, at the height of a personal and professional financial crisis, George's family, friends, and business acquaintances band together to bail George out, both financially and socially. Through this experience, George and the audience alike learn that meeting basic material and social needs through cultivating human relationships can ultimately be more valuable than commercial wealth.

It's a Wonderful Life is an enduringly popular movie during the American holiday season, but can the story's core ideas and lessons possibly amount to more than just a feel-good story for the last month of the year? The contention of this chapter is that the fundamental distinction between human value and commercial value expressed in *It's a Wonderful Life* can actually help us understand economic interactions in a surprising variety of contexts. One example can be found in government attempts to "formalize" land tenure arrangements throughout the Global South (i.e. Latin America, South Asia, and Africa).

Land tenure refers to the organization and governance of property and how this organization and governance affects the way that land is held and used by individuals or groups (Acheson 2015). Land tenure can be determined and governed by states, markets, local communities, or some combination of these institutions (Acheson 2015; Ostrom 2010). In many areas in the Global South, land tenure arrangements exist outside state purview and are often governed by traditional systems based, at least in part, on community management and common property. Governments often have difficulty translating these traditional systems into their bureaucratic structures. The bureaucratic demarcation and titling of land claims has therefore been a popular strategy throughout the Global South. This process is called land tenure formalization.

The basic idea behind land tenure formalization (described in more detail below) is that demarcating, and titling will secure individual land claims and unlock the wealth generation potential of free markets and commercialization (de Soto 2003). However, by adopting an overly narrow understanding of land tenure arrangements and economic relationships, studies of formalization miss important information about human freedom—what people are actually able to do—within different social, political and economic contexts.

This problem can potentially be remedied by analyzing land tenure related freedoms from a social mode of production (SMP) perspective. In particular, existing tensions in land tenure formalization analysis can be approached with the question "how does the social structure of economic exchange impact people's land tenure-related freedoms, that is, what are people actually able to do given their land claims?" Although this is a social science question, its thrust goes beyond dry academic inquiry and intersects with one of the basic themes in *It's a Wonderful Life*—that human relationships might somehow meet basic needs in ways that commercialization cannot.

Of course, like all parables, a good critic can poke various holes in the "Wonderful Life" story by comparing it to actually existing reality. We should be careful not to draw out any conclusions too far (interestingly, the same can be said about economic models and equations, but this is somewhat a different topic for another piece). Nevertheless, this chapter takes the position that George Bailey's experience provides a useful starting point for understanding the ongoing process of land tenure formalization throughout the Global South, and the implications that this has for understanding human economic relationships.

Section 2 briefly reviews the concepts and evidence surrounding land tenure formalization. It is argued that a dichotomous market-state approach to understanding tenure-related economic interactions is too narrow. Section 3 discusses some alternative conceptualizations of well-being that transcend the market-state dichotomy, especially as it pertains to land tenure and tenure-related freedoms. In particular, the contention is that analytical focus should be placed on human freedoms of action and that a social mode of production perspective can facilitate this approach. Section 4 closes with a rudimentary proposal for future research on land tenure formalization using a social mode of production perspective.

Land Tenure Formalization: A Survey of Concepts and Evidence

Land tenure formalization—the legal demarcation of land and titling of land claims—has been promoted throughout the Global South by the World Bank and mainstream economists as a mechanism that integrates individuals from the industrializing world into the wealth-generating potential of free markets (Deininger, Ali, and Alemu 2011; de Soto 2003). Scholarly critiques argue that land tenure formalization schemes often contradict stated stability and wealth-generating goals by disrupting pre-existing tenure arrangements, entrenching the previously contested claims of powerful actors, facilitating land appropriation by outside business interests, and displacing non-sedentary or non-intensive land users (Borras and Franco 2010; German, Unks, and King 2016; Lastarria-

Cornhiel 1997). Formalization proponents counter that while "change is rarely smooth or linear," formalization ultimately generates market-based financial wealth, provided that there is sufficient government support and societal willingness to forsake economically inefficient traditional practices (Ali, Deininger, and Goldstein 2014). A recent meta-analysis of land-tenure formalization found that formalization generally leads to increased incomes overall, but also tends to increase land disputes as well as reduce land access (Lawry et al. 2017).

Proponents of land tenure formalization generally point to increasing incomes associated with tenure formalization and argue that extending well-crafted state and market mechanisms will advance human freedom to obtain desirable levels of well-being (Ali, Deininger, and Goldstein 2014; Deininger, Ali, and Alemu 2011). This imagined path of economic freedom and well-being begins with steps toward demarcating and documenting land claims in areas where state bureaucracy has not yet been fully extended. In other words, the path toward economic freedom and well-being is thought to begin with land tenure formalization. Great efforts were made in the late 20th century to put parts of Latin America and Asia on this path and recent efforts have been made to place Africa on this road as well (Bromley 2008; Deininger, Ali, and Alemu 2011; de Soto 2003).

The basic argument behind land tenure formalization is that undocumented land rights, particularly in the Global South, lead to insecure and uncertain property claims, making it impossible to determine who has rights to what and thereby undercutting individuals' ability to leverage capital and benefit from the wealth-generating potential of markets. Formal land titling, it is asserted, will remedy this situation, turning land into commercial wealth and thus reducing poverty (de Soto 2003). The expectation is that when the state documents and recognizes previously undocumented land claims, individuals grow increasingly willing to invest in productive and sustainable land use practices due to state-backed tenure security (de Soto 2003).

It is further expected that individuals will become able to leverage their land wealth for financial credit by rent land, selling land, or borrowing against the value of land. According to this narrative, traditional land claims typically exist informally (that is, without being written down or recorded by the state), throughout the Global South. However, states and financial institutions cannot understand these informal claims. States are therefore less able to protect their citizen's land claims and without the ability to clearly demonstrate secure land holdings to a financial institution, claims are essentially "dead capital" (de Soto 2003).

Formalization, as conceived by its proponents, can therefore be understood as a state-based mechanism that unlocks the opportunities of a free market in land. By recognizing basic rights to particular parcels of land, the state protects the individual freedom to put land to the best possible use, including selling that land to those in a better position to put land to good use. In this model, the state guarantees individual freedom against complicated traditional systems that are conceived as typically patriarchal, gerontocratic, and ethnocentric. The state is also conceived as protecting against the chaos, violence, and uncertainty that is expected to exist when a local system is not recognized by a larger group of people (Cf. e.g., de Soto 2003; Millar 2016).

While empirical evidence certainly supports the existence of traditional property arrangements outside direct state purview, this evidence also indicates that traditional arrangements are often self-sustaining and productive in the long-term without being fully integrated into formal state or commercial market systems (Ostrom 2010). This calls into question assumptions about illegibility and chaos in traditional systems. Nevertheless, skepticism about the effectiveness of traditional systems is deep-rooted and, as previously indicated, the logic of formalization remains popular among development economists and World Bank policy makers (Ali, Deininger, and Goldstein, 2014; Deininger; Ali, and Alemu 2011).

Traditional systems of tenure often include some sort of community management or common property (Ostrom 2010). Although traditional land tenure arrangements in places as geographically distant as Europe, south Asia, and Africa do sometimes include private property arrangements, such systems also tend to include areas of common property and employ community resource management strategies alongside individualized land tenure (Netting 1993). Many of these systems have existed sustainably, both socially and environmentally, for hundreds or even thousands of years (Netting 1993; Ostrom 2010). However, the prevailing view developed among environmental and social scientists in the early second half of the 20th century was that common property arrangements are generally inefficient and unsustainable.

Hardin (1968) formulated that in an open-access regime, the cost of individual resource extraction is externalized to all users while the benefit of individual use is fully internalized by the individual, thereby incentivizing resource depletion. This is the famous "tragedy of the commons." Avoiding tragedy requires "mutual coercion mutually agreed upon" (Hardin 1968). According to Hardin (1978), mutually agreed coercion can take two forms—private property or state control and regulation. A parallel analysis by Demsetz (1967) asserted that while a group of users could potentially recognize the benefits of common management, such an arrangement is unlikely to succeed due to coordinating costs.

These assumptions have since been nuanced by the numerous case studies and empirical meta-analyses conducted by Ostrom and others. While it is true that the tragedy of the commons does often occur in ways described by Hardin, subsequent analyses reveal that many self-governed, collective tenure arrangements are viable and sustainable in the long-term (e.g. Berkes et al. 1989; Ostrom 1990; 2010). Additionally, as previously mentioned, a combination of private and collective tenure and labor arrangement often persist in conjunction with mixed subsistence and market activities (Acheson 2015; Netting 1993). These studies contribute to a robust analytical framework that moves beyond private-public and market-state dichotomies to include common property managed by a community of users. One element of this framework is the view that property is a bundle of rights rather than simply ownership or non-ownership (Ostrom 2010). Sustainable common property is more likely to occur when a community as a whole has secure ownership, that is, securely possesses a full bundle of rights (rights of use, access, management, exclusion of others, and sale) and individual community members possess secure use, access, and management rights (Ostrom 2010).

Despite existing analytical frameworks for understanding collective resource arrangements, customary collective tenure arrangements continued to be viewed as illegible and chaotic by policy makers and some social scientists such as de Soto (2003) and Millar (2016). Formalization remains a favored policy solution to perceived chaos and illegibility under traditional tenure arrangements (de Soto 2003, Renner-Thomas 2010). For example, in the West African nation of Sierra Leone, the new National Land Policy (2015) pursues the formalization of customary collective tenure arrangements. Despite various on-the-ground evidence to the contrary, (see, e.g. Bonanno and Bonanno 2017; Bottazzi, Goguen, and Rist 2016; Leach 1997) customary collective tenure arrangements in Sierra Leone are viewed as illegible and chaotic by the national government, intergovernmental organizations, and transnational corporations (Millar 2016; Sierra Leone National Land Policy 2015; UNEP 2010).[1] It is thought that formalization in Sierra Leone will secure the rights of women and younger men against relatively powerful male elders while encouraging orderly marketization and capitalization of property rights that will in turn facilitate a transition from subsistence to commercial agriculture (Renner-Thomas 2010).

This perspective echoes de Soto's (2003) arguments that documenting land rights will secure property claims and allow individuals to leverage capital, thereby integrating individuals into the wealth-generating potential of markets. Even economic analysis that takes this formalization perspective, however, indicates that market integration is multifaceted, and formalization alone does not necessarily lead to full commercialization (Ali, Deininger, and Goldstein 2014).

Consider, for example, the cross-sectional analysis conducted by Ali, Deininger, and Goldstein (2014) in a densely populated agricultural region of Rwanda. This analysis compares plots within a

---

[1] See Section 4

pilot area where titling is mandatory to plots outside the pilot area where titling is voluntary. It was predicted that formal titling would encourage long-term investment in soil conservation due to increased tenure security.

Ali, Deininger, and Goldstein (2014) found that being within the pilot area did have modest but statistically significant positive effects on soil conservation investments. However, women in titled areas who are in traditionally sanctioned polygamous marriages (not recognized by the state) experienced a decrease in tenure security. Changes in market participation (i.e. the sale of land) and credit access were also not statistically significant overall. Ali, Deininger, and Goldstein (2014) argue that land market and credit expansion will require further institutional reforms beyond land tenure formalization. Additionally, conservative tendencies such as maintaining polygamous marriage are seen as barriers to a smooth transition toward the economically efficient and politically secure private property that would otherwise emerge in a sedentary agrarian setting (Ali, Deininger, and Goldstein 2014)

While Ali, Deininger, and Goldstein, (2014) cite mid-twentieth century analyses framing land privatization as more or less a naturalistic economic transition given increasing population density and agricultural sedentism, their contemporary investigation recognizes that the state, through formalization policies, inevitably plays an active role initiating and guiding the privatization process. This calls into question whether formalization should be primarily conceived as a process of market integration or as an extension of state power. Indeed, it can be argued that throughout history, the extension of states and commercial markets are mutually dependent (Graeber 2011). It might therefore be more accurate to conceptualize formalization as a process of bureaucratic commodification, whether directly initiated through market-based or state-based mechanisms.

An example of bureaucratic commodification initiated through a state-based mechanism is the Mexican government's payment for ecosystem services (PES) program in a northeastern Oaxaca rainforest community (Ibarra et al. 2011). PES programs determine a monetary exchange value for the services provided by an environmental system (Buscher et al. 2012). A distinction can be made between market payments for ecosystem services and public payments for ecosystem services (e.g. Kallis, Gómez-Baggethun, Zografos 2013), but in either case, a monetary value is determined and exchanged for a set of environmental services.

In the Oaxaca rainforest PES program, community members are paid by the government to refrain from hunting and shifting cultivation in a newly demarcated state-owned forest area that was previously collectively owned and managed by the community. Although community members are allowed to forage within the protected area, foraging had previously occurred during multi-day hunting forays. This, combined with restrictions on shifting cultivation, contributes to an increased reliance on lower quality processed foods. While the PES program has increased cash income, the percentage of income spent on lower quality, processed food has also risen, leading to a potential reduction in embodied well-being. Additionally, community members perceive that ecological knowledge and social cohesion associated with hunting and gathering has decreased (Ibarra et al. 2011).

While the case described above differs from other examples of formalization in that land is commodified through a PES program and the state—rather than a private entity—is the landowner, the general impacts are not unusual. Recall the recent meta-analysis mentioned earlier that found formalization tends to increase incomes overall, but also tends to restrict land access and increase land contestation (Lawry et al. 2017). While formalization advocates assume that increasing incomes due to market integration indicates improved well-being (e.g. Ali, Deininger, and Goldstein 2014; de Soto 2003), the intertwined state-market relationships inherent in formalization and the mixed effects of this process warrant a reconsideration of how well-being is conceptualized and measured. This, in turn, has implications for how we understand the nature of economic interaction and human freedom to act given different types of economic relationships.

In the following section, different conceptualizations and measures of well-being are briefly explored. It is argued that a useful well-being indicator must account for both material and social elements at individual and institutional levels and that a social modes of production perspective can be used to understand how processes such as land tenure formalization affect well-being.[2]

Conceptualizing and Assessing Well-Being

Increased incomes or increased capital access through credit mechanisms are often cited as indicators to gauge land formalization success (de Soto 2003; Ali, Deininger, and Goldstein 2014; Lawry et al. 2017). Accepting the logic of formalization proponents, restricted land access or exacerbated power asymmetries are undesirable results insofar as they restrict widespread financial acquisition. However, to the extent that humans value certain social, political, and ecological outcomes apart from direct financial gain, using financial or monetary metrics to gauge well-being or to judge economic outcomes can obfuscate the assessment of non-financial goals (Kallis, Gómez-Baggethun, and Zografos 2013). On the other hand, while ecological sustainability, social equality, and deliberative community-based decision-making might be desirable policy goals, the determination of what qualifies as meeting these goals can be subjective, particularly if there are tradeoffs between these goals. Direct case-to-case comparisons are therefore difficult. The advantage of monetary valuation is that it allows quantifiable analysis that is widely comparable (Gsottbauer, Logar, and van den Bergh 2015). This does not mean, however, that all valuation must be converted into monetary terms; there is no reason that quantifiable bio-physical characteristics could not be used to assess the impacts or economic, environmental, political, or social processes (Godoy et al. 2009; Gsottbauer, Logar, and van den Bergh 2015).

Ostrom (2010) uses the criteria of long-term sustainability in her analyses; if an identifiable system of environmental management and

---

[2] Institutions are conceived here as processual rules in-use that guide human behavior. Conceptualizing institutions as processual recognizes that they are formed by repeated actions that can be either change-inducing or regularizing (see Moore 2000; North 1990).

economic activity has existed over the long-term, it can be said to be sustainable. Ostrom's work identifies systems that are sustainable and explores the common institutional design elements in these systems. While the evaluative specifics for sustainability can be debated, "sustainable," as defined by Ostrom, is a relatively simple general criterion that can be measurable using quantifiable bio-physical indicators. This is important because once a discernable criterion has been established, empirical evidence can be gathered to understand how this criterion is or is not met in a variety of contexts.

Ostrom (1990; 2010) focused her analysis on social and economic systems of environmental management that operate outside direct state purview. In addition to showing that such systems of common property and management are often sustainable, this work ultimately provides a robust analytical framework for understanding the institutional principles that perpetuate sustainable systems[3]. However, while this work can be incredibly useful at the institutional level, it provides less analysis regarding socially disaggregated actors and their relative positions within economic, political, and human-environmental systems and hierarchies (Agrawal 2014). A sustainable resource management or social system is not necessarily an equitable system, nor does system-wide sustainability in-and-of-itself indicate

---

[3] Elinor Ostrom was awarded the 2009 Nobel Memorial Prize in Economic Sciences for her work on common property and common resource management. This work includes eight intuitional design principles for successful common resource management based on extensive empirical analysis by Ostrom and colleagues. These principles of design are paraphrased below based on Ostrom 2010: **1) Boundaries:** there are clear resource boundaries as well as clear boundaries between resource users and non-users; **2) Congruence Between Rules and Resource**: resource management rules are congruent with social and environmental conditions and provide a proportional distribution of costs and benefits; **3) Collective Choice Arrangements** allow most individuals affected by resource use to participate in making and changing resource-use rules; **4) Monitoring** of the resource and resource users is done by individuals who either are resource users themselves or accountable to resource users; **5) Graduated Sanctions:** punishment for rule violation starts low and grows more severe with repeated infractions; **6) Conflict Resolution Mechanisms** for conflicts between users or between users and officials are local, effective, affordable; **7) Minimal Recognition of Rights:** the rights of local users to govern their own resource in recognized by the state; **8) Nested Enterprises:** local resource governance is nested within multiple layers of governance at increasingly larger geographic levels.

the freedoms of action available to individuals or sub-groups within the system (Agrawal 2014).

There has been some work exploring multi-dimensional elements assessing individual well-being in contexts of traditional land use systems in which people engage in a mix of horticultural, foraging, and market activities. Godoy et al. (2009), for example, measure well-being among indigenous peoples in the Bolivian Amazon using a set of quantifiable indicators based on monetary, physical, and social aspects. These indicators include the monetary value of weekly consumed food items and physical assets, body-mass index, and the level of participation in traditional drinking groups (Godoy et al. 2009).

The metrics employed by Godoy et al. (2009) recognize that well-being is multi-faceted and goes beyond material or financial possessions. While such indicators might be useful for a more comprehensive measure of well-being than relying exclusively on income or material possessions, they are still subject to the critique made against an over-reliance on monetary-based measurements. That is, relying on individual well-being metrics may obscure political motivations, systematic power asymmetries, and ecological impacts (Kallis, Gómez-Baggethun, and Zografos 2013). Yet, how can these institutional aspects be incorporated into well-being analyses? And how can such analyses take into account both the individual well-being and the larger institutions in which individuals act? One possible way to systematically incorporate institutional and environmental factors into well-being analyses is to focus on how individuals approach freedom to act, that is, approaching well-being from the perspective of what an individual is able to do given their access to available goods and services.

The idea that well-being can be conceived as the freedom to act was developed by Sen (1981) to help explain the social causes of famine. While famine can be caused by an overall lack of food, famine also occurs at times when there is an adequate food supply, but individuals or households lack the legal means to obtain the food that is otherwise available. These means are what Sen refers to as "entitlements" and include production, trade, and government support—any legitimate and legal command over resources that allows individuals or households to realize the benefits of their "endowments," or resources such as land or labor (Sen 1981). The actual freedoms that are possible given existing entitlements are referred to as "capabilities" (Sen 1981).

Leach, Mearns, and Scoones (1999, 233) extend this concept to include "environmental entitlements," that is, "environmental goods and services over which social actors have legitimate effective command." In this extended conceptualization, entitlements are taken to include forms of command sanctioned through customary institutions in addition to those sanctioned by a modern nation-state. Institutions, in turn, are understood as "regularized patterns of behavior that emerge from underlying structures or sets of 'rules in use'" and are repeatedly formed through ongoing human practices within and external to a given community of actors (Leach, Mearns, and Scoones 1999, 237). Leach, Mearns, and Scoones, (1999) apply an analytical framework in which environmental goods and services are derived from endowments, entitlements are socially constructed from endowments, and entitlements create different capabilities for individuals. In their examination of the livelihood capabilities that women in southern Ghana derive from bush-foraging rights, Leach, Mearns, and Scoones (1999) find that the high market value of foraged leaves (traditionally use to wrap food for transportation and storage) allows women to purchase food for themselves and their children during scarce times before harvests.

Some analyses that explore local wealth and poverty conceptualizations in areas of East Africa with a mix of market, horticulture, gathering, and hunting activities show that individuals tend to think of their own wealth or poverty in terms that generally correspond to the capabilities concept (Knapp, Peace, and Bretchel 2017; Tucker et al. 2011). In other words, individuals conceive their own wealth and poverty in terms of what they are able to do with their resources rather than their level of monetary income or material possession. Such "folk models" (Tucker et al. 2011) of wealth and poverty parallel Sen's (1983) argument that wealth and poverty are best understood in terms of capabilities.

Wealth and poverty, according to Sen (1983), are not determined by material possessions, the characteristics of material possessions, or the utility one gets from material possessions. Rather, wealth and poverty are determined by what one is able to actually do with their material possessions. This "capability view" of poverty and wealth includes the ability to meet basic life-maintaining needs, but also includes the ability to maintain dignity through basic social conventions and to participate in community activities. The capability approach therefore views poverty itself as both objective and absolute while the condition of poverty is viewed as relative. Whether or not an individual has the freedom to take one action or another is an observable and objective reality. Capabilities are also absolute; either a person has a particular capability, or he/she does not. However, whether or not a person possesses a capability depends on his/her relative position within society, and certain capabilities, such as the maintenance of dignity or social participation and acceptance, are by definition dependent on cultural context. Therefore, it is relative from place to place (Sen 1983).

Although further empirical studies are warranted, the explorations of African "folk models" mentioned above indicate the potential usefulness of applying a capabilities approach to formalization analyses, particularly in Africa. The recent push for land tenure formalization throughout Africa (Bonanno & Bonanno 2017; Ali, Deininger, and Goldstein 2011; Doss et al. 2013) and the reality of mixed market, horticultural, hunting, and foraging strategies in various parts of the continent (Fraser, Frausin, and Jarvis 2015; Frausin et al. 2014; Netting 1993) make the application of a capabilities approach all the more salient.

However, the previously discussed measurement problem remains. How does one determine which capabilities are the most important? If capabilities of social status and participation depend upon a person's relative position within society and are by definition dependent on cultural context, aren't such capabilities incommensurable from culture to culture? While the capabilities approach may be a useful framework for understanding the social and economic interactions of individuals and sub-groups within a larger institutional structure, the framework seems to lose its analytical power if particular sets of capabilities are not directly comparable from case to case. Nussbaum (2003) therefore argues that a flexible but definitive set of essential capabilities must be determined to assess economic and political outcomes throughout the world. This solves the problem of case-to-case comparison, but it does not solve the problem of deciding which capabilities are most important. It reintroduces a new problem—a globally applied, definitive set of capabilities for every case obfuscates the more culturally contingent capabilities such as dignity and community participation. This obfuscation, or what Sen (1983) refers to as an "informational constraint," is the very thing that a capabilities approach ideally avoids.

It could be argued that intangible, socially embedded capabilities such as basic dignity and participation in community life are destined to be casualties of social science analysis, or at least in analyses of economic well-being. Nevertheless, anthropologist David Graeber (2006; 2011) asserts that such intangible relationships are what economic activity is fundamentally about. In fact, Graeber (2006; 2011) argues that all economic activity can best be understood in terms of social relationships. Of course, these relationships are ultimately rooted in material reality and exchange and exist within particular political contexts. However, it is the social relationships intrinsically tied to economic activity that lie at the heart of economic systems—economic value is ultimately about human beings, who they are, and what they can do in a given social, economic, and political context. This focus is what Graeber (2006) calls social modes of production (SMP).

Applying a broad SMP perspective, Graeber (2011) generalizes all economic activity into three types of relationships: communal relationships, exchange relationships, or hierarchal relationships. All of these relationships exist to some extent in any economic system and are not mutually exclusive. However, some economic systems recognize the human element of these relationships while others abstract this human value into a particular means of exchange or financial instrument such as a commodity or formal credit system.

Graeber (2011) refers to the first kind of economic system as a human economy and the second as a commercial economy.

This distinction is somewhat reminiscent of George Bailey's "people as humans" versus Mr. Potter's "people as cattle." The former idea ultimately places economic value in humans as social creatures while the latter places value in dollars and cents—a human might as well be perfectly interchangeable with livestock, or at least, one could calculate the value of a particular human in terms of an equivalent number of cattle without any sense of moral irony. The irony here is that, as Graeber (2011) argues, in many societies that routinely determine how much one human is worth in terms of cattle for purposes of marriage payments or to settle a blood feud, such calculations are typically done with the sense that no amount of cattle, or anything else, can ultimately be interchangeable for a particular human life.

If one were to apply Graeber's SMP perspective in terms of capabilities, it would lead to the prediction that shifting from a human economy to a commercial economy will restrict the livelihood options for non-elites by limiting the capabilities derived from human economy relationships, such as the ability to access land based on community membership rather than formal title acquired through commercial exchange. Elites, however, can expect increased capabilities as they leverage their position toward newfound commercial wealth and power. This shift is expected to be particularly detrimental when hierarchies within human economies are alienated from their social context through socially disembedded exchange in a commercial economy (Graeber 2011).

Graeber's narrative is compelling if true, but it has yet to be systematically validated from the perspective of social science. It remains only an intriguing hypothesis. This hypothesis can potentially be tested using a capabilities framework. The SMP hypothesis, if confirmed, would not solve the problem of what particular capabilities are most important, but it could provide a way to understand the process of capability creation, preservation, and deprivation. In other words, while the SMP does not tell us which capabilities are the most important, it does potentially tell us what kind of capabilities will emerge from different types of economic relationships in different types of economic systems. If well-being can be conceived as the capability to act—that is, as freedom—then the SMP perspective can potentially tell us how well-being is enhanced or constrained based on the nature of the economic systems in which we act.

The approach outlined above can potentially elucidate our understanding of land tenure formalization. Land tenure formalization is unambiguously a bureaucratization project, whether vested in private or state ownership. Land bureaucratization facilitates land commercialization. Does it therefore follow that land tenure formalization will tend to restrict well-being for non-elites by limiting the capabilities derived through human economy relationships? Will well-being increase for elites as they gain new commercially-derived capabilities? These are questions that can potentially be answered through empirical analyses of emerging formalization projects in places such as Sierra Leone, West Africa. Below, I present a rudimentary research proposal for studying formalization in Sierra Leone. Given the socially constructed nature of customary tenure in Sierra Leone and prospect of formalization, the SMP may be particularly useful for understanding land tenure in rural Sierra Leone and the unfolding impacts of formalization.

Rudiments of a Proposal for Future Research

It is clear that formalization studies will miss important information if they adopt overly narrow understandings of land tenure arrangements and economic relationships—and by extension, human freedom and well-being. Emerging land tenure formalization policies in African countries such as Sierra Leone highlight the importance of new, appropriately conceptualized formalization analysis.

Land tenure formalization is currently being pursued in Sierra Leone as a tool for increasing commercialization and overall well-being. Sierra Leone's new National Land Policy (NLP) calls for the bureaucratic demarcation, registration, and taxation of land under

115

customary tenure in rural Sierra Leone (National Land Policy 2015). Customary land tenure in Sierra Leone is determined by a series of locally navigable social relationships that give people operative claims to use and manage land. These claims are primarily based on patrilineal descent, but maternal ancestry and a dynamic system of hierarchical and hierarchical family alliances also provide a basis for claims, albeit secondary to patrilineal claims (Bottazzi, Goguen, and Rist 2016; Maconochie, Dixon, and Wood 2009; Leach 1997).

It is thought that formalization in Sierra Leone will secure the rights of women and younger men against relatively powerful male elders while encouraging orderly marketization and capitalization of property rights that will in turn facilitate a transition from subsistence to commercial agriculture (Renner-Thomas 2010). However, this approach places undue emphasis on formal ownership and does not fully consider how land is routinely accessed, used, and managed—in other words, it does not take into account the full bundle of rights (Doss et al. 2013). Viewing land tenure as a bundle of rights, as briefly explained in Section 2, will help analysts identify existing land entitlements and capabilities.

A full bundle of rights includes rights to use, access, manage, exclude others, and sell land. Possession of the full bundle implies ownership, but it is possible to possess rights short of full ownership (Schlager and Ostrom 1992). Formalization proponents assume private ownership best incentivizes sustainable land use as is the case with Ali, Deininger, and Goldstein (2014). However, as previously mentioned, empirical analyses indicate that sustainable common property arrangements can, and often do, occur when a community as a whole possess secure ownership and individual community members possess secure use, access, and management rights (Ostrom 2010). From a capabilities perspective, a bundle of rights in land tenure analyses can be conceived as constituting different environmental entitlements from which various capabilities can be derived.

This has implications for understanding potential capability differences between individuals and groups of individuals. For example, given the relative lack of outright land ownership among women throughout Africa, it might be assumed that women possess nearly complete capability depravation regarding land, and any formalization effort that recognizes women's right to own property, however imperfect otherwise, is at least a step toward greater gender equity. However, by not adequately accounting for land rights other than full ownership, formalization schemes may unexpectedly restrict certain existing rights. This could arguably be the case in Rwanda's formalization process that restricted access for women in traditional polygamous marriages (see Section 1). Examples such as this might also be indicative of a shift from human to commercial economies. Regardless, it is important to better understand the bundle of rights in Africa. Doss et al. (2013) analyze existing demographic and land rights databases and find that while women in Africa almost always have less control over existing bundles of land rights, this gap is subject to wide geographic variation and gendered inequalities surrounding use, access, and management rights are typically smaller than inequality for full ownership claims.

In addition to gender, it is helpful to have a nuanced understanding of the role that social, political, and kinship status plays in the distribution of various land rights. In Sierra Leone, ownership is vested in the collective unit of an extended family. Adult family members have the right to use, access, and manage parcels of family land (Leach 1997; Oakerson, Bonanno, and Bonanno 2017). In some cases, past market integration in Sierra Leone has reduced the capabilities of politically less powerful actors. For example, while regional chiefs had previously appropriated the labor of young men from less powerful lineages to an extent, commercial plantations developed in the mid-1900s gave these chiefs additional control over youth through wage labor (Peters and Richards 2011). Although land was not bureaucratically demarcated and titled, this process could perhaps be considered soft formalization in that the British colonial government formally recognized the political power of compliant regional chiefs—thereby entrenching previously contested power— and later encouraged these chiefs to develop commercial plantations. These commercial plantations were also subsequently encouraged by the independent national government and the World Bank (Peters and Richards 2011). Nevertheless, others argue that market-oriented changes such as various infrastructure improvements have given women and young men greater opportunity to leverage their existing rights to cultivate or extract from land and then generate an independent source of livelihood through market income (Fanthorpe 2006; Leach 1997).

Exploring the production of social systems in Sierra Leone and examining the causal relationship between formalization and socially constructed land tenure claims can help us analyze the processes described above with greater clarity and precision. It can also allow us to test the SMP as a theoretical perspective for understanding economic interactions more generally, and thereby advance our understanding of fundamental economic relationships and how these relationships impact what individuals and groups are actually able to do in given social, political, and economic structures. To that end, the following questions can be asked in Sierra Leone and similar contexts:

> What are the freedoms of action related to land claims in rural Sierra Leone? In other words, what are different people—men, women, elders, youths, chiefs, land-holding family members, non-landholding family members—actually able to do with their land claims?

> To what extent do land-related economic transactions involve directly leveraging human relationships versus using a commercial instrument such as money or financial credit? Land-related economic transactions include access, labor, the application of human knowledge, and the input and production of material elements such as seeds, fertilizer, and crops.

> How do different freedoms related to land claims change given different extents of government land documentation (that is, formalization) and commercialization?

As mentioned at the close of the previous section, a SMP perspective predicts that increasing commercialization and formalization will restrict land-related freedoms for non-elites by limiting their ability to access and manage land based on leveraging human relationships. An SMP perspective also predicts that increasing commercialization and formalization will expand the land-related freedoms for elites by increasing their ability to access and manage land through commercial instruments.

While the confirmation of both hypotheses might suggest that the SMP is a useful lens through which anthropologists and other social scientists can analyze land tenure formalization and market integration more generally, the rejection of these hypotheses might indicate that an SMP perspective inaccurately understands social interaction within certain changing economic realities. Regardless, continuing appraisals of formalization in Africa and throughout the Global South must take a view that transcends narrow market-state dichotomies to include common management regimes and must understand human freedom of action within appropriate institutional contexts.

Of course, the hypotheses mentioned above are not mutually exclusive. It is possible that one will be confirmed while the other is rejected, or that one or both will be confirmed within a limited scope. If so, this would suggest that the SMP as currently articulated provides a starting point that can be re-worked to advance our understanding surrounding global efforts towards land tenure formalization and commercialization, and what this means for fundamental economic relationships and human freedom. Whatever the ultimate findings, this is the promising task for future research.

References:

Acheson, James M. 2015. "Private Land and Common Oceans: Analysis of the Development of Property Regimes." *Current Anthropology* 56(1): 28-55.

Agrawal, Arun. 2014. "Studying the Commons, Governing Common-pool Resource Outcomes: Some Concluding Thoughts." *Environmental Science and Policy* 36: 86-91.

Ali, Daniel, Klaus Deininger and Markus Goldstein. 2014. "Environmental and Gender Impacts of Land Tenure Regularization in Africa: Pilot Evidence from Rwanda." *Journal of Development Economics* 110: 262-275.

Berkes, Fikret, David Feeny, Bonnie J. McCay, and James M. Acheson. 1989. "The Benefits of the Commons." *Nature* 340(6229): 91-93.

Bonanno, A.V. and A.M. Bonanno. 2017. [Presentation] "Family Farms, Family Land: National Land Policy, Customary Tenure Arrangements, and Change in Northern Sierra Leone." Paper presented at the Southeastern Regional Seminar in African Studies Fall 2017 Conference, Auburn University (Auburn, AL, USA).

Bottazzi, Patrick, Adam Goguen and Stephan Rist. 2016. "Conflicts of Customary Land Tenure in Rural Africa: Is Large Scale Land Acquisition a Driver of 'Institutional Innovation'?" *The Journal of Peasant Studies* 43:1-19.

Bromley, Daniel. 2008. "Formalizing Property Relations in the Developing World: the Wrong Prescription for the Wrong Malady." *Land Use Policy* 26: 20–27.

Buscher, Bram, Sian Sullivan, Katja Neves, Jim Igoe and Dan Brockington. 2012. "Towards a Synthesized Critique of Neoliberal Biodiversity Conservation." *Capitalism Nature Socialism* 23(2): 4-30.

Deininger, Klaus, Daniel Ali and Tekie Alemu. 2011. "Impacts of Land Certification on Tenure Security, Investment, and Land Market Participation: Evidence from Ethiopia." *Land Economics* 87(2): 312-334.

Demsetz, Harold. 1967. "Toward a Theory on Property Rights." *The American Economic Review* 57(2): 347-359.

de Soto, Hernando. 2003. Listening to the Barking Dogs: Property Law Against Poverty in the Non-West. *Focaal–European Journal of Anthropology* 4: 179-185.

Doss, Cheryl, Chiara Kovarik, Amber Peterman, Agnes Quisumbing and van den Mara Bold. 2013. "Gender Inequalities in Ownership and Control of Land in Africa: Myths Versus

Reality." *International Food Policy Research Institute Discussion Paper 01308*.

Fanthorpe, Richard. 2006. "On the Limits of Liberal Peace: Chiefs and Democratic Decentralization in Post-War Sierra Leone." *African Affairs* 105(408): 27-49.

Fraser, James, Victoria Frausin and Andrew Jarvis. 2015. "An Intergenerational Transmission of Sustainability? Ancestral Habitus and Food Production in a Traditional Agro Ecosystem of the Upper Guinea Forest, West Africa." *Global Environmental Change* 31, 226–238.

Frausin, Victoria, James Fraser, Woulay Narmah, Morrison K. Lahai, Thomas RA Winnebah, James Fairhead, and Melissa Leach. 2014. "God Made the Soil, but We Made It Fertile: Gender, Knowledge, and Practice in the Formation and Use of African Dark Earths in Liberia and Sierra Leone." *Human Ecology* 42: 695-710.

German, Laura, Ryan Unks and Elizabeth King. 2017. "Green Appropriations Through Shifting Contours of Authority and Property on a Pastoralist Commons." *The Journal of Peasant Studies* 44(3): 631-657.

Godoy, R.A., Victoria Reyes-Garcı́a, Clarence Gravlee, T. Huanca, W. Leonard, Thomas McDade and Susan Tanner. 2009. "Moving Beyond a Snapshotto Understand Changes in the Well-Being of Native Amazonians. *Current Anthropology* 50(4): 563-573.

Graeber, David. 2006. "Turning Modes of Production Inside Out: Or, Why Capitalism is a Transformation of Slavery." *Critique of Anthropology* 26(1): 61-85.

Graeber, David. 2011. *Debt: The First 5,000 Years*. Brooklyn: Melville House.

Gsottbauer, Elisabeth, Ivana Logar and Jeroen van den Bergh. 2015. "Towards a Fair, Constructive and Consistent Criticism of All Valuation Languages." *Ecological Economics* 112, 164-169.

Hardin, Garrett. 1968. "The Tragedy of the Commons." *Science* 162: 1243-1248.

Hardin, Garrett. 1978. "Political Requirements for Preserving Our Common Heritage." In *Wildlife and America*. Edited by H.P.

Brokaw, 310-317. Washington, D.C.: Council on Environmental Quality.

Henrich, Joseph. 1997. "Market Incorporation, Agricultural change, and Sustainability Among the Machiguenga Indians of the Peruvian Amazon." *Human Ecology* 25(2): 319-351.

Ibarra, Jose Tomas, Antonia Barreau, C. Del Campo, Claudia Isabel Camacho, Gary J. Martin, and Susannah R. McCandless. 2011. "When Formal andMarket Based Conservation Mechanisms Disrupt Food Sovereignty: Impacts of Community Conservation and Payments for Environmental Services on an Indigenous Community of Oaxaca, Mexico." *International Forestry Review* 13(3): 318-337.

Kallis, Giorgos, Erik Gómez-Baggethun, and Christos Zografos. 2013. "To value or not to value? That is not the question." *Ecological Economics* 94: 97-105.

Knapp, Eli, Nathan Peace and Lauren Bretchel. 2017. "Poachers and Poverty: Assessing Objective and Subjective Measures of Poverty Among Illegal Hunters Outside Ruaha National Park, Tanzania." *Conservation and Society* 15(1): 24-32.

Lawry, Steven, Cyrus Samii, Ruth Hall, Aaron Leopold, Donna Hornby, and Farai Mtero. 2017. "The Impact of Land Property Rights Interventions on Investment and Agricultural Productivity in Developing Countries: A Systematic Review." *Journal of Development Effectiveness* 9(1): 61-81.

Leach, Melisa. 1997. "Shifting Social and Ecological Mosaics in Mende Forest Farming." In *The Ecology of Practice*. Edited by E. Nyerges, 135-167. Amsterdam: Gordon and Breach Publishers.

Leach, Melissa, Robin Mearns and Ian Scoones. 1999. "Environmental Entitlements: Dynamics and Institutions in Community-Based NaturalResource Management." *World Development* 27(2): 225-247.

Maconachie, Roy, Alan B. Dixon and Adrian Wood. 2009. "Decentralization and Local Institutional Arrangements for Wetland Management in Ethiopia and Sierra Leone." *Applied Geography* 29: 269-279.

Millar, Gearoid. 2016. "Knowledge and Control in the Contemporary Land Rush: Making Local Land Legible and Corporate Power Applicable in Rural Sierra Leone." *Journal of Agrarian Change* 16(2): 206-224.

Moore, Sally Falk. 2000. *Law as Process: An Anthropological Approach.* LIT Verlag Münster.

National Land Policy of Sierra Leone. 2015. Government of Sierra Leone Ministry of Lands, Country Planning, and the Environment. Freetown. http://extwprlegs1.fao.org/docs/pdf/sie155203.pdf

North, Douglass. 1990. *Institutions, Institutional Change, and Economic Performance.* Cambridge: Cambridge University Press.

Nussbaum, Martha. 2003. "Capabilities as Fundamental Entitlements: Sen and Social Justice." *Feminist Economics* 9(2-3): 33-59.

Netting, Robert. 1993. *Smallholders, Householders.* Stanford: Stanford University Press.

Oakerson, R.J., A.V. Bonanno and A.M. Bonanno, 2017. [Field Report]. *How Subsistence Farmers Hold and Access Land in Sierra Leone.* Houghton College.

Ostrom, Elinor. 2010. "Beyond Markets and States: Polycentric Governance of Complex Economic Systems." *The American Economic Review* 100(3): 641-672.

Peters, Krijn and Paul Richards 2011. "Rebellion and Agrarian Tensions in Sierra Leone." *Journal of Agrarian Change* 11(3): 377-395.

Renner-Thomas, Ade. 2010. *Land tenure in Sierra Leone: The Law, Dualism and the Making of a Land Policy.* Milton Keynes: Author House.

Schlager, Edella and Elinor Ostrom. 1992. "Property-Rights Regimes and Natural Resources: A Conceptual Analysis." *Land Economics* 68(3): 249-262.

Sen, Amartya. 1981. Ingredients of Famine Analysis: Availability and Entitlements. *The Quarterly Journal of Economics* 96(3): 433-464.

Sen, Amartya. 1983. Poor, Relatively Speaking. *Oxford Economic Papers* 35(2): 153-169.

Tucker, Bram, Amber Huff, Jaovola Tombo, Patricia Hajasoa and Charlotte Nagnisaha. 2011. "When the Wealthy Are Poor: Poverty Explanations and Local Perspectives in Southwestern Madagascar." *American Anthropologist* 113(2): 291-305.

Chapter 6

Migration, Dependence, Freedom and Independence in Ifeoma Chinwuba's *Merchant of Flesh*

Elisabeth N.M Ayuk-Etang
University of Buea

Humankind, from time immemorial, has depended on migration as a liberating aspect that would warrant autonomy, independence, freedom from oppression and the constraints of sedentariness. Migration is a fundamental issue in the 21st century, which is heartwarming worldwide, as intimated by Ashcroft et al. With the advent of globalization, humankind dependency on immigration and emigration has regained currency in discourse as it further shifts from physical to psychological. Here, nobody in the world is left out. The world is a moving world, or so to speak, the world is on the move. However, the reason behind emigration and migration is what makes the difference. Westerners migrate for the sake of exploration, pleasure, and business. People from formerly colonized countries, i.e. those from the South, migrate in and out of their societies in search of greener pastures i.e. wealth that would guarantee them independence, freedom, liberation. Paradoxically, migration ends up becoming their enslavement bait. They end up in the West without the requisite immigrant or resident status that would allow them to have the freedom/independence to circulate freely. Homi K. Bhabha, in his *Location of Culture* expresses, this view on migration when he argues that the idea of migration is an issue which is difficult to combat in this post-colonial age. He says,

> Unlike the dead hand of history that tells the beads of sequential time like a rosary, seeking to establish serial causal connections, we are now confronted with what Walter Benjamin describes as the blasting

of a nomadic moment from the homogenous course of history…"
(Bhabha 4).

This nomadic attitude of the post colonists is attached to social and financial empowerment. To attain their goals, their nonimmigrant/non-resident status must be changed to immigrant and resident. Better still, a complete change of identity will be called for as seen in Athol Fugard's *Sizwe Bansi is dead*, Chimamanda Ngozi Adichie's *Americanah*, NoViolet Bulawayo *We Need New Names*, Samuel Selvon's *The Lonely Londoners* including the Ifoema Chinwuba's *Merchant of Flesh*, the object of the present paper as well as most travelogue literatures.

Nigeria, like most postcolonial societies, is confronted with political, economic and social challenges which have resulted in poverty and the culture of dependence on foreign aid. This insufficiency is at the center of the characters' displacements and Human Trafficking as highlighted by Chinwuba in her novel. The state of Nigeria, as presented by Chinwuba, is lacking in their legal framework. Consequently, there is total lack of autonomy and her citizens live as if they are in a jungle where the bigger animals depend on the smaller ones as food. The inability of these states to provide the necessary tools for independent/autonomous survival to their citizens push the people to move from place to place in search of a more fulfilled and fulfilling life and a sense of independence. Some human traffickers gained favor because of their sophistication in the midst of desperate and frustrated people who they deceivably trafficked abroad and forced into prostitution to enrich none but the traffickers. Interestingly, the traffickers are at the "centre" back home in Nigeria when they return from the West and make a public show of their ill-acquired dollars and pounds. Meanwhile, the trafficked victims and their family remain at their beck and call or on the margin. Trinh T. Minh-ha describes the margin as "our site for survival which becomes our fighting ground and their site for pilgrimage" (Minh-ha 216). Anxiously, these victims sought all ways to join their "madams" i.e. the traffickers, as Chinwuba calls them. They do so with the intention of picking fruits on the streets or washing plates in restaurants in the metropolis. Unfortunately, their dreams are deferred when they are pushed into prostitution by the so call "madams" who tender exorbitant bills to their victims for the "madams" role in bringing them abroad. In such situations, those who comply with this task end up with HIV/AIDS or are killed on the streets of Europe or deported because of their illegal status. Meanwhile those who disobeyed are killed by their benefactors and their relations back in Nigeria are also wiped out. This frightening mindset of human trafficking is Chinwuba preoccupation in *The Merchant of Flesh*. However, there are other variants in opinion as far as this trafficking of persons is concerned.

The UN has identified different ways of human trafficking, "One form is that of agricultural slavery" whereby migrants are transported from one place to the other to work on plantations. According to the UNODC Report, the most common form of human trafficking (79%) is sexual exploitation. The victims of sexual exploitation are predominantly women and girls. In some parts of the world, women trafficking women is the norm. (UNODC Report, 2018) Chinwuba's major concern in *Merchant of Flesh* centers on this obnoxious practice of female sexuality which is traded as a commodity. In "Combating Forced Labour[sic] in Africa: The Role of Endogenous and Exogenous Forces", Ambe J. Njoh and Elisabeth N.M. Ayuk-Etang (2012) argued that forced labor and human trafficking are rapidly growing problems throughout the world, especially in Africa. They established that this problem is greatly enhanced by endogenous and exogenous forces. The study identifies the advent of Islam and Christianity, colonialism and imperialism, as well as the imposition of the capitalist mode of production as elements that conspire to breathe new life in human trafficking. Chinwuba in *Merchant of Flesh*, sturdily highlights poverty as the root from which human traffickers tap their victims.

Poverty eradication, which is the first of the Millennium Development Goals, is at the center of human trafficking. The phenomenon has caught and is catching most people in Africa off guard. There is a variant in the interpretations of poverty. The World Bank in Development Education Program (DED - 2000) considers poverty as hunger, lack of shelter, being sick and not being able to see a doctor. Poverty is not having access to schooling and not knowing how to read. Poverty is not having a job. It is fear for the future. Poverty is losing a child to illness brought about by unclean water. It is lack of representation and lack of freedom. It argues that the "notion of poverty varies…the richer a country is, the higher its poverty line… It established an international poverty line of $1 a day per person in 1985 purchasing power parity (ppp) prices". Conversely, Gareth Rees and Charles Smith in *Economic Development*, distinguishes between relative and absolute poverty. In this division, relative poverty is defined in relation to the situation of another. Its measurement is a matter of social equity, reducing social inequalities and differences in wealth, living conditions and opportunities. Absolute poverty refers to poverty defined according to income which provides a minimum set of resources a person needs to survive. In this definition, the poverty line is determined and anyone that falls below this line is poor. All of the trafficked victims in *Merchant of Flesh* seemingly fall within this category as intimated by Chinwuba in *Merchant of Flesh*

With a diplomatic eye in Italy and Canada, Chinwuba has witnessed these trafficked victims' quandary. *Merchant of Flesh* gives an irreversible image of lack in Faith's neighborhood which is "thickly populated with a long corridor that has single rooms on each side, known in their daily parlance as "face-me-I-face-you" (33). These "rooms together housed over sixty souls," (33) with barely two pit latrines at the end of the building. There is also a common cooking room, whereby the flavour [sic] from food blends the smoke and the odour from the toilet. The "smell joined the urine and toilet odour to form an acrid permanent airlessness that threatened to suffocate the occupant of the house" (34). This unhealthy smell "was a smell of poverty: a mélange of kitchen and septic tanks smells, which meant that one was too poor to keep the two apart" (34). This squalid and polluted environment is injurious and detrimental to the health of the inhabitant of this locale. Faith Moses' fate places her at this peripheral line where "a mixture of the clutter accompanying the lowest of this world in their mistaken existence called life" (34) should be. As subalterns, to reiterate Gayatri Spivak, Faith Moses and her cohort are oppressed, commodified, and exploited because of their social and economic handicapped. Their destiny is left in this dungeon with acrid smell and environmental injustice. They are at the mercies of purported "helpers" such as human traffickers whose promises are sugary at first sight.

However, Chinwuba's *Merchant of Flesh* constitutes a strong feeling of lack and helplessness by the subaltern populace in the narrative. Faith explains: "Sister, you are talking of flushing toilet, […] what of ordinary water to drink? If rain does not fall here, some of us will not be able to catch water to drink. This is in a big town like this. Imagine in the villages. Half of the thing killing our people is dirty water, lack of clean water" (51). Faith's tone here is sorrowful as she expresses regrets to the poor conditions her people lived in. The post independent state of Nigeria does not pay attention to the welfare of its citizens. A good number of people in this community cannot afford pipe borne water because of their limited resources. As a result, some die of diseases contracted from dirty water. The state's failure to provide pipe borne water and other basic necessities like free education to its citizens is a hindrance to the development of that state. Consequently, students drop out of school; there is unemployment, and young girls are lured into prostitution and other irresponsible activities such as human trafficking.

Faith highlights her state of poverty in retrospect; "I am poor, poor, poor. How can I not be when I am an ordinary ward-maid in a third rate, rundown clinic?" (36). Faith becomes a ward maid after she loses her father, who was the only bread-winner in her family. "If anyone had told her that she would end up a ward-maid in a third-rate hospital, she would not have believed it." (39). As a dropout from the academia, Faith "had searched and searched for a job for months and months, pleading, kneeling, begging" in order to work her way out of misery and wretchedness. In her distress and probing how good and successful Lizzy and the rest of the traffickers are, "Faith was not jealous. She was only curious and anxious to learn how to escape from her misery …" (48). With such mindset, she and the rest of the victims are deceivably migrated from Africa to Europe. Lizzy arouses Faith's curiosity to travel abroad thus:

> Well, Faith, I can promise you a better life than you have now. As you can see from that card, I live in Italy now. I can get you a job there. […] I can get you a job in a hospital doing what you are doing now. Otherwise, you could wash plates in a restaurant. Of course not a restaurant like this poor ramshackle one. I am talking about a big, posh, executive restaurant. The tips alone from customers can be more than your salary. People can also pick tomatoes or fruits in a farm. There are many possibilities. The interesting thing is that the salary is good. The white man has what they call minimum wage that is the smallest amount any worker can receive. Right now it is … let me see. (50)

Lizzy uses flowery words to brainwash and lure her victims into her web of prostitution and frustration by giving them false impressions about Europe. The presentation of her card to Faith seems to depict her superiority over Faith since she is now a "been-to". The card is not only a mark of advertising her business but represents an identity for her; it stands as a trope for her belonging whether in Italy as a migrant or in Nigeria. As a "been-to" and trafficker Lizzy's style is indirectly persuasive because she needs trafficked victims to ferry abroad to work for her. According to Esohe Aghatise, "most victims are induced to travel abroad by promise of high effortless earnings in a short period of time" (1129). Aghatise's argument reveals that Africans are always deceived and presented with a wrong image of Europe. This colonial mentality remains in the minds of Africans who think that everything Europe/West is good and vice versa. Faith, who is elated with Lizzy's westernized lifestyle, is motivated to travel abroad and see her dreams come true. The constant use of the personal pronoun "I" by Lizzy indicates that she may belong to the Italian space which she is projecting. There is a contrast between Lizzy, who sounds superior because she is coming from Europe, and Faith, who feels inferior because she is based in Africa. Also, Lizzy's consistent use of the word "now" is to impress Faith and make her see her present life as worthless, thereby, creating the impression of a better life for her in Europe. Calculating the minimum wage, a worker earns in Europe, Lizzy, the internal focalizer, uses the adverb "now" to emphasize that the salary of the least wage earner in Italy is far better than what Faith could imagine. Lizzy's deceit and exaggeration spur Faith's anxiety and excitement to travel to Europe and make her dreams come true.

Lizzy, like other traffickers, is dependent upon her reckless invention of new ways to import and export "the girls" abroad for the ever-vainglorious purposes of amassing wealth. This wealth is demonstrated through the amount of money they (the traffickers) send to Nigeria, and the gigantic buildings they erect. This socio-economic development motivates many parents who oblige their children to travel abroad and make money to improve on their living conditions.

Some parents in this society are in dire need of money to the extent that they seem not to care about the ways through which their children make the money they bring home to them. Faith's mother, Ma, reprimands her daughter because of the thought that some of the outstanding wealth from Europe might come as a result of trafficking drugs. According to Ma, anything that could be done abroad to raise money, "as long as he does not kill anybody … anything short of that was acceptable for survival sake" (100). Ma's words are very important as they show the degrading attitude/mentality of Africans as usurpers due to poverty. The fact that Ma posits anything except murder to make money illustrates, by inference, that she is an unconscious trafficker. In this connection, some parents who are blinded by money from abroad simply wish to undertake this journey to quick wealth. As such, they desire to have female children who will go to Italy and grace their lives with money:

Now people were praying for female children that would eventually go to Italy when they reached puberty. People now wished pregnant women to "born" females, baby girls that would go to Italy, twelve years later, and take over the baton from a sister or aunt or cousin before them. "Go and make money for me, my dear. Good daughter. Good pikin, what would I do without you? Go, the genitals have no measurement, no ruler. It does not finish. When you finish making money, you can marry". (73)

Poverty has created a different mindset to the people of this community that like Faith's mother, they have the awful need to walk out of their present impoverished state. The adverb of time "now" in the quote above is an indicator of urgency to have female children who will go to Europe and make money. Notice the shift in the mind of the postcolonial man whereby a girl child is preferred to a boy child; the reverse is true as postulated in the works of some previous writers like Buchi Emecheta, Juliana Makuchi and Tsitsi Dangarembga. In "Feminity, Sexuality and Culture: Patriarchy and Female Subordination in Zimbabwe, Maureen kambarami holds strong to this patriarchal view when she says the male child is preferred to the female child. In fact, males rule females by right of birth and even if the male child is not the first born in a family, he is automatically considered the head of the household who should protect and look after his sisters". The woman's marginal space is brought to the centre for vainglorious purpose because she still remains an object of exploitation. She is not considered a human being but is valued because of the wealth she will bring to the family. The wealth expected from her is no longer through her bride price, but from her daily bodily sales.

The parents of these trafficked victims, especially the men, do acknowledge prostitution as a necessity which has no defect. That explains why parents could urge their children to use what they have i.e. their bodies, to get what they want, after all, "the genital has no measurement, no ruler. It does not finish." (78) Prostitution has been connoted positively. A child that prostitute and sends money to her parents is known as "good pikin" i.e. a good child and vice versa.

Moreover, Italy has a better and ready market for this 'unhealthy act'. The idea of the producer/consumer dependency is highlighted whereby the Italians are the consumers who are endowed with goods and services. They determine the prices. Given the high demand of "sex" for financial gain in Italy, a man insults his daughter who wants to uphold the mores of womanhood by getting married in these words:

> Stupid girl. You are here entertaining your boyfriend for free. Follow your mates to Italy. Go and meet the white man and make money. Foolish girl. Stupid fool. You want to bring disgrace to me? Don't you see my mates riding cars sent by their children? You are here befriending men for free. You say you want to get marry. If I hear that out of your mouth again, I will slap okra seeds from your smelly mouth." (73)

The tone of the speaker is bitter. He is angry with the daughter. He calls her "stupid girl" without mentioning her name to illustrate her invisibility and lack of identity. This bitterness, here expressed by the speaker, results from his disgust of the fact that his daughter is in a love relationship with somebody the speaker considers worthless. The African boy is acclaimed with nothingness, but the little girl is urged "to go and meet the white man who is supposedly rich, thus exposing the postcolonial binary of black/poor and white/rich. Marriage, which is an honorable institution to the black woman, has become stupidity. Apparently, there is a shift in discourse here, whereby the black man feels he can exploit the white man through his daughters. Little wonder, this "exploitation" is to the detriment of the young girl whose individuality is stifled and her health is also at risk. As a result, the black woman's body is nothing but a consumer product as considered by the white.

Black prostitutes seem to play a vital role on the Italian community. When they stayed off the street, nine rape cases were registered in one week. "Four by family members. Even a teenage immigrant student was gang-raped by a group of boys" (227). Before a fortnight, "more rape cases were reported all over Italy including that of a woman of eighty in Reggio Emilia" (229). These rape cases become a call for concern to the Italian medical institution. It's in that light that a medical expert calls on the immigration officials to regularize the prostitutes' stay, purporting that "medically speaking, medically, I repeat, these girls play an important role in our health system" (228). The black woman's presence in Italy safeguards the welfare of the Italian woman, as well as the entire populace. Her absence is important, because while on the street, these girls are vulnerable to rape. This shows the white man's high libido towards African women. Again, the disappearance of the prostitutes pushes the Italian men with high sexual desires to harass even their own women.

Despite the "protective roles" these black girls play in the Italian community, they are rampantly found dead in the street of Italy and no investigation is carried out because they are dead, prostitutes and black. So, "the police never seemed to follow up on these incidents. No attempt is made to catch the perpetrators. It's like the victims count for nothing" (4). The idea of nothingness is associated to the postcolonial man. His/her existence to serve the white man is acceptable, but his/her absence through death is insignificant.

Chinwuba further highlights mismanagement of the state's estate, bribery, and corruption as spectacular in Nigeria. This state of affairs has made the leaders to amass wealth for themselves while the masses wallow in misery. Chinwuba confirms that Nigeria is "a rich oil-producing country; the sixth world producer of petroleum." but that money goes into private bank accounts and finally there is always fuel shortage in the country. Mismanagement has led the people of this giant petroleum producing country to lament thus: "Where is this country headed?" This question can only be answered by those in possession of public funds. The bus driver and his passengers, who are a representation of the masses worries thus: "Our rulers are only interested in lining their pockets. They have huge accounts in all the banks in the world. Nobody cares for the poor" (114). Italians cannot imagine how a country which is so rich in oil production can breed a group of people living in abject poverty, so their conclusion is that "there was a lot of bribery in business circles in Third World countries and in fact, it would be possible to have a head of state siphon money of that magnitude without any question asked" (140). With this in mind, the Italian knows that the postcolonial African man has no place in and out of his land because the siphoned money is kept abroad and the masses struggle to go abroad for a better livelihood whereby they are exposed to frustration, desperation, exploitation and colonization.

Mismanagement in this community breeds corruption. A classic example is the security officer at the immigration office who does not pay attention to the girls he is supposed to control, but "would be leafing through the documents until he came across the green notes in the middle. … the officer will slide these notes down into a waiting carton placed on the floor under his table, then stamp the papers vigorously, waving them through, without so much as a glance at the girls" (67). Lizzy recounts the intricacies of owning a passport when it's being issued at the 'back door'; this means using illegal and/or corrupt means to acquire a passport. That is the immigration officer issues the passport without taking cognizance of the bearer because his pocket has been filled with money. "Once you were able to pay the bribe demanded by the passport issuing officer, he would process the document" (69) without any supporting documents such as birth or marriage certificates. Corruption does exist at every stage of the trafficking business. It is practiced by those issuing passports, those issuing of visas to the victims, those helping victims to cross the borders in order not to be identified and, finally, the *"Carabineers"* who are friends to the traffickers.

However, once the girls get to Italy, their self-esteem and dignity are defiled, and they become sex machines in order to pay back the exorbitant debt imposed on them upon their arrival in Italy. Faith Moses is asked to pay "ninety million in Italian money" (267). An amount she is supposed to pay within two years. My Ufot, a Nigerian, working at the Nigerian embassy in Italy, "did some elementary arithmetic and concluded that for her to pay that amount as stipulated in the contract, she has to sleep with at least three to four thousand men." (20) A woman who sleeps with this number of men is equated to an animal and her lifespan is shortened. Nonetheless, before getting to their destination (Italy), some of the trafficked victims from Nigeria pay their "tolls" to the "madams" i.e. the intermediaries who pursue their travelling documents. These tolls are usually harsh, unprotected sex or money.

The migration process is also very risky, be it by land, sea or air. Chinwuba recounts a situation whereby one of Lizzy's girls, Doris, is being held at the Charles De Gaulle International Airport because of her behavior at the airport. Such behavior resulted in her detention at a psychiatric hospital. Faith recounts:

> I went first, [...] next was Doris. Poor Doris. Ordinarily she did not understand English, did not speak it well. Now here was this French man who spoke through his nose. I believe Abu made a sign to her and she let out a scream, a loud scary scream that startled all the people around us. She threw her hands in the air, tore her hairpiece out of her head and let her mouth hang out wide open. ... Just then Abu intervened and explained to the officer that Doris had a history of mental illness. For this reason, he was taking her to her brother in Italy for medical attention. ... They brought a stretcher and strapped Doris onto it. Then they told Abu that they were taking Doris to the psychiatric hospital that she was not in a good state to travel" (261).

Doris's retention by the immigration officers is frustrating both to Doris and Lizzy. It is frustrating to Doris who is impeded in the cause of pursuing an unknown future, and also to Lizzy whose business was disturbed and capital detained.

Eventually, Chinwuba presents a bevy of girls who are prostitutes, hitting the streets of Italy in search of clients to enable them accumulate money, pay off their "madams" and buy their freedom and or independence. Lizzy recounts her experience thus: "I worked two good years for Aunty Rose. Go and ask. She is there. Not one day did I give trouble, knowing that, one day, I will finish paying her and set up my own business" (81). Lizzy, a onetime trafficked victim, could pay off her debt and is presently a trafficker. Having bought off her freedom, she indulges in the obnoxious practice of trading human beings. Lizzy's act confirms Frantz Fanon's view in *Black Skin White Mask* (1952) that when a black man is freed from slavery; he starts by enslaving his own counterpart. It is in this light that Lizzy told her girls that "there is no holiday in this job. ... Time is money" (80). As such, Lizzy trains the girls on "how

136

to stuff cotton wool and tissue paper up their system when they were seeing red, to be able to work with the lower outer part" (80). Since these girls are answerable to Lizzy as their "madam", they follow her instructions fervently. She instructs:

> You have a debt to pay. And remember, you are not doing this for love or for fun. It should not last more than three minutes. Once the man has released, leave him; go, start hustling again for the next client. The money the client pays is for one come, not two. If he wants a second round again, make him pay first. If he does not pay, no do. Remember to bend down forward, let him do from back. That style is faster for them. No need for underwear. Time is money. Do not waste time on foreplay. Any extra service attracts extra charge. This is business. (80)

From Lizzy's instructions, the female body is sold as a commodity and is used as a sex machine by the colonizers. Lizzy's instructions are specific because she has lived the experience as a former victim of trafficking who is now a trafficker. She understands the terrain so well that she knows what it will take for her to recuperate her money and amass wealth from these girls. In retrospect of her days of servitude, she threatens, oppresses and eventually kills Tina who does not want to succumb to her orders. Of course, as a "madam" who masters the trade of trafficking girls from Africa, she keeps them subjected to her whim and caprice. "It was slavery all over again. The girls will be under bondage to pay back millions of liras, supposedly spent in bringing them out of their poverty-stricken lives in Nigeria" (197).

Lizzy and the other "madams" reflect Edward Oben Ako's assertion in "Between and Within" that post colonialism is not only a problem between blacks and whites but also within the black community. The trafficked victims not only experience exploitation from the European/Italian sex market, but also from their black counterpart from Nigeria: "Most of the girls did not know what types of jobs awaited them abroad until they got there. However, it was too late for them to turn back. Their travelling documents would have been taken from them and perhaps used them to ferry in other girls" (197). This business in human trafficking is a whole program with consistent follow-up lessons in *Merchants of Flesh*. Since most of the girls are stranded abroad, they finally embrace the unexpected street life because, at that point in time, they have no choice. The silencing of their voices pushes them to work tirelessly day and night. For that reason, the job has no season and no break. No winter or summer. During winter, the girls cling to each other round a fire waiting for their clients. The job knows no sickness or seasonal break as is the case with Roli who "for over two weeks, has been nursing a wound in her genitals. In spite of that, madam had forced her to work" (219).

This inhuman training has made the girls to lose their sense of self. They sleep with their client on a patch at each joint. This patch "costs ten thousand extra to use. There is a blanket there" (275). Of course, the patch is uncomfortable, for that reason; there is no foreplay, what Faith calls "touch bobby", i.e. breast caressing. The prostitutes consider that as waste of time. Lovette reminds Faith: "Remember, we do not do this for fun. The client is not your boyfriend so do not waste time. Lovette re-echoes Lizzy's declaration to Faith sequentially to emphasize the fact that time is money. This money is needed to settle their "madams" in turn for them (the victims) to be settled. Consequently, the victims look for all avenues to payback their debts. They do take-home which fetches them more money but is risky. "Many girls have not come back alive. The clients kill them and dump their bodies in the bush" (276). The consular officer from Nigeria counted about seven dead cases of prostitutes in a week. However, no "attempt is made to catch the perpetrators. It's like the victims count for nothing" (4). No investigation for such deaths is warranted because these victims are blacks and prostitutes. As blacks, in a foreign land, they are debased. This observation confirms Frantz Fanon's view in *Black Skin, White Mask* that "a woman of color is never altogether respectable in a white man's eyes" (42). Though black and white do co-exist all over the world, Fanon considers their relationship as built on hatred for the blacks, when he says "that is why the Americans have substituted discrimination for lynching" (53).

The constant attack and killing of prostitutes on the street of Europe has made the prostitutes to build a defense mechanism towards their clients. Chinwuba informs readers that the girls too have learnt new ways to work at their different joints: They do not do "take away" alone. They come together and fight a client who wants to subdue them; they collect their complete money before the commencement of the business. Also, for the men who come to steal their money, they spray acid into the (the thieves') eyes and run away. Notwithstanding, all these measures are less protective to the girls. Some of the gentle men still infect them with HIV/AIDS. Meanwhile others are repatriated after having completed their debt and are about to start their own investment. A handful of them is harassed and exploited sexually in the name of police patrols. Faith recounts her first experience:

> It was while we were standing by the arena, [...] that two policemen approached us and all I heard was 'documenti' [...] They led us to their car packed around the corner. Lovette explained to me that she had told them our papers were at home. ... We were bundled into the police car. [...] We raced through the streets of Verona. [...] We were now at the outskirts of Verona. The sirens were switched off. Only the lights flashed silently. Suddenly, the police driver veered off the main road into a dirt path. [...] they were my first clients in the oldest profession on earth, which had now become mine, and they paid nothing. They took Lovette and I in turns and afterwards abandoned us there to hike our way back to town. (283 – 284)

These girls also experience sexual harassment and exploitation from the colonizers; those who pay and use them as sex machines; others pay for them to sleep with their dogs, and some arrest and rape them like the two police officers who had them in turns. The rape that Faith and Lovette experience from these two men can only be compared to the rape experiences that black women encountered from their slave masters in the days of slavery. Faith and Co are trafficked victims who are voiceless, and "usually end up as forced labourers [sic] abroad" (Njoh and Ayuk-Etang, 2013). They cannot resist this obnoxious treatment from their masters, otherwise, they might be repatriated for lack of documents or they might be killed. In this light, depending on travel out of home for greener pastures without authentic documents would leave one hapless and at the mercy of others for one's freedom i.e. the worst kind of dependence. Thus, as the saying goes: a cock at home becomes a chick out of home. This insinuates a loss of identity. Chinwuba's female characters experience exploitation at different levels, thus they have no other life but that of servitude.

From the foregoing discussion, one will realize that reliance on migration for liberation, freedom, independence, etc. by the post-colonial citizen in the 21th century is nothing short of a euphemism for eventual servitude, i.e. living (in)dependence. This is because these citizens do not only experience suffering, but they live it in their migrated world. Their exploitation results from their status as voiceless carnal objects. Dependency renders them powerless, as observed in *Merchant of Flesh*. The traffickers were once victims who have been liberated through (hard work). Their financial autonomy commands power and authority back home amidst their crime. Their diasporic status makes them seemingly important in the same society where they were once upon a time subjugated to poverty and social challenges. The authorial ideology, as constructed from the text, is that migration is not a liberating force for the postcolonial woman or man and neither is it a solution to his/her problems. It is apt to re-emphasize the often remembered saying that a "cock becomes a chick" in a strange land. Consequently, reliance on migration for liberation, freedom, independence, etc. is a form of escapism. The postcolonial man should instead struggle and fight to change the situation in his country and not struggle to escape from it – for as the saying made famous by Bob Marley goes, "he who fights and runs away will live to fight another day" (Bob Marley Web).

WORKS CITED

Adichie, Chimamanda Ngozi. *Americanah*. Alfred A. Knopf, 2013.

Aghatise, Esohe. "Trafficking for Prostitution in Italy" *Violence Against Women*, Vol. 10. No. 10. 2004.

Ako, O. Edward. (Ed.) *Between and Within: Essays in Commonwealth and Postcolonial Literature*. Editions Saargraph, 2003.

Aschroft, Bill et al. (Eds.). "Introduction." *The Post-Colonial Studies Reader*. Routledge, 1995.

_____. *Key Concepts in Postcolonial Studies*. Routledge, 1998.

Bhabha, K. Homi. *The Location of Culture*. Routledge, 1994.

Chinwuba, Ifeoma. *Merchant of Flesh*. Spectrum Books, 2003.

Dangarembga, Tsitsi. *Nervous Conditions*. The Women's Press, 1988.

Emecheta, Buchi. *Second Class Citizen*. Alison and Bushy, 1974.

_____. *The Bride Price*. Heinemann, 1976.

Fanon, Frantz. *Black Skin, White Mask*. Grove P, 1968.

Fugard, Athol. *Sizwe Bansi is Dead*. Oxford U. P., 1986.

Kambarami, Maureen. "Feminity, Sexuality and Culture: Patriarchy and Female Subordination in Zimbabwe, *African Regional Sexuality Resource Centre*, 03/08/2006, www.arsrc.org/download/uhsss/kambarami/pdf. 06/02/2010.

Makuchi, Julianna. *Gender in African Women's Writing*. Indiana U. P. 1997.

Minh-ha, Trinh T. "No Master Territories." *The Post-Colonial Studies Reader*. (Eds.). Bill Ashcroft et al. Routledge, 1995, 428 – 430.

Njoh, J. Ambe and Elisabeth N.M. Ayuk-Etang. "Combating Forced Labour and Human Trafficking in Africa: The role of Endogenous and Exogenous Forces". *African Review of Economics and Finance*. Vol. 4. 1. 2012.

Selvon, Sam. *The Lonely Londoners*. Longman, 1956.

Spivak, Gayatri Chakravorty. "Can the Subaltern Speak?" *The Post-Colonial Studies Reader*. (Eds.). Bill Ashcroft et al. Routledge, 1995, 24 – 28.

UNHC (Online). "The Protocol to Prevent, Suppress and Punish Trafficking in Persons Especially Women and Children." Accessed, Nov. 24, 2011 from:

http://www2.ohchr.org/english/law/protocoltraffic.htm

World Bank Poverty Net: www.worldbank.org/poverty

World Bank Development Education Programme, *Beyond Economic Growth: Meeting the Challenges of Global* Development 22/09/2014 www.**worldbank**.org/depweb/beyond/**global**/chapter6.htm. 2ooo.

Chapter 7

African Immigrants in the United States: Perspectives on Acculturative Stress and Religiosity

Christson A. Adedoyin
Samford University

Mary S. Jackson,
East Carolina University
&
Kayode Julius Ayeni, MA
Independent Scholar

Introduction

Scholars have observed the unique religious mosaic, religious practices, and the wealth of spiritual capital that African immigrants bring along to North America (Akintunde, 2007; Clarkson-Freeman et al., 2013; Okpewho & Nzegwu 2009; Olupona & Gemignani, 2007). The World Bank long ago acknowledged spiritual capital as a mechanism for human development (Clarke, 2007; Deneulin & Rakodi, 2011; Ryan 1995). Surprisingly, spiritual capital has been understudied and underutilized by healthcare professionals in better understanding how African immigrants deploy spirituality/religiosity in attaining healthy life-styles, and coping with life's challenges in North America. Unsurprisingly, however, the spiritual/religious capital of immigrant congregations have persistently been identified as sources of social support, acculturation, healthy living, education, and employment hubs to mention but a few (Ebaugh & Chafezt, 2000; Okpewho & Nzegwu 2009).

Hitherto, African immigrants' health profiles have been assumed and subsumed into the African American culture. Thus, extant literature focusing on health promotion, and coping strategies among

African Americans have been erroneously applied to, or suggested as best practices for African immigrants. With an estimated 1.65 million African immigrants living in the United States of America (Zong & Batalova, 2017), African immigrants and their religious institutions are no longer perceived as appendages, or amalgams of African Americans. Consequently, African immigrants are establishing a new paradigm of healthy immigrant effect (Venters and Gany, 2011) and the intersection of this paradigm with the indigenous and "imported brand" of religion and spirituality capital to address health, and acculturation challenges (Okepwho & Nzegwu 2009; Olupona & Gemignani, 2007).

While scholarship is burgeoning on the roles of spirituality/religion in health promotion, and coping strategies of African immigrants in North America across disciplines there is no research endeavor that has attempted to synthesize the array of extant scholarship describing how African immigrants use spirituality (or religiosity) to cope with the challenges of acculturation, and to maintain a healthy lifestyle. Moreover, no research compendium exists to showcase how spirituality or religiosity influences healthy behaviors and enhances coping skills among African immigrants North America. From the foregoing therefore, an observable gap and opportunity for scholarship exists in the literature.

The main purpose of this chapter is, therefore, to provide a review of extant literature on the role of spirituality (or religiosity) in improving the health and coping strategies of African immigrants in North America. Secondly, it is our expectation that this chapter will jump-start additional scholarly discussion, and prompt further research exploration of the nexus of health, acculturation, and spirituality/religiosity coping mechanisms of African immigrants in North America. Succinctly, this chapter seeks to contribute to the emerging scholarship of the spiritual/religious capital of African immigrants and the intersections of health, acculturation, and the deployment of religion/spirituality as coping strategies in the global north.

144

Challenges of Acculturation

Immigration comes with the challenge of adaptation to the new homeland. This adaptation or acculturation process leads to conflict in the original cultural patterns of the immigrant (Gitterman 2001). The multiple anxieties and uncertainties which accompany the acculturation process induces stress. Stress is the response of individuals to the circumstances or events that threaten their coping ability as either psychological discomfort or social distress (Santrock 1997). Gitterman (2001) posited that stress is the imbalance experienced between external demands and self-defined capability.

For instance, among African immigrants, the lack of recognizing their homeland educational credentials, otherwise termed de-skilling or de-credentialing (Grant & Nadin 2007; Gou, 2015) causes a lot of acculturative stress, frustration, and socioeconomic immobility. The consequence of deskilling catalyzes status reversal for most or some African immigrants from a higher status in country of origin, to a lower economic status in receiving countries. This experience no doubt accentuates and contributes to acculturative stress. This, further, triggers inner conflict and anxiety in qualifying for similar licenses and jobs in the new homeland (Grant & Nadin 2007; Gou 2015). Climbing the high-status ladder could be fraught with diverse challenges. This transitioning phase presents psychosocial challenges for which African immigrants often seek solutions and professional help (Berry 1997).

Berry (1997) also stated that high socio-economic status is protective against life stressors. Therefore, if an immigrant's economic status prior to migration is relatively higher, any reversal through deskilling or acculturative stress can be counterproductive to the overall health and wellbeing of immigrants. Individuals who migrate to new environments often forego financial resources, experience status loss, and lose social and professional mobility status in new homelands. Berry further asserted that that majority of immigrants in the lower social status are more likely to experience high stress. Thus, stress may manifest as anxiety, depression, psychosomatic symptoms and identity confusion (Berry, Kim, Minde, & Mok 1987).

Theoretical Speculations

The United Stated of America, as a nation of immigrants, has been very accepting of immigrants who can easily assimilate into society. Assimilation was not a choice for black Africans in America because American cultural norms had successfully enslaved them, and they did not give up many of their African traditions (norms). In addition, immigrants such as Africans find it more difficult, not only because of the historical link, but also primarily because they look different from the majority (White) population. Acculturative process and challenges are therefore, an imperative experience for African immigrants.

Gungor, Fleischmann, Phalet, and Maliepaard (2013) research on immigrants in Europe reported that acculturation stress has an impact on the immigrants' health, and therefore, religion can be a coping strategy. Acculturation occurs when individuals and/or groups take on cultural norms of another group whilst simultaneously attempting to maintain their own particular cultural norms as well (Gungor et al., 2013). Acculturation differs from assimilation in that acculturation allows for the uniqueness of each groups cultural norms to remain distinct (Kottak, 2007).

Whereas, assimilation is the integration of cultural norms to the extent that features of only one culture are dominant. Assimilation can lead to extinction of one's cultural norms as is in the case of Native Americans in America who have assimilated to the point where their culture and practices continue to decline in mainstream America. Redfield, Linton, and Herskovits (1936) discussed the "psychic conflict" that may develop as a result of the acculturation process. The experiences of emotional stress bring about a fundamental psychological distress that may affect the African immigrants upon arrival in America.

146

The Role of Spirituality and Religiosity in the Acculturation Process

Religiosity is interchangeably used as spirituality in literature. Spirituality is defined as the ability to give meaningful outlook to a precarious situation, by having inner convictions that there is some greater purpose or force at work for a favorable outcome and then finding solace and strength in these outlooks (Walsh 1999). The thin line between religion and spirituality exists to the layman as an academic exercise just like the difference between the chick and the egg. Spirituality is considered one of the many coping tools for immigrants. For instance, over 1000 empirical studies on religious coping were published between 1997 and 2011 (Pargament, Mahoney, Exline, Jones, & Shafranske, 2013). However, many questions remain unanswered, especially as they relate to the use of spirituality in the acculturation of African immigrants. For example, a major question, which needs answers, is: How do African immigrants utilize their spirituality in coping with acculturative stress in the United States. It is equally important to identify factors that contribute to acculturation stress and provide best practices to dealing with attendant emotions and stressors.

Religion and Spirituality as Coping and Resilience Factors in Acculturation

Religion and spirituality are both coping mechanisms in attenuating acculturation stress. Studies have shown an inverse relationship between trauma and religiosity (Adedoyin, et. al., 2016; Chen & Koenig, 2006; Hook, 2016). Spirituality contributes to resiliency, while religious coping was identified as being significant in times of stress (Pargament & Raiya, 2007). From the reviewed research studies there is no doubt that religiosity and spirituality contributes to the healing process, fosters acculturation adapting and compensates for the attendant socio-economic losses of migration (Adedoyin, et. al., 2016; Walsh 1999). Pargament and Raiya also noted that religion is reported to be relatively available part of the orienting system, as thus a compelling way of coping. The submission of the aforementioned scholar undergirds the influencing relationship between religiosity involvement either at organized and private levels (spirituality) and surmounting the daunting problem of acculturative stress.

In his combined religious moderator-deterrent model, Pargament (1997) as cited by Xu (2016, p. 1399) affirmed that "religious coping serves a moderating function and protects religious people from the harm of stress". This implies that African Immigrants who actively engage in religious or spiritual practices at private or organized levels might cope with acculturation stress in their residing or sojourning countries. Concurrently, religious coping performs a deterring function because it is a reliable predictor of more favorable outcomes no matter how intense the stress is (Xu, 2016). The implication of this is that religious intervention has a moderating influence on stress, as it provides strength and comfort in such critical times. The aforementioned evidence in the literature, therefore, provides justification for understanding the mechanism of religious coping and acculturation among African immigrants in the United States. Without doubt, religion can be described as helping to address the problem of human insufficiency in trauma or vulnerability by providing solutions such as spiritual control, explanation for difficult life events, and a sense of control.

The Paradigms of Positive and Negative Religious Coping Strategies

- **Positive Religious Coping and Acculturative Stress**

Researchers have identified positive religious coping strategies which appear to promote healing and reduce traumatic acculturation stress. Spiritual coping is a means of dealing with such stress when triggered in the adjustment phase of settlement in the new homelands. Positive religion seeks to reinterpret the stressor as salutary by treating God as partner, seeking and appreciating God's love and care (Xu 2016). This partnership is what Pargament et al.

(2011) meant when they asserted that when spirituality or religiosity is applied to an African immigrant, "a secure relationship with a transcendent force, a sense of spiritual connectedness with others, and a benevolent world view" (p. 51).

Thus, acculturative stressor can be reinterpreted, or reframed as treating God as the partner, seeking, and appreciating God's love and care. All these imply that acculturative stress and spirituality are inter-related, in that an immigrant experiencing disequilibrium, will seek spiritual means of appeasement or finding meaning to the multifarious challenges besetting his immigration experience. It could be from a supportive standpoint or understanding the mystery behind perceived misfortune in the new enterprise. Such perception or belief is common among African immigrants who see every challenge or blessing from purely a spiritual lens. Doubtlessly, positive religiosity/ spirituality stimulates spiritual awakening, offers hope, and opens possibility for growth (Vis & Boynton, 2008). Spirituality also helps people overcome their pain by redefining the event as God's plan, finding something beneficial in their experiences as well as turning to church or God for guidance and support (Fallot & Heckman, 2007).

Acculturation and Negative Religious Coping

However, the negative religious coping mechanism, "reinterprets the stressor as a punishment given by God, passively depending on God to resolve the stressor, attempting to cope on one's own without relying on God's help" (Xu 2016, p. 1399). Whereas negative spiritual coping involves individuals struggling with their faith in a God who allowed negative, hurtful things to happen to them, leading them to denounce the existence of God and take a distance from spiritual beliefs (Hook, 2016). This is detrimental and potentially increases stress and deleterious effects resulting in negative psychosocial behavior. This perspective mirrors "underlying spiritual tensions and struggles within one's self, with others, and with the divine". (Pargament et al. 2011, p.51). Hook also identified negative religious coping strategies, which are associated with an increase in distress

(Hook 2016). Therefore, it will be instructive to have a better understanding of the role of positive religion on the acculturation experiences of African immigrants in the United States. Concurrently, it will be appropriate to also understand if immigrants utilize negative spiritual coping strategies and the intersections of acculturative stress.

From the foregoing therefore, religion/spirituality reduces the sense of powerlessness or abandonment of being without support and worthlessness which can erode confidence or trust in God or the higher power. Religious practitioners who view traumatic events as part of God's judgment further their sense of self-blame. Spirituality is therefore transpersonal beyond the person's self and ego.

The next section discusses specific health and emotional challenges associated with acculturative stress among African immigrants in the USA. The section also offers insights into the deployment of religious, and or spiritual capital to mitigate health challenges among African immigrants in the USA.

Health and Emotional Challenges that Assail African Immigrants in the USA

-   Health Needs

Many black African immigrants have migrated to the USA from African nations with very limited, or even non-existent preventive healthcare systems. Therefore, many enter the USA with limited knowledge about health care resources coupled with language and cultural barriers many live with untreated illnesses. Many black African immigrants who are treated by American physicians may be unclear about medical protocols due to culturally insensitive communication, language barriers, and differences in healthcare practice between the USA and immigrants' countries of origin. The following section delineates some of the common health challenges African immigrants encounter in the USA.

- **Trauma**

African refugees and asylees have unique national and cultural identities and stories behind their resettlement in the United States. Many of these class of African immigrants have stories that are filled with sadness, violence, and horror. Theirs are difficult and complex stories for many in the USA to understand. Refugees have endured significant amounts of trauma, rape, beatings, discrimination, tortures, humiliation, and mutilation as well as having witnessed the murder of a loved one. Witnessing the destruction of one's country, home, family and friends can leave refugees traumatized and at a higher risk for mental illness (Matheson, Jorden & Anisman, 2008). Refugees once had to live in constant fear for their lives. This fear has stemmed for a variety of reason from persecution or random brutal acts. Unfortunately, it is impossible to completely forget their trauma experiences, leaving African refugees with the only option of attempting to cope.

Matheson et al. (2008) examined the impact of traumatic experiences on resettled African refugees. They specifically looked at a sample of 90 Somali refugees' ability to successfully cope with stressful situations created by the stressors associated acculturation. The study found that trauma experienced before a refugee's migration was more likely to have an impact on the formation of mental illness, such as anxiety, depression and PTSD.

However, African refugees continue to experience incidents of trauma upon resettlement, such as traumatic news from family still in their homeland, loss of social support, threats, discrimination, and the overall impact of acculturation. Matheson et al. (2008) also identified differences in the amount of impact and coping style used based on the type of trauma experienced. It is important to understand the varying impact of trauma, it can be altered in all different ways including: severity of the event, the individual's temperament, number of traumatic events, whether the trauma was experienced in a collective group or individually. Assault was the traumatic event most associated with the formation of psychological disturbances (Matheson et al., 2008). However, refugees' ability to cope with traumatic experiences are associated with better mental health outcomes and ability to handle future stressors. Overall, religious faith was reported as the most commonly used coping strategy and resiliency factor for protecting African refugees' acculturation stressors (Adedoyin et al., 2016; Matheson et al., 2008). These findings are important because it demonstrates the naturally occurring protective factor of religion and spirituality engrained in African culture. The collective beliefs held by African refugees in regards to their religion promote a strong, shared sense of grand design. This sense can give African refugees the strength to find meaning and hope from their traumatic experiences, allowing them to successfully cope with new stressors faced with resettlement (Adedoyin et al., 2016; Matheson et al., 2008).

Mental Health: The Trio of Post-Traumatic Stress Disorder, Anxiety, and Depression

- Collectivist versus Individualistic Cultures

Most African culture is a collectivist culture whereas the United States is an individualistic culture. The individualistic culture of the United States radically contrasts with the collectivist culture to which African immigrants are accustomed. The collectivist culture is based on its population members thriving on group-cohesion. Members in the collective society view themselves as a member of specific groups all connected by culture. Individuals can belong to multiple groups such as family, friends, community, ethnicity and nationality. The members of this culture prosper and advance through their alliances, therefore much of an individual's self-esteem, identity, happiness and purpose is derived through the groups' view of the individual and how the group as a whole appears to be thriving.

Since African refugees and immigrants are accustomed to the collectivist culture, moving to the United States, an individualistic culture-based society, can have a traumatic impact on their physical and emotional wellbeing. It is not uncommon for depression to strike after an African individual moves from one culture to another, especially one that is halfway around the world. The different relationship patterns and societal views can leave immigrants and refugees vulnerable to low self-esteem, loneliness, anxiety, and depression.

Post-Traumatic Stress Disorder

Researchers believe that post-traumatic stress disorder (PTSD) is the most common mental illness experienced by resettled refugees, and new immigrants whose migration have been stressful (Rasmussen, Hawthorne, & Keller, 2007). There is no exact record to date of how many refugees suffer from this disorder; researchers have discovered a wide range of percentages while researching the topic. However, Gladden (2006) in his literature review stated an average of 30.6 per cent. There are also significant symptoms associated with PTSD, which can include "hyper vigilance, flashbacks, nightmares, ex- aggregated startle response, concentration problems, and avoiding traumatic cues (Rasmussen et al., 2007, p.171)".

Rasmussen et al. (2007) also described African symptoms involving social problems and a variety of clinical disorders. This is a mental illness that can drastically take hold of an immigrant or refugee's life until treated. Rasmussen et al. (2007) research examined 400 male and female African refugees resettled in America. Their results found symptoms of numbing and avoidance in African refugees with PTSD (Rasmussen. et. al., 2007). They additionally discussed the limitations of comparing African refugees to the assigned symptoms of the Euro-American population. The Rasmussen et al. (2007) sample also reported feeling less interest in daily activity, feeling hopeless, and feeling angry. All of these symptoms and the usual symptoms of PTSD make living a normal productive life nearly impossible.

However, recent studies have reported hope as being a significant coping skill needed by African refugees to overcome the past and thrive in the future. Many African refugees' feelings of hope can be directly connected to their religious beliefs (Adedoyin et. al., 2016). Some refugee's feelings of hope are related to their religious belief in God having a specific plan for the life. This belief in hope and God is used as a coping mechanism for understanding the traumas they have overcome. However, it is clear that this mental illness puts extreme limitations on the refugee, making the numerous obstacles (racism, isolation, acculturation, etc.) of resettling in America even more difficult. For these reasons it important for African refugees to maintain their religious beliefs as coping mechanisms in their new life.

The impact PTSD can become very evident when resettled African immigrants are faced with obstacles in the United States such as finding employment. The natural anxiety and fear associated with exploring an unknown place can become too overwhelming for the refugee, or immigrants suffering from PTSD. Employment is already a huge issue for African immigrants in general and refugees in particular. It is therefore, not surprisingly that the research shows that nearly 30 per cent of the refugee population appear to have this illness. Thus, PTSD negatively impacts unemployment related stressors among migrants. Guenther, Pendaz, and Makene (2011) identified employment as being a major stress factor for African refugees and immigrants. They describe the difficulties that African immigrants encounter in obtaining a decent career path. In addition to the difficulties associated with finding a job, Makene et al. (2011) also added the issues of over-employment and under employment. Over employment means that some African immigrants or, and refugees are forced to work two, three, and even four jobs in order to make ends meet in the United States. Contra wise, under employment means that well educated Africans refugees have to take jobs for which they are over qualified. Therefore, it is not uncommon to see an African immigrant or refugee who was once a doctor of an engineer in his/her home country having to take a job as taxi driver (Makene et. al., 2011). Unfortunately, hard earned degrees in Africa does not necessary mean that such credentials are recognized and transferable for employment and career advancement in the USA. Consequently, deskilling or unrecognized credentials of African immigrants' causes extreme stress and can amplify underlying issues of PTSD.

Depression

When individuals move from a familiar environment to an unfamiliar one they tend to experience increased levels of anxiety and apprehension. New environments can also leave individuals feeling fearful, agitated and confused about what they might encounter. It is a natural human instinct to remain cautious when entering unknown environment. African immigrants experience all of these emotions as they face resettlement, and acculturation in another country. Every year thousands of African immigrants and refugees resettle as aliens in the United States. One of the initial challenges for African immigrants is to piece their lives back together. Some immigrants have the comfort of family or friends from their hometown. However, many begin their new lives with uncertainty about their future success, especially in relation to support structures and relationships (Owaka, 2015)

Since depression is thought to be incurable or untreatable to some African immigrants, the migration from one nation to another is devastating to immigrants since depression is not uncommon with resettlement. This research demonstrates that depression education is necessary to the African immigrant population in the United States (Ezeobele, Malecha, Landrum, & Symes, 2010). The education on depression needs to be tied into the spiritual beliefs and religion of African immigrants so that it can be received and respected as a viable alternative (Ezeobele et. al., 2010).

Educators need to recognize African spirituality as a valuable tool for coping with depression (Beagan & Etowa, 2011). By incorporating African immigrants' religious beliefs and spiritual leaders into mental illness treatment educators would be able to maintain natural coping mechanisms and further assist African refugees suffering from mental illness. In order to provide care for a person, a health care professional needs to know the interconnectedness between the person's culture and social stigma (Ezeobele et. al., 2010). Health care is not a Band-Aid that can just be applied to anyone, anywhere and anytime; it is a complex system that differs from person to person, country to country, and from culture to culture.

Clarkson-Freeman, Penney, Bettman, and Lecy (2013) found that spirituality was used as a coping mechanism for depressive illness among African immigrants and refugees. The researchers identified beliefs unique to African immigrants and refugees' spirituality. These beliefs are used to understand and cope with mental and physical illnesses. The first theme involved the use of the Quran in healthcare and diagnosis acceptance (Clarkson-Freeman, et al., 2013). The guidelines expressed in the holy book mold African immigrants view of physical and mental illness. They can view diagnosis as punishments from God and find meaning through it (Clarkson-Freeman, et al., 2013). The Bible and Quran are utilized for their power of healing (Adedoyin, et al., 2016; Clarkson-Freeman, et al., 2013). This means that African immigrants will reflect upon scripture and seek God's guidance through prayer. Studying sacred books is also used or believed to be a treatment in itself. So, many African immigrants seek answers and healing of their medical diagnosis through the holy book.

The second theme identified was the "God's Will" (Clarkson-Freeman et al., 2013), Muslims belief in the almighty power of God determining the outcomes of mental and physical illness relate back to the study by Ezeobele et al. (2010) in how African immigrants view mental illness. African refugees and immigrants' spiritual identities can conflict with the ways that doctor's present diagnosis; this shows the importance of healthcare professional understanding religious and cultural barriers (Ezeobele et. al., 2010). The final theme was "religious prohibition to healthcare" (Clarkson-Freeman, et al., 2013). This involves having the patient's religion and religious leader becoming an active part of the treatment process (Clarkson-Freeman, et al., 2013). African immigrants hold significant religious view that is very important to their identity. Their religious views and coping mechanisms for mental and physical illnesses can also be seen as natural protective factors for African refugees in particular (Clarkson-Freeman et al., 2013). Their strong religious beliefs combined with religious leaders working alongside doctors on refugees' treatment plans can promote resilience and excellent mental health. Believing that you can be cured through God gives medical professionals the natural protection of hope (Clarkson-Freeman, et al., 2013).

Anxiety

Stress can have a severe negative impact on African immigrants' mental and physical health. It increases the likely hood of negative health outcomes and disease (Matheson, Jorden & Anisman, 2008). However, many African immigrants are unaware of the negative impact that stress can have on their individual mental health due to cultural health literacy barriers. The daily stressors of African refugees and immigrants can easily ware away at the psyche, leaving immigrants vulnerable to anxiety disorders.

However, the psychological effects of stress can be counteracted by an individual's spiritual practices. Beagan and Etowa (2011) examined African immigrant women and their use of spiritual occupations such prayer, bible studies, choir, or teaching Bible school as effective ways to counteract daily stressors and add meaning and hope to their lives. African immigrant women also participated in the spiritual occupations of joining committees, volunteering, and becoming an active member of their spiritual community (Beagan & Etowa, 2011). By becoming involved in these religious activities, African immigrant women received psychological protection through social outlets. This spiritual activity gave those women the strength to overcome one of the most common immigrant stressors, racism (Beagan & Etowa, 2011). Women were able to reinterpret and better understand racism; in turn, they formed a strong sense of "identity" and a greater motivation to rise above the shackles that racism causes in society (Beagan & Etowa, 2011).

Pargament, Koenig, and Perez (2000) examined the use of spiritual coping as a means of overcoming anxiety. This means is readily applicable to the current discussion on the experiences of African immigrants. The researchers identified over 21 different spiritual activities used as coping mechanism. These were then broken down into five specific categories of religious coping: identifying meaning in events, gaining or maintaining control, achieving closeness to God, and achieving closeness to others through the use of religion with hopes of obtaining transformation in life. Pargament, Smith, Koenig, and Perez (1998) then took these categories and identified the differences between positive and negative religious coping for anxiety and daily stressors. Pargament et al., (1998) examined the use of these coping strategies across very diverse samples and identified that each sample used more positive religious coping strategies such as forgiveness, prayer, collaborative coping, etc. This study shows the importance of religion and spirituality and these findings can also be applied to African immigrants who are experiencing anxiety and mental illness due to past traumas and resettlement stressors.

Religiosity/Spirituality and Coping with Health Challenges of African Immigrants

Without debate, religion and spirituality always have dominant role in African cultural life. It is the center of African values and a key ingredient to how Africans interact with people and their environment. Spirituality is also the way Africans maintain their overall well-being. African immigrants and refugees use spirituality to heal both the physical body and the mind. The importance of spirituality and the unwavering faith associated with their beliefs provides African immigrants with initial physical and mental health benefits. Overall, African immigrants just entering the United States are healthier than those who have been living here. This phenomenon is called the "healthy immigrant effect" (Venters & Gany, 2011). Unfortunately, this natural protection vanishes the longer that African immigrants stay in the United States (Venters & Gany, 2011). Spirituality has been shown to be one of the highest coping mechanisms used by African immigrants while overcoming the countless struggles they face being emerged in American culture (Gladden, 2013). Spirituality is a necessary coping skill that can help African immigrants to endure and overcome both mental and physical illness, racism, unemployment, isolation, vitiation, and acculturation (Gladden, 2013).

Between 1996 and 2004 nearly 325,000 Somali refugees resettled in the United States (Clarkson-Freeman, Penney, Bettman, & Lecy, 2013). Almost all of these refugees were Muslims. An estimated 99.8% of the population in Somalia is Muslim (Clarkson-Freeman, 2013). The Muslim belief system has a huge impact on its follower's daily lives. Tradition and the use of the "Quran", the holy book of Islam, are seen as the focal point for coping with difficult situations and living a righteous life (Clarkson-Freeman et al., 2013). Since spirituality is so important to Muslim African immigrants, the United States healthcare and social service providers must learn to adjust their assistance and messages to align with these populations' religious views in order to serve them better.

Implications for Healthcare and Human Services Providers

The United States glorifies its medical services and accomplishments. As a nation, the cultural norm is to place modern health care on a pedestal and to seek modern medical intervention whenever someone is physically or mentally ill. The American population and the modern world's ways of idealizing modern medical interventions leave no room for belief in another culture's way of healing. The American healthcare and its professionals need to further embrace culturally sensitive healthcare needs of African immigrants. America's modern medicine is seen as the civilized way of providing individuals with cures while folk medicine is largely seen is ineffective and barbaric. The medical field's negative view towards African immigrant's traditional way of healing can be very harmful to African immigrants' health. The rejection of the traditional beliefs which they originally utilized to stay healthy, leave them more vulnerable to physical, mental illness, and especially stress caused by acculturation.

Most African refugees and immigrants come from areas where modern healthcare by American standards are either very limited, inaccessible or do not exist at all. Instead, African culture has always embraced their traditional form of healing known as folk medicine or homeopathic care (Murray, Mohamed, & Ndunduyenge, 2013;

159

Orjiako & So, 2014). Therefore, folk medicine is still popular and acceptable among some African immigrants and refugees. Some African refugees and immigrants have limited medical knowledge just as many people in main street America. This knowledge gap known as low healthcare literacy has implications for some African immigrants who are yet to fully comprehend the healthcare system of the USA.

In some African countries, preventative screenings are very costly and prohibitive. This may have denied some refugees or immigrants' access to fully appreciate the complexity of a healthcare system. For such medically disadvantaged African immigrants coming to America and interacting with the American healthcare system could pose a significant culture-shock and acculturative stress. Many African immigrants do not know how to navigate the healthcare system, receive the care they need, or understand the diagnosis given to them. African immigrants can also be untrusting of the healthcare system and its professionals. This fear comes from trauma and poor experiences in the past. Some of these issues including fear, religious beliefs, and cultural barriers can cause African immigrants to act in ways that health professional's view as uncooperative and disrespectful. Consequently, African immigrants must learn more about American culture, the medical system, and social services available to them. This knowledge can reduce the stress of acculturation. Research has also demonstrated that African immigrants want more knowledge about illnesses, symptoms, and treatment options through educational seminars, support groups, or through the religious congregations (Adedoyin et al. 2016; Orjiako & So, 2014).

The healthcare system and medical professionals also have difficulties that they must overcome in order to successfully work with the African immigrant population. Medical professionals need to be able to respect and consider indigenous health beliefs from the traditional African cultures in order to serve this population better. African indigenous healthcare beliefs and interventions can serve as complimentary by acknowledging such knowledge-base to American healthcare professionals required cultural sensitivity education.

Medical professionals must also acknowledge the importance of religion in African immigrants' health and work alongside with the African immigrant religious leaders. Incorporating religion, folk medicine, and modern medicine would create an environment where African immigrants can heal and flourish whilst acculturating in the United States.

Conclusion

The population of African immigrants in the United States will most definitely grow in coming years. Whether these immigrants come by choice or to seek political refuge, the United States healthcare system should be more prepared to serve African immigrants in culturally sensitive ways. This involves having a culturally sensitive social service programs, government assistance, and healthcare practices that meet these specific population needs of African immigrants. Incontrovertibly, there is limited research on the nexus of acculturation, health, and religiosity among African immigrants in the USA. For example, ethnographic study may shed more light on whether African utilize traditional or contemporary (or both) healing methods when faced with health challenges in the USA.

Furthermore, it would be instrumental and vital to better understand African immigrants' traditional medical practices before considering the significance of enhancing the overall health care initiatives and quality of life for all and sundry. Moreover, research endeavors are further needed to understand comparative practices between American folk medical practices and African immigrant traditional folk medical practices. Folk medical practices are utilized extensively among some segments of the American population and are considered legitimate health care strategies in some instances. Folk medical practices may play a vital role in healthcare among African immigrants as well.

With the continued influx of black African immigrants into America, there is a desperate need for more research that will assist policymaking decisions as well as healthcare program design and implementation that will yield measurable outcomes. Finally, research is needed to advance the notions of acculturation theory. There are opposing perspectives dealing with acculturative stress experienced by immigrants. However, very limited research on the topic is related to black African immigration. Our research overview has clearly demonstrated that the USA Health and Human Services (HHS) systems needs to embrace the growing population of African immigrants by becoming better informed on their cultural and spiritual belief systems in order to make our public programs more accessible to them.

Religiosity or spirituality is a strong part of African immigrant culture and identity. The majority of African countries have both Christian and Muslim beliefs as their dominant religions. African immigrants use their spirituality as a coping mechanism for overcoming the many difficulties accompanied with immigrating to the United State such as acculturation, racism, healthcare literacy, physical health, mental health, domestic violence, underemployment, and family issues.

References

Adedoyin, A. C.A., Bobbie, C., Griffin, M., Adedoyin, O. O., Ahmad, M., Nobles, C., & Neeland, K. (2016). Religious coping strategies among traumatized African refugees in the United States: A systematic review. *Social Work and Christianity*, *43*(1), 95-107.

Akintunde, A. (2007). "Non-western Christianity in the western world: African immigrant churches in the Diaspora" in Olupona, Jacob K. and Gemignani Regina African immigrant religions in Americas. USA: New York University Press.

Beagan, B. L., Etowa, J. B. (2011). The meanings and functions of occupations related to spirituality for African Nova Scotian women. *Journal of Occupational Science*, *18*(3), 277-290.

Berry J.W., Kim, U., Minde, T., Mok, D. (1987). Comparative studies of acculturative stress. . *International Migration Review.*, 21(3):491–512.

Berry, J. W. (1997). Immigration, acculturation, and adaptation. . *Applied psychology*, 46(1), 5-34.

Chen, Y. Y., & Koenig, H. G. (2006). Traumatic stress and religion: Is there a relationship? A review of empirical findings. *Journal of Religion and Health*, 45(3), 371-381.

Clarke, G. (2007). Agents of transformation? Donors, faith-based organizations and international development. *Third World Quarterly*, 28(1), 77-96.

Clarkson-Freeman, P. A., Penney, D. S., Bettmann, J. E., & Lecy, N. (2013). The intersection of health beliefs and religion among Somali refugees: A qualitative study. *Journal of Religion & Spirituality in Social Work: Social Thought*, 32(1), 1-13.

Ebaugh, H. R., & Chafetz, J. S. (2000). Religion and the new immigrants. Continuities and adaptations in immigrant congregations. Walnut Creek, CA: AltaMira.

Ezeobele, I., Malecha, A., Landrum, P., & Symes, L. (2010). Depression and Nigerian-born immigrant women in the United States: a phenomenological study. *Journal of psychiatric and mental health nursing*, 17(3), 193-201.

Fallot & Heckman. (2005). *Spirituality, Religiosity, and Trauma in Women who Have Experienced interpersonal violence*. Azusa, California: ProQuest.

Gitterman, A. (2004). *Handbook of Social Work Practice with Vulnerable and Resilient Populations*. New York: Columbia University Press.

Gladden, J., (2013) Coping skills of East African refugees: A literature review. *Refugee Survey Quarterly*, 31(3), 177–196.

Grant, P. R., & Nadin, S. (2007). The credentialing problems of foreign trained personnel from Asia and Africa intending to make their home in Canada: A social psychological perspective. *Journal of International Migration and Integration/Revue de l'intégration et de la migration internationale*, 8(2), 141-162.

Guenther, K. M., Pendaz, S., Makene, F. S. (2012). The impact of intersecting dimensions of inequality and identity on the racial status of eastern African immigrants. *Sociological Forum*. 26(1), 98-120.

Guo, S. (2015). The color of skill: contesting a racialized regime of skill from the experience of recent immigrants in Canada. *Studies in Continuing Education, 37*(3), 236-250.

Hook, M. P. (2016). Spirituality as a potential resource for coping with training. *Social Work and Christianity Journal*, 43(1) 7-25.

Kottak, C. (2007). Windows on Humanity. New York: McGraw Hill.

Matheson, K., Jorden, S., & Anisman, H. (2008). Relations between trauma experiences and psychological, physical and neuroendocrine functioning among Somali refugees: Mediating role of coping with acculturation stressors. *Journal of Immigrant and Minority Health, 10*(4), 291-304.

Murray, K. E., Mohamed, A. S., & Ndunduyenge, G. G. (2013). Health and prevention among East African women in the US. *Journal of health care for the poor and underserved, 24*(1), 233.

Okpewho, I., & Nzegwu, N. (Eds.). (2009). *The new African diaspora.* Indiana University Press.

Olupona, J., & Gemignani, R. (Eds.). (2007). *African immigrant religions in America.* NYU Press.

Orjiako, O. E. Y., & So, D. (2014). The role of acculturative stress factors on mental health and help-seeking behavior of sub-Saharan African immigrants. *International Journal of Culture and Mental Health, 7*(3), 315-325.

Owaka, M. (2015). *Black African immigrants' acculturation and psychosocial functioning: A clinical literature review.* Doctoral Dissertation. Azusa Pacific University.

Pargament, K. I., & Abu Raiya, H. (2007). A decade of research on the psychology of religion and coping: Things we assumed and lessons we learned. *Psyke and Logos,* , 28, 742–766.

Pargament, K. I., Koenig, H. G., & Perez, L. M. (2000). The many methods of religious coping: Development and initial validation of the RCOPE. *Journal of clinical psychology, 56*(4), 519-543.

Pargament, K.I., Mahoney, A., & Shafranske, E.P. (2013). From research to practice: Toward an applied psychology of religion and spirituality. *APA Handbook of Psychology, Religion, and Spirituality, 3-22.*

Rasmussen, A., Hawthorne, S., & Allen, S. K. (2007). Factor structures of PTSD symptoms among West and Central African refugees. *Journal of Traumatic Stress, 20*(3), 271–280.

Redfield, R., Linton, R., & Herskovits, M. J. (1936). Memorandum for the study of acculturation. *American anthropologist, 38*(1), 149-152.

Ryan, W.F. (1995). *Culture, spirituality and economic development: Opening a dialogue.* IDRC.

Santrock, J. W. (1997). *Human adjustment.* . Brown & Benchmark.

Walsh, F. (1999). *Religion and spirituality: Wellsprings for healing and resilience.* NY, US: Guilford Publications.

Venters, H., & Gany, F. (2011). African immigrant health. *Journal of Immigrant and Minority Health, 13*(2), 333-344.

Vis, J. A., & Marie Boynton, H. (2008). Spirituality and transcendent meaning making: Possibilities for enhancing posttraumatic growth. . *Journal of Religion & Spirituality in Social Work: Social Thought,,* 27(1-2), 69-86.

Xu, J. (2016). Pargament's theory of religious coping: Implications for spiritually sensitive social work practice. *British journal of social work, 46*(5), 1394-1410.

Zong, J., & Batalova, J. (2017). Frequently requested statistics on immigrants and immigration in the United States. Retrieved from http://www.migrationpolicy.org/article/frequently-requested-statistics-immigrants-and immigration-united-states.

Chapter 8

Emmanuel Fru Doh's *Boundaries:* Pre-emptive Framing of Freedom and or Autonomy and Independence

Bill F. Ndi
Tuskegee University

At the origin of everything material is something immaterial; i.e. the unseen, the unspoken, the unwritten, the unheard of, the never thought of or, in short, the unimagined. In any good piece of literature, these immaterial elements become the central pieces that make all the difference. In the grand scheme of things, Emmanuel Fru Doh's *Boundaries* mentions the word freedom only once. Besides, there is neither mention of the words independence, autonomy, and sovereignty nor is there any mention of dependency, subjugation, repression, enslavement nor slavish mentality. It is in this regard that in his introduction to *Secret, Silences, & Betrayals,* Ndi hammers home the idea that, "what is unsaid (in a written piece) weighs equally on the scale of semantic construction as that which is said" (5). It is therefore, no surprise that this brilliant novel, from the point of view of cover design, caption, dedication, plot structure, themes, characterization, style, motif, tone and overall mood, is anchored to the hybridity of living (In)Dependence, freedom, and or the lack thereof, autonomy/sovereignty and colonial/imperial domination. This approach to writing makes Emmanuel Fru Doh (EFD), "a great [novelist] and great critic [who] is like a mule who can smell fresh water ten miles away" to quote Robert Bly as cited in Donald Hall when talking about poets. Also, EFD writes "with a sense which tells the reader where the water of [his narrative fiction] is, abroad or at home, west or east, even under the earth" (Bly qtd. in Donald Hall, 35).

EFD takes the reader through an inward journey from the microcosm of Southern Cameroons within *La République du Cameroun,* to a macrocosm of Africa and the entire world. This he does to affect all life as a special gift to his country in particular and to his reader in general. "Boundaries", one must note, delimit, frame, as well as they form lines one should not dare to cross. Yet, it is common knowledge for humans to conceive independence, freedom, autonomy, sovereignty, etc. as boundless or limitless. However, we live in a world with structures and systems wherein repression runs roughshod. Social, political, cultural, psychological, etc. are common forms of repressions humans deal with frequently. Thus, examining the binary of dependence and independence as in— (In)Dependence—would situate EFD's *Boundaries* in its rightful context of an inward narrative in a world where there is much noise about freedom, independence, and autonomy and one in which the authorities would rather have all silent and dependent upon their whims and caprices. Yet, geopolitically, the world is not one without boundaries. Hence, there are various forms of restriction in EFD's novelistic universe: linguistic, physical, social, cultural, political, emotional, spiritual, psychological, etc. Recognizing and elaborating on these aspects would warrant a holistic appreciation of EFD's novel as, "[t]hey translate what is externally present into the realm of mental representation, thereby bringing the outer into the inner— just as the [novelist] works up the stuff of his own sensation into images for our minds." (Hegel 3). Such appreciation will permit the elucidation of the otherwise intricate and inexplicable fusion of aspects—mostly revealed through the inward/outward dependence binary for freedom—which would push any inattentive reader further into the heart of the noisy confusion of life. This, in EFD's world, tends to be so at variance with Dickens's lifetime attitude to politics, which, according to William Long, '… is said to have been… "neither consistent nor particularly coherent"' (Long qtd. in *Dickens Quarterly*, vol. 34, n° 4 Dec. 2017. p. 303).

How then does EFD in his novel frame the freedom/subjugation, and the independence/dependence binaries to safeguard their fruitful and symbiotic interaction? Does EFD's work come across as an outright advocacy for independence, freedom, autonomy, and sovereignty or as a total denunciation of coerced dependency? Could a critic conveniently view this work only from the lens of physical, imaginary and or imposed boundaries? Answering these questions, and much more, through the exploration of the aforementioned narrative techniques used by EFD in *Boundaries* would establish the novel as a pre-emptive framing of Freedom and or Autonomy and (In)Dependence as can be seen from the lines of demarcation—in the cover design—between a large body of water and the landscape, and between the landscape and the sky. Is it not true as Judith Stewart Shank—in "Interpreting Poetry: The Literary Habitus"—would have it, that "[a literary work of art] is understood through contemplation of its images and their interrelation—the way in which the individual images come together to form a single thing, a unity"? (Shank *Web*)

Were any critic interested in commenting on or judging a book by its cover image or design, then EFD's *Boundaries* would be the perfect book to start its review from the cover. At the foreground is a lake, river, sea or ocean, or again simply a large body of water. In the middle ground, a landscape can be clearly seen with residences surrounded by trees to the point of even obscuring the human habitats. While in the background, the eyes embrace the blue skies with some clouds. All put together, the foreground, a body of water is considerably larger than the middle ground, host of human habitats, but not the boundless skies. Also, worth noting is the fact that the human habitations seem to be buried in a forest of obstacles on which humans depend for their survival. With the preceding observation, the critic could infer a universe in which humans are caught in the middle of things they would rely on for their freedom, autonomy, and independence. The literary merit of the cover design is both in its symbolic and allusive as well as metaphorical representations. Symbolically, the reader, holding this book and willing to plunge into it or read it, would be embarking on a symbolic biblical crossing of the Red Sea or the River Jordan. There is a sense in which this allusion would be of interest as it pre-empts the streaks of narrative techniques through which EFD reaches to clarify and give meaning to the forced subjugation of the Southern Cameroons and the turbulence rocking a freedom/independence seeking people.

EFD's *Boundaries* alludes to this biblical happening and thus becomes a metaphor for the Southern Cameroonian's long-awaited crossing of a large body of water into freedom after many years of bondage reminiscent of that of their Jewish counterparts who suffered captivity in Egypt before their journey to the Promise Land. For a number of reasons, such an allusion is important. EFD stands tall as an heir of dissenting trails of previous generations of committed writers, desirous of freedom for their people in which quest a holy experiment cannot be excluded. Furthermore, the clouds at the background, while signaling the temporal/temporary obstacles to visibility, seem to suggest a possible realization of freedom/independence through a dependence on dream or daydreaming. The realization of such freedom is symbolized by the blue sky, which seems to echo the all too familiar cliché, "the sky is the limit". In this holy experiment, EFD seems to go against the popular wisdom of the saying that having the head in the clouds is to be out of touch with reality. He crafts a universe with a stifling environment in which the only hope to attain freedom is to discard and annul dependency, subjugation, enslavement, bondage, servitude, etc. and focus on that which is beyond the clouds shielding the skies.

As if to confirm *Boundaries* is a holy experiment, EFD's opening sentence in the novel captures it all. The narrator opens the book with a portrait of a fervent and devout catechist, Ndzem, taking in the skies of his local as he walks back from a meeting with his parish priest, Father Alphonsus Freegan. Through this cosmic sweep, linking man to the sky, EFD seems to imply that in the face of wanton abuse, one in which denizens are hapless, only the power beyond the clouds and or the horizon can set man free. The Narrator states:

> The fervent and devoted catechist, Ndzem, looked up at the revealing face of the sky above the Bamenda Station hill as he walked down to the doctrine class from the Reverend Father's house where Father Alphonsus Freegan had summoned and reminded him of the upcoming First Holy Communion (EFD 1)

Ndzem, the opening character's first action is to "… look up at the revealing face of the sky…" (EFD 1). Could this be the revealing face of a higher authority? All in all, Ndzem comes across as a man of action and one on a mission with both his action and mission reinforcing the idea of freedom, identity, community, education, and coded educational discourse geared towards the binaries: Dependence/Independence, repression/resistance, subjugation/freedom, exclusion/inclusion, imperial domination/liberation struggle, subordination/insubordination. The fact that Reverend Father Freegan Alphonsus summons Ndzem to remind him of the upcoming event he is supposed to make run smoothly reinforces the dialectic co-dependence of Father and Catechist in the proper execution of the church's mission. Nonetheless, what Ndzem sees upon looking up in the skies is a "revealing face". This phrase is highly charged with meaning, as it could be a reference to the white clouds on the cover image. Could this be a play on color "depletion" which is "white"? Implicitly, could it be the revealing face of Father Alphonsus who happens to be white? In choosing *Boundaries* as the title for this novel, EFD seems to sound a warning note to the oppressors, letting them know there are lines they cannot cross no matter how repressive they are and no matter the tactics they use to subvert the sociopolitical structures to maintain their citizens in a state of perpetual subjugation. Up above is a powerful force that oppression cannot subdue, and up to which man must look before hoping to communion with Him like Ndzem.

Besides analyzing the cover as has been done, it is worthwhile making another stop at EFD's rather illuminating dedication before delving into the analysis of the novel proper. In the words of author and journalist, Tim Dowling writing for *The Guardian* of June 21, 2007:

> "A dedication remains, however, the first thing the reader sees after the title. As an author, one wants it to be reflective of the contents, or at least reassuring and inviting. The perfect dedication would also be immediately moving, or funny, or both; timely but also timeless" (*Web*).

Admitted, dedications do not generally constitute an object of literary analysis. The claim is, "[i]t is not part of the text; it is just some soppy, private transaction of the heart tacked on at the last minute. Or is it?" (*Web*.) Nonetheless, EFD's speaks to his pre-emptive framing of freedom and thus worthy of analysis as some have posited. Again, Tim Dowling, quoting Kevin Jackson, writes: "… many of the bits of books we tend to disregard – epigraphs, acknowledgements, indexes, bibliographies – are actually "paratextual", in other words, worthy of analysis in their own right" (qtd. by Dowling *Web*). The dedication starts with a friend, the memory of a mutual friend, and the cause of the suffering people of Southern Cameroons. EFD uses his dedication to echo the woes that corrupt and selfish politicians—with sole desire to repress citizens— heaped upon these people. This dedication could not be clearer. It summons the living, vis. his friend Robson Sama, the dead vis. the mutual friend, Pong George Pong and himself to stick together and "make our point or let belly-politicians divide and maintain us as national bastards in our fatherland" (EFD).

This dedication is explicit on the level of lack of care that politicians espouse. EFD's dedication cannot be said, as Edwin McDowell would have it in his *New York Times* article that dedications: "[…] seem little affected by political or ideological distinctions" (*Web*). Politicians in EFD's novelistic universe are not those who protect and serve a free people. They would rather be served by those that they have forced into subjugation. All the politicians care for is their belly. So EFD's dedication is everything but what Bloomsbury talks of in relation to dedications. In *Bloomsbury Dictionary of Dedications*, he describes it as "a catalogue of favourite[sic] aunts, perfect spouses and the profoundest platitudes. Dedications really do bring out the worst in authors." (qtd. in Dowling). All in all, EFD's dedication aligns very much with what Lizzie Einfield writes in her article captioned: "Book dedications: so few words, but such big stories" (*Web*). In this article, Enfield writes: "… many authors tell tales far more complex and varied than we might initially imagine with their brief, staccato dedications" (Einfield *Web*). EFD does exactly this in *Boundaries* and eloquently pleads for the oppressed of

The Southern Cameroons just like "Charles Dickens, the large hearted, whose works plead so eloquently and nobly for the oppressed of his country" (Slater 516). EFD uses his dedication page to erect a permanent memorial that he has crafted with care to usher his readers into the narrative proper of *Boundaries* and to pre-emptively frame freedom, autonomy, sovereignty, and or independence.

EFD's multi-layered holy experiment is a spiritual odyssey of freedom, independence, autonomy, and sovereignty journeying from subjugation, dependence, imperial domination and colonization. The journey starts with the grounding of young Southern Cameroonian pupils on the art of reliance on the Almighty for absolute freedom. This holy experiment is articulated around the story of younger generations of Southern Cameroonians whose love, passion and desire for each other supersede any kind of hatred and animosity that their parents' generation might have engendered. The novel ends on a note of love trumping hate as well as love blurring boundaries. EFD uses the tale of Musang and Etonde, their growing up, their encounter and falling in love, their background as young lovers, their struggles to maintain their newfound love forever, and the challenges that society and cultures impose on them as well as their attempts at resolving the problems to construct the intrigue of the plot of his novel. This intricate storyline avails itself as a profound meditation on destiny. As aforementioned, the plot is held together by the multiple subplots serving as the fiber to the fabric of boundaries. Thus, doing what Hegel holds as that which historians do. These subplots "bind together what is vanishing down the stream of time, and place it all in the Temple of Memory to give it immortality" (Hegel 4). EFD weaves a suspenseful plot, which takes the reader through a thrilling emotional roller coaster ride to a narrative dealing with bigger and invidious social and political trauma lived by contemporary Southern Cameroonians. What then is the story of the main plot?

The main plot traces Musang's trajectory. He is the son of Ndzem, a Roman Catholic catechist on the one hand and that of Etonde, Mola Ngomba's daughter. The reader follows them from their falling in love to their getting married. However, when the plot unveils, Musang and Etonde are rarely seen or heard of. The reader is introduced to Ndzem, Musang's father through whose pivotal role young minds are groomed in the art of reliance. They must master this art to the satisfaction of their spiritual master, Reverend Father Alphonsus, under the guardianship of the Catechist to whom the Father has entrusted the teaching of the doctrinal classes. *Boundaries* comes across as a spiritual odyssey through which the protagonist's humanity, blended with both dependence and independence, is brought to light. From the beginning lesson, the Narrator highlights man's purpose and mission on earth: to love and work as well as rely on God to be free. *Boundaries* seems to underline that there is no true freedom/independence without dependence. From the spiritual to the physical, this ambivalent relation exists. The doctrine classes that the children take are aimed at paving their way to freedom and independence through their total dependence on God. EFD brings to the fore children being trained in this art through the doctrinal class pupils reciting their lesson and chanting:

"*Na who make you?*"
"*Na God make me.*"
"*Why God make you?*"
"*God make me for sabi yi, for like yi, and for work for yi.*"

The class of twenty-eight had been split into two groups: one asking the questions and the other answering in return. (EFD 3).

Even though the reader does not see the protagonist amongst the pupils in this class, it is evident that as the saying "charity begins at home" goes, his father Ndzem has already taken care of this for his first son. The Narrator probes into Ndzem's psyche as he walks home from the doctrinal classes. He reveals his thought:

… he thought of the thousands of children he had prepared for communion all through his career with an air of humble satisfaction, but his mind was heavy; it occurred to him the Lord did not seem to be keeping his own part of the bargain. It is His promise that the house of the honest man will want for nothing, but his children did not seem to be thriving, especially his first son, his cane in old age. (EFD 4)

When he gets home, the reader is introduced to Mojoko, Ndzem's wife. These two are involved in a game of intimacy and it is one in which they are concerned about their first son, Musang, and his future. Lest the reader forgets, Ndzem and wife depend and count on their first son, whom they see as their "... cane in old age" (4) i.e. independence. Dwelling on this worry, EFD seems to be less concerned with societal restraints and taboos as he discusses the topic of sexuality and or sexual orientation. He broaches the topic with alacrity.

> Unlike other children in the neighbourhood[sic], they had never heard him talk seriously about what he would like to become as an adult besides moving from school to school for one strange reason or another, nor have they seen a single girl come around to visit with him as they have established with other boys whose friends at school or former school mates in primary school do stop by from time to time for a visit. They could not help wondering if their son was all right or if he was someone who could not interact with the opposite sex. (EFD 5)

Capturing this moment of change in contemporary Southern Cameroons life, the novelist shares Leslie S. Simon's common view of "a novelist as [himself as] a historian of a given sort, [who] works to carve out the space of the private in the midst of the public." (Leslie S. Simon in *Dickens Quarterly* vol. 34, n° 4 Dec. 2017. 310). Like novelists writing in the 1830s, EFD seems to capture this episode "[i]n moments of heightened self-awareness, we might assume too that narratives emanating from this era [feels] unusually burdened "with a sense of time that exceeded the limits of plots..." (Leslie S. Simon in *Dickens Quarterly* vol. 34, n° 4 Dec. 2017. 310).

From Musang's parents' anticipated concern, the Narrator walks the reader through Musang's journey to and from his paternal uncle in the beautiful coastal city named after Queen Victoria of England.

While at his parents' he would go out for walks and would stroll pass his father's doctrinal classes and by the cemetery where he contemplates the meaning of life and death. During one of these walks he hears the children in his father's doctrinal classes singing the *"Tantum Ergo"* which is normally sung during veneration and benediction. This nurses the seed of priesthood in the young protagonist. Also, during one of these walks the idea of visiting the South West Province is born. From thence, the reader meets Musang planning to obtain permission from his parents to visit his "old haunts in all those South West townships: Buea, Tiko, Kumba, and Victoria especially" (EFD 9). Relying on the parents' permission to bathe in his new-found freedom far away from mother and father; he planned to talk about it to his father:

> "He was going to talk about it to his father today that he seemed to be in a better mood. First though, he was going to try winning over his mother before confronting his father so that in case of any resistance on the part of his father, his mother would side with him." (EFD 9)

On the above note, the narrator takes the reader through the exchanges between mother and son, husband and wife, etc. After these exchanges, a deal is in the making as the narrator highlights that "Ndzem never gave in to his wife directly, but Musang knew better that when his father postponed issues raised by his mother, he was indirectly giving in to her request" (EFD 13).

The narrator operates a shift in space, place and time. He takes the reader through the city of Victoria from Musang's arrival and his meeting with Bandon and Etonde to the brief dialogue that ensues between Musang and Etonde. The said brief dialogue ends up being a full-blown love affair that would culminate into an aborted marriage proposal.

The culprit of this abortion is none other than the would-have-been father-in-law, Mola Ngomba. He simply turns down the effort Musang's family has made to set the record for the traditional asking of a hand in marriage straight. This episode is clearly captured in a dialogue between Etonde and Mrs Musongo. She tells her: "… only for my father to storm out of the house after insulting me in front of the man I love. He left me embarrassed and stranded with my guests who had come all the way from Bamenda to ask for my hand in marriage" (EFD 162). This incident frustrates Musang to the point where the priesthood he once thought of just as a child's play seems to be resonating with him now. He finally joins a major seminary only for his priestly dreams to be squashed after six years. The plot thus reaches a culminating point with suspense full as the protagonist seems to be walled in by frustration and desperation from every angle: left-right, top-bottom, front-back. With no hope in sight, the resilient Musang endeavors to get even a teaching job with the denominational school system and to no avail. To handle this terrible situation in writing would call for the kind of author Hegel highlights when he writes that "… authors must actually be of high social standing. Only from a superior position can one truly see things for what they are and see everything, not when one has to peer upward from below, through a narrow opening" (Hegel 5-6). Indeed, EFD, from his moral and social standing, brings about rescue just about a week to a major competitive exam to recruit air force pilots.

Musang enrolls for this exam, takes the test, and passes. He then goes off for training in Arizona USA where he spends four years before returning. Upon return, Musang visits Brandon and the two friends revisit the old conversations about Etonde. They arrange for Musang and his lieutenant friend Mbonge to go and visit Etonde. During this visit, Mola Ngomba who had adamantly rejected Musang when he came with the family to ask for Etonde's hand, now recognizes him and welcomes him with: "Eei! Eei! Eei! My in-law, is it you?" (EFD 176). After a long evening during which Mola Ngomba tenders his apologies, the two lovebirds leave hand in hand as the narrator captures Brandon seeing them through the window: "Brandon saw Etonde and Musang approaching hand in hand, he ran out and hugged Etonde; they held onto each other tightly, rocking from side to side for what seemed like forever" (180). Finally, the two finish their evening with Etonde hushing Musang not to talk, but to hold her. The narrator then captures through a vivid imagery, the moment Musang and Etonde had long awaited. He says: "[i]n the silence that followed, they could hear their hearts thumping against each other, along with the sounds of nocturnal insects screeching outside in the darkness oblivious of the minutes ticking by" (EFD 182). This is, in short, the storyline of a narrative brought to us by a cast of characters brought together as a narrative technique to tell a bigger tale than that of some isolated individuals in a smooth running and functioning society.

Beyond some of the characters mentioned while discussing the storyline, EFD relies on multiple character accounts—which he uses as ingredients only—to avoid the problems with a single narrative. Novelists, like Hegelian "... historians rely on the reports and accounts of others, since it is not possible for one person to have seen everything. But they use these sources as ingredients only, (just as [they] already [possess] the civilized speech ...)" (Hegel 3-4). The life of the characters from the protagonist, the protagonist's father, major and minor characters to the antagonist is woven around the binary of dependence and independence. This leaves all the characters desirous of independence while relying on dependence for total freedom. Ndzem dwells on the borders between dream and reality as he struggles to grapple with his faithfulness and his service to God; yet the outcome of his life always seems to contradict his hopes and aspiration.

Drawing from a cast of characters whose *Modus Operandi* and *Modus Vivendi* are marked by the repressive forces of imposed boundaries, virtual, surreal, etc. EFD upholds living (in)dependence as the central element that grounds the conflict that almost transforms the lives of two loving and free born citizens into a living hell of parentally imposed boundaries. Nonetheless, both their dependence on each other's love and trust for each other as well as their desire to break the chain of dependence and parental control and be independent, underscore the happy-ever-after ending. Hence the characters' interdependence on dependence for independence. This is made clearer when Musang meets Brandon in Victoria, the narrator depicts him as "enjoying the newfound freedom" (EFD 16). This newfound freedom is all dependent upon the generosity of his friend, Brandon. It is also associated to his being away from his father and mother as the narrator intimates: "just he and his friend out in the South West without his parents or people who knew him" (EFD 16). Again, he is free of his everyday concern of moving from school to school in pursuit of certificates.

As for Etonde's life and attitude towards the challenges she faces in life, hers offer insights into a free-minded, principled, and idiosyncratic life. Her attitude, like EFD's, is a resonant take on blind hatred, tribal allegiance, and political manipulation of the populace. This attitude challenges traditional perception, norms, and reliance on offences and grudges to take revenge. Etonde is an upholder of morality. In a conversation between Brandon and Musang, Brandon emphasizes Etonde's moral rectitude. He states that, "Everyone here has tried and failed, even our comptrollers from Douala with all the money they show up here willing to spend. We cannot seem to tell what she wants in a man or if she's even thinking about men" (24). In a society rife with corruption, the powerful and rich depend on their money to have access to what they desire, i.e. oppress the poor. EFD, in setting this example, takes a swipe at the corrupt who think by flashing all the money they can achieve or get all what they want. Etonde is a character the narrator pits as difficult to decipher to the point that she is not moved by material things. She seems to camp ferociously on uncompromising grounds.

Her role and take are a gentle reminder of a woman's fight to pursue her dreams in a hostile environment created by an establishment with which collaboration is impossible. It is through Etonde's dependency on love that the author shows how such breeds transformation in human relations. Etonde goes from a people-oriented person to a loner who avoids even those same things and people that once characterized and symbolized her source of pleasure, freedom, and autonomy. After her father botches Musang's attempt at asking for her hand in marriage, Brandon highlights the transformation she undergoes. According to him, "Etonde barely greeted her colleagues anymore and she ate alone at a different location instead of where they used to eat as a group. She rarely smiled and no longer went to nightclubs" (EFD 70).

Again, other characters pitched, in EFD's narration, as an ingredient of his plot structure and development are Ndzem and his wife, Mojoko. When Musang is about to leave for overseas, Mojoko, reliant upon tradition, would want Ndzem to say something about their son getting married before the son's departure. Ndzem understands times are changing as well as the dynamics. Hitherto, young men depended on their parents to pick and choose their wives whereas, these days, young men are ascertaining their independence with claims of knowing everything and making the choice for themselves. As the voice of reason and an advocate for young men's pre-emption of their freedom, Ndzem refuses to meddle in the life of his son whom he now considers as a young adult. EFD employs rhetorical questioning as a device to make this refusal. Pursuant to this, Ndzem asks:

> What do you want me to say? Am I the one to get a woman for him? Don't children these days claim to know everything? Why then should I bother getting a girl for him when he would only turn her down? I do not intend to bring that kind of pain to somebody's child; not me. (EFD 50)

This position very much echoes the plight of Southern Cameroons/Ambazonia in her union with *La République du Cameroun*. Southern Cameroons in her desire for independence forced herself on to *La République du Cameroun*, the latter turned her down and in the present dispensation, all it does is, "bring that kind of pain…" (EFD 50). This kind of pain cannot let its sufferer to be free, independent, autonomous or sovereign. Adopting this stance transforms EFD's *Boundaries* into an eloquent and noble plea for the oppressed. Ndzem, whose life is entirely dependent on the service of the Lord, is an epitome of the oppressed. And each time he does this, he comes alive and adopts as favorite slogan: "God works in strange ways…" (EFD 4). Also, Ndzem does not hesitate to do the right thing. The reader learns of how he comes about with just Mojoko as his sole wife in a society where polygamy is the order of the day. What he does shows his love for human freedom and independence. He

180

leaves each former wife well off, as illustrated by this excerpt from the narrator:

> After completing his training to become catechist, he did not hesitate returning two of his three wives back to their parents when the Church preached against polygamy and warned polygamists that they were continuing the tradition at the risk of losing their souls after death. He built a house for each wife back at her father's compound and left each well off with a little money and a field farmed and planted with different food crops before walking away. He was left with his first wife, Mojoko, a woman from the coast. (EFD 5)

Finally, Mojoko, Musang's go-to parent reveals to Ndzem, Musang's hopes and aspiration of intending a girl before his first attempt to leave for the United States. She intimates dependency on marriage as the bedrock of responsibility, freedom, and autonomy.

In another literary twist, EFD sheds light on Southern Cameroons past through characterization. Using the character, Mola Ngomba, EFD paints a tableau showing how tenaciously holding on to past grudges and offences can quickly become a recipe for hurting the very people an individual loves and wishes to protect. Mola Ngomba holds on to his past, thus shackling himself down and standing in the way of embracing and exercising his own independence and freedom. His refusal to accept Musang as son-in-law can only be understood in the light of his wife's explanation. His wife, Iya laments to Ndzem after her husband's refusal to entertain the asking of her daughter's hand by saying:

> … my husband has suffered in one way or the other in the hands of Bamenda people. He lost his position at work to a Bamenda man, and then he feels his oldest brother should have been one of the first Bishops in West Cameroon, but it went to a *Graffi* man; to add insult to injury, when one of our daughters was denied a position in Our Lady of Lourdes College, Mankon, he failed to see it was because of the competitive nature of the interview, with over a thousand students from all over the country vying for not up to a hundred positions; to

181

him, it was *Graffi* people refusing to admit his daughter into Lourdes, even though he knows white reverend sisters are the ones running the school. So just like that, *Mola* has developed an aversion for Bamenda people which is personal rather than cultural. After all, as you yourself have rightly pointed out, your wife is Bakweri and there are many Bakweri men around who are married to women from Bamenda. Go to all these CDC (Cameroon Development Corporation) camps and see all the mixed couples that are thriving there. Honestly, *Mola*, I had never foreseen anything like this else we would have dealt with it before today. Please give us time to talk to him. (EFD 58-59)

The above excerpt makes of Mola Ngomba someone from Hebert Blumer's playbook of Symbolic Interactionism. Mola Ngomba's action and behavior is tapped from Blumer's theory. His action and behavior are based on the result of meanings which he ascribes to action and things. Besides, his meaning is constructed, as well as arrived at, by the participants, like Musang, Ndzem, etc. on the scene. In short, Mola Ngomba constructs his meaning from social processes. He thus sees the marrying of his beloved daughter by yet another *Graffi* born as a possible privation of his freedom. It is through this reckless behavior of Mola Ngomba's that Musang takes a split-second decision which EFD seems to use subtlety to chastise the fact that two wrongs have never made a right. His choice of a Seminary over human love seems to be EFD's leitmotif to critique the attitude of those who would shun to love fellow humans and yet, try to show love for a higher power. EFD displays his understanding that no man in his incapacity to love a fellow human being can love God to the rightful measure.

Using Musang's enrollment into a seminary in a remote locale, EFD further demonstrates that the remoteness of one's hiding place does not change the design and desire of a heart destined to love, for love, and or to be in love. Though seminarians live in a world apart, in Musang's case this would be short-lived; they have time to go back home to parents, they are also sent to other parishes for field experience. Though Mola Ngomba fails to observe himself from the standpoint of others, he is redeemed down the narrative line when in an ironic twist he is challenged by the facts that his wife has left home, his daughter will not speak to him for a long time. They will not depend on a husband and a father who would rather deprive mother and daughter of their freedom and independence. It is then it dawns on him that his thoughts and actions, as well as the meaning he has constructed from the events in his life, are all adversely affecting his own family on whom he depends for happiness, freedom and independence as a family head. Thus, Mola Ngomba embraces redemption, a thematic frame EFD uses to round the edges of a character who could have been flat.

Stylistically, the novel opens with a vivid description of the St. Anselm's Parish at Big Mankon with an interaction between Ndzem, the Catechist and the parish priest, Reverend Father Alphonsus Freegan. The priest has just convoked Ndzem and instructed him on getting his catechumens ready for their first holy communion. The narrator points out: "The children had to be ready for their First Holy Communion Examination within the next two weeks. This … group … would receive First Holy Communion on Big-Day Maria, the feast of the Assumption of the Blessed Virgin Mary into heaven" (EFD 1). Also, EFD hints on all other dependent parishes. St Anselm's at Big Mankon "… was the main parish with other satellite parishes in surrounding neighbourhoods [sic] like Bayele in Nkwen, Small Mankon in Azire, and Ntambeng Parishes" (EFD 4). This depiction of a main parish and its satellite parishes brings to the fore the dependent/independent relations between parishes as well as between the Father and the Catechist.

Dependence through contrast brings out the beauty of anything cf. "It was the same Cameroon Bank stone building, just freshly painted, the stones black and the network of cement between the stones white" (EFD 17). Through artistic description, EFD skillfully plays with colors to bring out the beauty of the would-be source of Musang and Etonde's dependence and independence. In a dialogue that follows between Musang and Etonde, she introduces herself and states "My name is Etonde" (EFD 18) and Musang engages in an onomastic play—giving his full names—which highlights EFD's view on the need for regional and cultural interdependence as the true and veritable source of independence for a nation struggling with issues of national identity.

> She had on a cream white long sleeve blouse that vaguely revealed, in a tantalizing manner, the outline of her bra around her body. Each breast was the size of half a pineapple with pointed tips that seemed to crush against her breast-wear from within. (EFD 18)

The casual dialogue between Etonde and Musang, the latter in responding to Etonde's question if it were his first time in Victoria, reveals that is where he grew up. It is this seemingly casual dialogue that concludes with what the critic can assume to be the very beginning of a dependent<->independent relationship. Etonde adds after a brief pause, "it was good talking to you" (19). This statement betrays the beginning of Etonde's emotional attachment to Musang, with whom she has just had a brief conversation. However, EFD lays a foundation for more frequent conversation and contact in a creative way. He does this through Brandon who announces that Musang's Birthday will be an opportunity for "a lot of celebrating..." (19).

The Narrator, in describing Etonde's stride as she walks away from this conversation with Musang and Brandon, captures men's emotional dependence on women. This dependence is often initiated by the physique. It gives the physical appeal of relieving the would-be possessor of any constraint of wholesomeness i.e. possessing such a physique completes the desiring physique and imbues it with a sense of total independence. It could also be added that even on Etonde's part, the reaction is not different as revealed in the discussion that ensues between Brandon and Musang. Brandon points out that: "each time somebody asks her out, it's one excuse or another, until we've all given up. She claims we're her brothers. I've tried making her to understand that my sisters are all in Bamenda, but she just laughs at me instead" (20). EFD makes of the imagery of sexual freedom a cornerstone of the dependence/independence binary. Sexual freedom is only achieved by loving and having the real object of one's desire. Describing Musang's fantasy as he admires Etonde to and from the counter to get her drink at the nightclub, the narrator draws attention to the fact that,

Each time she walked to the counter to get herself a drink, Musang liked the way her hips would bulge seductively on the sides, causing the pleats to lose their disciplined lines temporarily, widening against her hips like the lines on a python's body after it has swallowed something really big. (22).

These lines subtly insinuate the female genitalia, which would eventually swallow Musang's manhood, one which the narrator claims to be "something really big" (22).

EFD weaves a nightclub into the narrative in a characteristic way of portraying a sense of independence that is totally dependent on either a thought and an act or a person, a place, a space, and an object. The youths depend on the Nightclub as a place and space to display or exude their youthfulness under the guise of "celebrating their youth and the weekend" (EFD 21).

Musang, having found a girl in whom he takes interest, EFD introduces a dialogue between mother and son in which he expressly makes clear that people may think freedom means having free rein in everything, decision and or action one wills. Clearly, this is Musang's thought as he does not fathom the idea that others should have a say in his choice. The following exchange between mother and son highlights EFD's conviction (with the mother, Mojoko, as his mouthpiece) of independence through dependence on tradition.

"Now that she is from the South West, I do not know what your father's people will think."

"What do you mean by what my father's people would think? What would they think? Are they the ones getting married?"

"My son, it is not as easy as it may seem. You know, tradition is something that runs really deep. For your father, he certainly won't mind, but his family is likely to think I am behind this—trying to carry their grandson away to the coast as I have carried their son."

"Mom, people still think like that these days?" (EFD 33).

In short, the narrator espouses the ideal of freedom without constraints, and one, which always depends on an antecedent, which most call tradition. This dialogue, in a way, foreshadows Musang's struggle to be accepted by his would-be father-in-law. This is for EFD, an excuse to express frustration over irrational concerns people in his universe have with intra- and inter-cultural marriages. While Mojoko has enjoyed her independence to choose whom she marries, she is still emotionally tied to the petty gossips and misgivings of her in-laws.

In yet another ironic twist, Mojoko makes a mockery of her husband's status from the perception of his family, her in-laws. He is not opulent. He is a struggling catechist who barely makes ends meet. EFD uses this instance to make clear his worldview regarding human overreliance on material things of the world. Still using Mojoko as his mouthpiece, the narrator elaborates on marriage as independent and dependent as well as predicated upon character and kind-heartedness rather than material wealth. She provides a lesson in human inter-dependence upon family. Mojoko is family oriented and reveals her willingness to win over the approval of other family members in all matters that would bring joy to all. She juxtaposes two cultures: hers and another, supposedly western culture, learned in her culture class. Here below the juxtaposed views:

No, Musang, it can never be like that. We are a family people, and so family always comes first. The thing to say is that we'll do all to win their approval, okay! Go now, go and get ready for your trip. With God, you will get a passport, and that visa will be given you unless He wishes otherwise for you. Make sure all your documents are together, and remember, as they say it, when you are talking to a white man look him in the eyes. Those people have no sense of respect: a child will be talking to the father and looking at him in the eyes as if they are equals. (EFD 34)

Their argument, I hear, and which we learned in our culture class, is that to them everybody is equal before the law, something that makes me laugh each time I hear it. If they believed in that, how come they went around buying and selling human beings as if they were selling animals and even their own courts could not get them to stop without a fight? In fact, it took the use of soldiers to enforce the laws that brought about a semblance of change to the slave era. (EFD 35)

She reinforces her advice to Musang by reminding him what his father has always said about those people. He says: "…those people hate liars…" (EFD 35). The deictic use of "those" emphasizes the distance between theirs and the group of human beings involved in the heinous trade in humans. However, those people are for the truth. To succeed with them, people must make truth their priority. At the end of this conversation the narrator brings to the fore the theme of falling in love and how love engenders emotional dependence. The reader finds out that "Musang fell asleep thinking of Etonde. He had spoken to her earlier on in the day and told her of his trip to the embassy and she was very happy for him, but she complained about how she was missing him" (35).

Furthermore, EFD uses Musang's anxiety before he goes to get his passport as a means of elucidating the travails of the Southern Cameroons. EFD in his reach to clarify the travails paints a part of the world living in a union intended to mark independence, but which turned out to be a life of dependence. Through Ndzem's monologue, the author predicates the acquisition of a passport as a herculean task, one which, through an allusion the reader learns, is a procedure "comparable to the biblical camel going through the eye of a needle…" (EFD 38). He notices there is something wrong as Musang seems happy but somewhat preoccupied. As a result, he wonders: "Maybe it was the approaching struggle to acquire a Cameroonian passport and the impending interview at the US embassy following which his application for a US visa could be accepted or rejected that was getting to him, [...]" (EFD 35).

It is as a result of a shift in setting that an emotional shift sets in to highlight the binary opposition of collective culture and attitude. In the symbolic representative cities—Yaoundé and Bamenda—of the French and English-speaking regions that make up the

187

Cameroons, the novelist subtly describes the attitude of the francophone vis-à-vis his English-speaking counterpart:

> He hated spending any time in Yaoundé with the rather disrespectful and somewhat chaotic attitude displayed by the characteristically distant occupants of the city as opposed to the calm, gentle, and respectful approach he is used to back home in Bamenda with people acknowledging each other. Back in Bamenda, people show they recognize someone even from a previous visit and can even chat, but this had not been his experience in Yaoundé each time he had visited. People just seemed preoccupied with one thing or the other and barely exchanged greetings. He had heard it was a disease of the cities. The result was that he unknowingly developed a dislike for the city as a whole. (EFD 36)

The chaotic scene in Yaoundé pushes Musang to see in it "madness!" (37) as he screams out loud in defiance. The vivid description of the environmental chaos, Musang's feelings, and take on the environment, as well as the narrator's and the protagonist's attitude, tone, etc. as far as Yaoundé is concerned, are all pre-emptions of freedom and autonomy for the English-speaking Southern Cameroons which has no business with the chaos and passivity that reigns in the French speaking parts of the Cameroons. This is very consistent with EFD, as noted by Bill F. Ndi in his analysis of EFD's *The Fire Within*. Therein, Ndi highlights the fact that "EFD does not also miss to seize any opportunity afforded him to castigate the rampant corruption and malpractices in all the echelons of the Caramenjuan [Cameroonian] society" (Qtd. in Fishkin, Ankumah, and Ndi 225).

The pre-emptions of freedom, independence, and autonomy become a true basis for conflict in this novel. Such pre-emptions illuminate the interaction between the francophone and the English-speaking Southern Cameroonian. Metaphorically, EFD transforms the movement of Musang's eyes in this disturbing environment into the "movements ... of the painter's brush..." (EFD 40). EFD uses Musang's passport and visa acquisition to expound on a bigger

188

narrative: the tale of subordination and insubordination in a brutal police state. Can one be free or independent in such a state? Musang wonders the use of policing which to him is nothing but privation of freedom and independence pure and simple. Using the example of traveling within a police state, the narrator reduces it to an adventure of probabilities. He intensifies his caustic critique of the police force by flagging the nature and state of police officers. The narrator points out: "A half-drunk police officer would hold one hostage for hours even just because one has refused giving him a bribe" (EFD 44).

Such a situation leaves the reader questioning why a police force should be constituted of bribe seeking drunks. EFD seems to tell the readers only fools would actually rely on these half-drunks for the maintenance of law and order. In this guise, Musang's prospective travel overseas becomes a kind of Dedalian flight, à la Joyce, transposed into reality that pre-emptively frames freedom from oppressive and regressive forces. Obtaining a passport and a visa shows all manner of privation with which Musang is not very pleased. The narrator tells us: "He was very disgruntled pulling out that amount of money for an application only" (45). Nonetheless, Musang's reliance on the visa to travel as well as dependence on another country to acquire his much-needed knowledge are the keys to his freedom and independence. Paradoxically, Musang reminds the reader that the visa issuance is also dependent on an individual whim: "Discretion" he says, "they call it" (46).

Moreover, the narrator captures a moment of epiphany for Musang who suddenly realizes that his life of a dependent—in a supposedly bi-jural federal/fraternal structure—is rife with subjugation, exclusion, suffering, abjection, dislocation, colonization, which are the great themes in EFD's universe (*Boundaries*) and they all unfold as contemporary as breaking news. The narrator depicts:

> As Musang walked on, taking in the noisy scene before him, marked by an unfortunate aura of chaos, confusion, and apathy, something welled up inside of him, leaving a bitter taste in his mouth. It was a feeling he always experienced each time he visited major French speaking towns, especially Yaoundé, the so-called capital city

of his country. The feeling is usually provoked by his repeated discovery that everything, except on government buildings, is written only in French whereas in all Anglophone cities or towns, virtually everything written in English is again repeated in French for the benefit of the French speaking Cameroonian. He had always wondered what this was all about: the simple fact that the Francophone population was the majority, or some idiotic way of hopefully turning Anglophones into third generation Francophones, recolonized this time by a state within their twin-state federation of Anglophone and Francophone Cameroon. Musang was still mumbling his dissatisfaction at the kind of bilingualism practiced in his country when his eyes landed on the sign on the front roof of a funny looking stone building on which appeared the letters *"Police des Frontières."* (EFD 39)

It is at the *"Police des Frontières?"* that Musang comes to the realization of "…those Francophones without knowledge of a single English word…" (40). This nameless francophone epitomizes the spite with which the francophone treats the English-speaking Southern Cameroonian within the *La République du Cameroun* dispensation. Bringing to the fore a spiteful police officer, he is pictured as angry and hateful which drastically contrast Musang's debonair composure. The physical description of this police officer betrays the undependable tie that such a character can knot: "he looked skinny, a kind of a drunk with cigarette stained lips and knuckles" (EFD 41). As Musang tries to make sense of this, he first thinks he must be a hen-pecked husband but then he comes to the conclusion that "it must be a combination of this and the man's hate for either English- or English-speaking Cameroonians" (EFD 41). This encounter brings to the fore the central idea of marginalization ingrained in the culture and conscience of citizens of *La République du Cameroun*. EFD seems to tell the readers only fools would actually rely on the half-drunks for the maintenance of law and order.

EFD further takes the reader into a reflective and introspective journey he uses to take a swipe at the passivity of the francophone masses. They encourage maintaining the status quo. Through introspection and reflective rhetorical question, the protagonist muses on this predicament. It is also with a pinch of salt that the author embraces the media sell of the US to the rest of the world. Could this be for EFD a way to shed light on US dependence on the rest of the world for her hegemonic posturing? The following extant quote takes us through the journey.

> It was then it occurred to Musang that lately he was no longer seeing those French men in Cameroon's military uniforms driving jeeps arrogantly along the streets. It was good he was planning on leaving Cameroon for a long time if he could get his visa from the US embassy. He was completely fed up with all the nonsense happening in his country with the people remaining as passive as if all was well. "How is it that a child is born, raised until he gets married and is having his own children and the same individual is in place as head of state with other morons ready to dance and fête with every opportunity of the buffoon's appearance in public?" Musang could not wait to see for himself how free the free world, as the United States of America is always presented in the news, would be, nor could he wait to experience the opportunities in the land of opportunities, another popular term of reference for the United States. The furthest the taxi could approach the immigration office was about two hundred metres away because of some repairs taking place in the street where the tar had come off leaving behind huge dusty undulations and deep potholes in certain areas. (EFD 38)

Further still, Musang muses on academic freedom and independence. He has convinced himself that there is only one reason for anyone to want to go to the United States; i.e. "an academic degree from the US would be recognized anywhere in the world" (EFD 43). This dependence upon a US degree is aimed at being free to be recognized anywhere in the world. This is an echo of dependency theory in history and sociology which upholds that "Third World [countries] are unable to control major aspects of their economic life, because of the dominance of industrialized countries in the world economy" (McLeish 193). That is the only reason for leaving someone like Etonde behind. In spite of this, he still weighs options to study in neighboring Nigeria which he views as a viable alternative. Just as Musang is about to leave the country for the United States, the writer introduces poetry through Ndzem. The poem that Ndzem recites is both prayer and invocation/incantation which he uses to call on "the ancestors of his family, the souls of his dead grandparents and parents as he prayed" (132).

> Wo-o-o-! Tabufor, Grandmother Atuakom!
> Tata Tuilui-ntong, Nemoue Shom!
> Here we are, gathered to send your child out
> To a world we do not know where it is located,
> All because of the blessings you all have heaped on him.
> We call you all then to keep him company as he travels
> Out, cleanse his face so that whoever looks upon it will
> Fall in love with him and accept him as a friend.
> Brighten his mien, open doors for him and let
> No harm come his way. Who is that parent who feeds his or her
> Child a scorpion? Then he or she is something else and
> Not a parent. Who is that parent who laughs at a child in pain,
> Then he or she is something else not a parent.
> We will go to sleep and sleep soundly because we know
> Musang is surrounded by you all. Our Father, Yesso,
> We call on you, bless this your child who is going out
> To hunt; may he thrive, may his days be full of joy,
> And after all is done, bring him back home like a true master.
> We ask all this in the name of our Lord and Master Yesso,
> *Amin?*

"Amen!" They all chorused after Ndzem. (EFD 132-133)
This represents a call to the higher power on whom humankind must rely for their absolute freedom.

Pre-emptively framing freedom, autonomy, and independence has been elucidated in EFD's *Boundaries* as coming from a writer who brings in a single genre a combination of the major literary genres viz. poetry, prose, and drama and even fine art. The novel comes across

192

as a syncretic piece written with the enthusiastic excitement, the enchanting commitment and dynamic verve of a poet. The vivid descriptions herein are gripping with the clarity of a novelist, and his character representations are enthralling and captivating as those of a dramatist. EFD's bringing together of the three major genres to explain the dependence/independence binary is highly imprinted by his own powerful vision. His synergy of walking the tightrope of the said binary aims at attaining the so much desired autonomy, freedom, independence, and or sovereignty within the context of *La République du Cameroun* which is befitting of being "a metaphorical prison …" (Ndi qtd. in *Secrets, Silences, and Betrayals* 204). In short, Leslie S. Simon's extant quote hereunder is an apt conclusion of EFD's pre-emption in framing the absolute that humankind aspires to, viz. freedom, independence, autonomy, sovereignty, etc. Simon writes:

> The novelist shares [his] concern: as [himself a] historians of a given sort, [he] work[s] to carve out the space of the private in the midst of the public. [Like a] [n]ovelist[s] writing in the 1830s, "a world [very] newly understood this concern in a particularly intensive way: not just the place of the person in the crowd, but the place of humanity in the ever-before and ever-after. In moments of heightened self-awareness, we might assume too that narratives emanating from [EFD feels] unusually burdened "with a sense of time that exceeded the limits of plots," wondering at the relevance of human storytelling, of considerations of the personal, when confronted with the earth's antiquity. (Qtd. in *Dickens Quarterly,* vol. 34, n° 4 Dec. 2017. 310)

Works cited

Stone, Harry. "Dickens and the Jews" *Victorian Studies,* vol. 2, no.3 March 1959, pp. 243-245

Doh, Fru Emmanuel. *Boundaries,* Langaa Research & Publishing, 2015.

Dowling, Tim. "This book is dedicated to ... who exactly?" https://www.theguardian.com/books/2007/jun/21/news.com ment Accessed 10/23/2018

Einfield, Lizzie. "Book dedications: so few words, but such big stories" https://www.telegraph.co.uk/culture/books/books-life/7073767/Book-dedications-so-few-words-but-such-big-stories.html Accessed, 10/23/2018

Fishkin, Benjamin H., Adaku T. Ankumah and Bill F. Ndi, editors. *Fears Doubts and Joys of not Belonging*, Langaa Research & Publishing, 2014.

Hall, Donald. *Claims for Poetry*. U of Michigan P, 2007.

Hegel, GWF. *Introduction to the Philosophy of History: an Appendix from The Philosophy of Right*. Translated by Leo Rauch, Hackett, 1988.

Long, William. "A Balance of Parties Took": Political Allusion in a 'Parish' Sketch." *Dickens Quarterly*, vol. 34, no. 4, Dec. 2017, pp. 293-305.

McDowell, Edwin. "To Those Who Read Book Dedications" https://www.nytimes.com/1982/09/06/books/to-those-who-read-book-dedications.html Accessed, 10/23/2018.

McLeash, Kenneth. *Key Ideas in Human Thoughts*. Prima, 1995.

Ndi, Bill F. *Secrets, Silences and Betrayals*, Langaa Research & Publishing, 2015.

Room, Adrian, *Bloomsbury Dictionary of Dedication*. Bloomsbury, 1990.

Shank, Judith Stewart. "Interpreting Poetry: The Literary Habitus." *Readings in Literary Criticism*, edited by Judith Stewart Shank, CSTM P, 2009.

Simon, Leslie S. "The De-orphaned Orphan: *Oliver Twist* and Deep Time." *Dickens Quarterly*, vol. 34, no. 4 Dec. 2017, pp. 306-330

Slater, Michael. *Charles Dickens: A Life Defined by Writing*, Yale UP, 2009.

Chapter 9

Foreign Aid Dependency and the African Continent

Dalal Alkordi
Tuskegee University

Foreign Direct Investment (FDI) is one of the ways that countries interact with each other bilaterally after foreign aid and trade. There are differences in the way countries conceive of their financial and trade interactions. Alesina and Dollar write that "while foreign aid responds to political incentives, foreign direct investments are more sensitive to economic conditions in the receiving countries."[1] Interestingly, while foreign aid responds more directly to "political" openness (democratization), FDI responds more to "economic" openness including general improvement in the investment climate, policies, trade liberalization, better and protection of property rights.[2]

It is important to set the tone for this chapter with the above-cited clear and clarifying distinction between Foreign Direct Investment and Foreign Aid—by Stephen Magu—since developing countries have suffered many serious economic setbacks since the 1980s. Central to this distinction is the fact that the motivational paradigms determine whether dependency is engendered or not. Also, one could add the following rhetorical question: who benefits from it? This question is important for the simple fact that Western theories and approaches to explaining and understanding foreign aid obfuscate the very role played by the West herself in perpetuating dependency.

---

[1] Alberto Alesina and David Dollar, "Who Gives Foreign Aid to Whom and Why?" *Journal of Economic Growth* 5, no. 1 (2000): 34, accessed January 15, 2018, https://dash.harvard.edu/bitstream/handle/1/4553020/alesina_whogives.pdf.

[2] Stephen Magu, *Peace Corp and Citizen Diplomacy: Soft Power Strategies in US Foreign Policy* (Lanham: Lexington books, 2018), 67.

Aid dependent countries thus find themselves in the role of puppets while the aid donors are the puppeteers. No wonder poor quality institutions, weak rule of law, absence of accountability, tight controls over information, and high levels of corruption still characterize many African countries today. Yet, the lions must tell their tale of the hunt to stop narratives that will only glorify the hunter.[3] The relations between foreign aid donor countries and recipient nations have given rise to a fertile area of literature on both foreign aid and economic growth.[4]

There are major reasons for the ongoing poor governances on the African continent. These reasons include economic crisis, unsustainable debt, civil wars, and political instability resulting from undemocratic institutional practices in recipient countries for many, many decades now. The roots of these problems are not separate from the potential impact of foreign aid. Foreign aid, in excess, goes into these countries year in year out, yet the inhabitants of these countries suffer from problems arising from the incurred debt. Recently, a number of studies have examined the impact of foreign aid on African development.[5] These studies concluded that generally foreign aid help African governments in relief from binding revenue constraints, enabling them to strengthen domestic institutions and pay higher salaries to civil servants. For more than three decades, a key feature of Africa and African relations with the outside world, has been foreign aid. Brautigam and Knack explain the history of foreign aid in African countries in their study "Foreign Aid, Institutions, and Governance in Sub-Saharan Africa." They explain that it began, as an institution, in 1947 with the Marshall Plan.[6] With the inception of the Marshall Plan, almost immediately, the impact of

---

[3] From an African proverb: "Until the lions write their own history, the tale of the hunt will always glorify the hunter" qtd. in Bill F. Ndi, *Secrets, Silences, and Betrayals* (Langaa Research and Publishing, 2015), 21.

[4] Williams Easterly, *The White Man's Burden* (Westminster, UK: Penguin Books, 2006), 44.

[5] Deborah A. Brautigam, and Stephen Knack, "Foreign Aid, Institutions, and Governance in Sub-Saharan Africa," *Economic Development and Cultural Change* 52, no. 2 (2004): 255-285, accessed January 19, 2018, http://people.ku.edu/~asiedu/FDI-in-Africa-WD.pdf

[6] Ibid.

large amounts of foreign aid on the behavior and attitudes of recipient governments raised concerns. Riddell describes the massive amount of foreign aid that continues to flow to Africa from the donor community. However, the end of aid in terms of absolute amounts of money transferred is certainly not in sight.[7] And one can ask—on the sidelines of Riddell's assertion—who stands to benefit, the donor or the recipient? In the same vein as Riddell, McKinlay and Little in their study view economic aid as a form concessional finance designated explicitly for the purposes of development. By providing a concessional supplement to foreign exchange holding savings, aid can increase investment and thereby accelerate development. It is in this guise that aid can be seen as a fund transfer designed to improve the economic and welfare problems of low-income countries.[8] There is relatively little attention for the evidence regarding the negative effects of aid dependence on state institutions. This explains why in 2005, The United Kingdom Chancellor of the Exchequer, Gordon Brown called for doubling the foreign aid, the Marshall Plan for the world's poor, and the International Financing Facility (IFF).[9] The record of aid to Africa is not encouraging. Although the positive achievements of aid are yet to be well recognized, aid should not be abandoned, but be improved upon.

It is in the light of the previously mentioned that this chapter explores the link between foreign aid dependency and the African continent. It examines the relationship between aid receipts, politics, economics, and autonomy. In addition, it reviews a number of studies in the literature i.e. studies all focused on the aid dependency relationship. It also considers the potential impact of aid dependence on the relationship between state and citizen. Yet, this relationship exists where one party relies upon the other without the reliance

---

[7] Roger C. Riddell, "The End of Foreign Aid to Africa? Concerns about Donor Policies," *African Affairs* 98, no. 392 (1999): 309-335, accessed January 9, 2018. http://www.jstor.org/stable/723522.

[8] Robert D. McKinlay, and Richard Little, "A Foreign-Policy Model of the Distribution of British Bilateral Aid, 1960–70," *British Journal of Political Science* 8, no. 3 (1978): 313-331, accessed January 11, 2018, http://www.jstor.org/stable/193645.

[9] Easterly, *The White Man's Burden*, 3.

commonly shared.[10] It is a one-way independence —> dependency or so to speak, donor —> recipient track or axis. Following Jürgen Habermas' *Theory of Communicative Action*, it is clear that there is a form of domination here, which prevents free and equal negotiation necessary for an equitable business transaction.[11] In this case, one of the parties can, at will, terminate the relationship with no cost, whereas the other can only do so at a considerable and negotiated cost. The dependent party, therefore, holds a subordinate position while the dominant party possesses the advantage. This potential for control constitutes the main advantage for creating dependency. Consequently, the donor is in a dominant position because he/she can terminate its aid freely and with little or no cost, while for the recipient to terminate the aid, it would involve the loss of concessional finance. The recipient is hamstrung; with hands and feet bound by strings attached to the aid. The dominant power also has the power to decide or to impose the ways in which the money is dispensed. The dependent party holds the shorter end of the leash and cannot but simply implement or go by the orders the donors impose. James C. Scott makes this evident in *Domination and the Art of Resistance: Hidden Transcripts*. He draws attention to the fact that, "…public activity between dominant and subordinate is nothing but a tableau of power symbolizing hierarchy."[12] Even though some studies have shown the positive impact of aid on economic development and improvements in quality of life, the impact of foreign aid nevertheless, varies from country to country.

In many countries, Foreign Aid has almost always had to produce negative effects in spite of the very positive outcomes donors sought to encourage by giving the aid. Policy ownership, fiscal unsustainability, institutional and economic stagnation, not growth, are amongst these adverse effects of aid.[13] In 1978, McKinlay and

---

[10] Michael Barratt Brown, *After Imperialism* (UK: Humanities Press Intl, 1970).

[11] Jürgen Habermas, *Theory of Communicative Action*, Translated by Thomas McCarthy (Boston: Beacon Press, 1985).

[12] James C. Scott, *Domination and the Art of Resistance: Hidden Transcripts* (New Haven, CT: Yale University Press, 1990), 56.

[13] T. J. Moss, G. Pettersson Gelander, and N. Van de Walle, "An Aid-Institutions Paradox? A Review Essay on Aid Dependency and State Building in

Little stated that it was necessary to examine the advantage or the distorting effect of foreign aid on recipient counties. Also, they highlighted that it was crucial to fit in an exploration of the relationship between international donors and recipient countries. For these two authors, the excess demand for aid places the donor in a strong bargaining position and may enable the donors to dictate a number of conditions under which the aid is provided. Moreover, the type of aid itself may allow the donor to intervene in the internal affairs of the recipient. Accordingly, the repayment would be an advantage to the donor and not the recipient. It might require the recipient to reschedule her debts.[14] However, considering the result of the Riddell study, it is important to ensure that the amount of granted aid will be made available for a considerable length of time for it to have a better chance of making a difference instead of aiming at increasing the amounts of aid. In addition, for a real difference, the focus needs to be more explicit on issues of power, politics, and interest groups.[15]

In view of the abovementioned, previous studies have shown that Africa is an aid dependent continent. Few countries in Africa can deliver basic public services without having recourse to external funding and expertise.[16] This has attracted the attention of aid donors who, in turn, have established that such states can raise a substantial proportion of their revenues from the international community. These states are less accountable to their citizens and are under less pressure to maintain popular legitimacy. However, they do not owe their citizens any loyalty for foreign donors constitute their financial mainstay. Moreover, this is a case in point to show how the international assistance negatively affects the recipient country. By influencing the decision-making in the country, it is certain that the

---

Sub-Saharan Africa," *The Mario Einaudi Center for International Studies*, paper no. 11-05 (2006), accessed January 11, 2018,
https://www.cgdev.org/sites/default/files/5646_file_WP_74.pdf.
   [14] McKinlay and Little, "A Foreign-Policy Model of the Distribution," 316.
   [15] Riddell, "The End of Foreign Aid to Africa?" 333.
   [16] Eveline Herfkens, and Mandeep Bains, "Reaching Our Development Goals, Why Does Aid Effectiveness Matter," *United Nations Millennium Campaign and Organization for Economic Co-operation and Development* (2008).

interest of the populace is not at the forefront of the aid donors' agenda. Equally, the donors' expected outcomes might be materially contrary and irrelevant to the desires of those in the recipient country. They are less likely to have the incentives to develop and invest in effective public institutions.[17] There is another important feature of foreign aid in Africa. In the short and long terms, it can save lives and reduce suffering. In the first place, the most disputed aspect of aid is that associated with economic development.

When talking of the art of domination, J. C. Scott is quick to point out that, "[t]he practices of domination and exploitation typically generate the insults and slights to human dignity that in turn foster a hidden transcript of indignation. Perhaps one vital distinction to draw between forms of domination lies in the kinds of indignities the exercise of power routinely produces."[18] However, dependency is assigned, more or less, equal emphasis to internal (national) and external (international) factors as sources of dependency. Emphasis falls more on such formal and institutional relationships as foreign aid, foreign investment, and trade relations than on class relations and class conflict, which are given attention but not prominence.[19] There are examples that aid has successfully supported economic development, including countries successfully emerging from aid dependency, such as, Rwanda, Mozambique, and Ethiopia. These countries are examples of countries that have successfully used aid to expand their economies and improve well-being of their citizens. Nonetheless, without aid, many countries cannot develop the abilities to produce the goods and services they need in order to be involved in the international trade market. According to Easterly, it is impossible to end world poverty. However, aid agencies can do many useful things to assuage the desperate needs of the poor and give them new opportunities. Apparently, Non-Governmental Organizations (NGOs) always lay emphasis on their efforts and

---

[17] Moss, Gelander, and Walle, "An Aid-Institutions Paradox?" 1.

[18] Scott, *Domination and the Art of Resistance*, 7.

[19] Louis A. Perez, "Dependency," *The Journal of American History* 77, no. 1 (1990): 133-142, accessed January 21, 2018, http://www.jstor.org/stable/2078645.

struggles in eliminating the poverty.[20] Moreover, Easterly gives one example, stating that, "instead of trying to "develop" Ethiopia, aid agencies could devise a program to give cash subsidies to parents to keep their children in school."[21] It is not surprising that some proponents of dependency theory hold strongly to the claim that the uneven development of global society casts the main core of the industrialized world in a dominant central role which renders the position of poor aid dependent countries peripheral and eternally dependent.[22]

The causes of underdevelopment in Africa is their propensity for aid dependency. However, Harvard University Alberto Alesina and the University of Mainz Beatrice Weder have found no evidence that aid donors give less aid to corrupt countries. In fact, in some of their statistical analyses they showed that donors gave these countries more aid.[23] Nevertheless, aid problems are well recognized and this has led to a variety of responses. This governance crisis in Africa has continued for more than 10 years after the World Bank (WB) identified it as a major contributor to Africa's development problems. The United Nations Millennium Project report in January 2005 claims that the main problem facing poor countries, is a lack of money and not bad government as it has been argued. Where many reasonably well governed countries, lack the fiscal resources to invest in infrastructure, social services, and even the public administration necessary to improve governance.[24] The Big Push of massive aid flow was supposed to get poor countries out of what the UN Millennium Project calls a "poverty trap," i.e. the idea that saving is very low for poor people, increasing only at some intermediate level of income and thus automatically preventing very poor countries from growing.[25]

---

[20] Sebastian Mallaby, *The World's Banker: A Story of Failed States, Financial Crises, and the Wealth and Poverty of Nations* (Canada, HC: Penguin Books, 2004).

[21] Easterly, *The White Man's Burden*, 11.

[22] Kenneth McLeish, *Key Ideas in Human Thoughts* (Rocklin, CA: Prima Publishing, 1995), 193.

[23] Alesina, Alberto and Beatrice Weder (qtd. in William Easterly, *The White Man's Burden*, New York: Penguin, 2006, 133.

[24] Easterly, *The White Man's Burden*, 153.

[25] Ibid., 38.

Despite the excellent job done by WB professionals and their vital mission, there is still a letdown from international organizations and financial bodies such as UN, IMF, and the WB in justifying their objectives to forge peace, banish financial instability, as well as lift people out of poverty.[26] Indeed, the WB has full control over both sides, the Africans (i.e. recipient nations) and the West (i.e. donor nations). The World Bank advises Africans on what to say to the donors. It also tells the donors what to give to Africans.[27] As such, aid dependency seems to explain neocolonialism in McLeish's view. Through African aid dependency, it is clear that previously formal administrative control (i.e. the colonial administration) has simply ceded its place to economic control over aid recipient countries. This is mostly achieved by dictating to the recipients, how, on what, and where they spend the aid dollars.[28]

Basically, Africa's dependence on the official creditors resulted from the first oil shock which brought about a lot of debt issues. Gradually, the region's debt became huger and huger. Accordingly, Mallaby points out that private lenders in the early 1980s refused to provide more cash. Thus, Africa was stuck in a spiral of servicing its debts. However, the WB made long-term loans to Africa so that the IMF's short-term loans could be paid back.[29] Moreover, Asiedu suggests that the negative effects on FDI for Africa was based on the perception that African countries are characterized as being risky. This conveys a lack of knowledge about the countries in the continent. Furthermore, Asiedu provides a description of policy implications to help African countries overcome some of these struggles and to perform more successfully.[30] However, no margin of income above that for survival can be invested for the future. This is the main reason why the poorest of the poor are most prone to becoming trapped in low or negative economic growth rates. This is

---

[26] Mallaby, *The World's Banker,* 4.

[27] Ibid., 91.

[28] McLeish, *Key Ideas in Human Thoughts,* 193.

[29] Mallaby, *The World's Banker,* 106.

[30] E. Asiedu, "On the Determinants of Foreign Direct Investment to Developing Countries: is Africa Different?" *World Development, 30*(1), (2002): 107-119.

so because, they won't be able to save for the future and be self-sufficient to get out of their existential poverty.[31] Moreover, Aart Kraay and Claudio Raddatz, in a January 2005 paper, studied the savings rate in all countries with data and found that saving does not behave as the poverty trap at low income. That explains the why those countries must stay poor.[32]

Even though, some public policy measures aimed at combating poverty and hunger succeed and some do not. According to Riddell, donors have given high priority to using aid resources to help solve Africa's poverty problems.[33] Despite this, some corporations come to Africa with the goal of trade not aid. Examples of such corporations abound. Shell, Elf, Schlumberger, BP, NNP-Paris-Bas, Credit Lyonnais etc. are a few that come to mind. Of these companies, Schlumberger, the largest oilfield company in the world was founded in 1927. It dominates the oil and gas exploration sector and employs more than 100,000 employees in more than 80 countries including Kenya, Mozambique, Cameroon, South Africa, Tanzania, just to name a few. This company's primary goal is to trade and add value. Although, trade is booming in Africa, the number of Africans living in poverty continues to grow.[34]

Moreover, the clarifications and justifications of aid challenge that aid levels are not based on meeting the needs of the poor and there is a growing gap between Africa's aid needs and the aid.[35] Sebastian Mallaby, in his book *The World's Banker: a Story of Failed States, Financial Crises, and the Wealth and Poverty of Nations,* draws attention to the fact that the more the World Bank lends money to bad debtors, the more indebted they become. He further highlights that the big disaster is when these bad debtors fail to repay. Consequently, the bank operation does not help in the battle against the poverty. The bank keeps forcing these countries into default if they cannot repay their loans. In addition, the bank's Structural

---

[31] Easterly, *The White Man's Burden*, 38.

[32] Aart Kraay and Claudio Raddatz qtd. in Easterly *The White Man's Burden*, 41.

[33] Riddell, "The End of Foreign Aid to Africa?" 309.

[34] Padraig Risteard Carmody, *The New Scramble for Africa* (UK: Polity Press, 2016).

[35] Riddell, "The End of Foreign Aid to Africa?" 313.

Adjustment Program (SAP) aims at getting fresh loans to aid receiving African nations so they can repay old ones. That means this program does not promote adjustment because the provided loans do not really help Africa.[36]

Besides, aid donors face several challenges and these lead to inefficiencies. Amongst these inefficiencies are the following: the widening gap between aid needs and aid provided; the hype of donor commitments to reduce poverty in Africa, which is not new; divisions among donors, and large gaps between the rhetoric of support for poverty alleviation, and the reality of sectoral aid allocations; all of these severely weaken aid programs and their endeavors. Again, the uncertainties about whether the development model within which aid funds are located will be able to deliver the growth and employment generation required. In addition, though donors have given increasing prominence to aid which reaches the poor directly, there are serious doubts regarding the scale and effectiveness of such aid. Furthermore, the growing emphasis which donors are placing on the results and effectiveness of aid risks shifting aid towards the less poor.

In recent years, aid donors have tended to place less emphasis on politics and the power of selfish elites interested in asset looting then in genuinely solving Africa's poverty problems. This is very similar to the Greek economic problem that started with the global financial crises of 2008. These themes were dominant in the mid-1970s when donors last focused strongly on aid for poverty reduction. Again, there is a big debate on the effectiveness of foreign aid. Reports on the number of successful projects across the leading agencies show that there has been some recorded improvement over time. More and more aid projects are now achieving their immediate objectives than they did in the past. Data from some agencies, including the WB and the Asian Development Bank for the period from the mid-1970s to the showed that the success rate of projects was pathetic. This notwithstanding, Riddell asserts that, three clear successes of aid are to be found on the European continent: The Marshall Plan, the example of Greece, Spain, Portugal, and Ireland in the 1970s, and the

---

[36] Mallaby, *The World's Banker*, 107.

1990s Eastern Europe where the European Commission investments changed both the socio-economic and democratic landscape for the better.[37]

Moreover, considering the UN's 2005 'Year of Microcredit', it marked the long journey of the microcredit from an obscure experiment in the mid-1970s to that of a worldwide movement, decades later. Microcredit has captivated not just the entire development aid industry, but journalists, editorial writers, policymakers and much of the general public in both the North and the South.[38] However, donor data still show that some projects have failed to meet their immediate objectives and that some have achieved only a limited success. This is particularly the case in sub-Saharan Africa transport projects. Nevertheless, in the case of Malawi, the combination of financial aid, technical assistance, and institution building contributed to growth in the 1970s. In East Asia, growth has been much larger over time than those in sub-Saharan Africa. However, it must be stressed that, in the 1960s and part of the 1970s, growth rates in most African countries were far superior to those in South Asia.[39]

Additionally, developing countries were encouraged to implement electoral democracies. Through this, Washington consensus emerged among Western leaders as to how to run the economy as a result of the supremacy of Margaret Thatcher and Ronald Reagan. Organizations, such as the WB, the IMF, and the WTO, imposed the same rules and laws on all countries, irrespective of their level of development. This was often to the detriment of the lower classes. Free trade, small government, lower taxes, and financial openness became the universal mantra for economic development. Therefore, from the mid-1970s, or at least from the beginning of the 1980s, most African governments stood under the

---

[37] Roger C. Riddell, "3 Does Foreign Aid Work?" *Doing Good or Doing Better* (2009): 47.

[38] Thomas Dichter, "Hype and Hope: The Worrisome State of the Microcredit Movement," The Microfinance Gateway (2006), accessed December 9, 2008.
http://
www.microfinancegateway.org/content/article/detail/31747?print=1.

[39] Riddell, "3 Does Foreign Aid Work?" 60.

surveillance of the IMF and the WB.[40] It is during this period that the IMF and the WB prescribed the Structural Adjustment Programs (SAP) to African governments. The SAP completely ignored areas in which emphasis should have been made viz. health, education, agriculture, and infrastructure. Instead, "disinvestment was the rule, and development assistance during those years was mainly used to keep Africa alive."[41]

Increasingly, during the 1990s, the donor community as a whole has focused on linking the aid directly or indirectly to the alleviation, reduction, and eventual elimination of poverty.[42] That again stresses that the important indicator of donor commitment to alleviate poverty in Africa depends on the level of funds provided. In his 2006 book, *The Whiteman's Burden,* William Easterly points out how donor nations set the priorities for nations they are keen on awarding aid to. This is generally done in a bid to "maximize benefits from the HIPC (i.e. Heavily Indebted Poor Country Initiative)."[43] He goes a step further to saying donors would do everything possible to put a diplomatic spin to facilitate aid to awful recipient governments. He points out the gerundive use of language in aid documents and highlights the ubiquitous presence of gerunds therein. It is therefore no surprise that the Cameroonian autocrat, Paul Biya, who had been in power for 24 years still received an evaluation from aid agencies which had a positive ring to it making it possible for him to be awarded the aid. Finally, he emphasizes that "[t]the weak but improving" line is popular among aid agencies in Africa."[44] Easterly's claims lead the international community to wonder what role aid dependency plays in underdevelopment.

Furthermore, examining the relationship between dependency and underdevelopment is a complex task. It has been noted that increasing growth broadens inequality and makes nations more

---

[40] Riddell, "3 Does Foreign Aid Work?" 343.

[41] Riddell, "3 Does Foreign Aid Work?" 126.

[42] Ibid.

[43] Interim Poverty Reduction Strategy Paper, Joint Staff Assessment, Ethiopia, 2001. (qtd. in William Easterly, *The White Man's Burden,* New York: Penguin, 2006, 138).

[44] Ibid.

dependent on foreign powers. Mostly, the various types of dependence; economic, military and political are directly related to one another. Economic dependence does not allow for fully independent policy positions in other areas. It is also assumed that economic dependence retards prospects for national economic development. A number of scholars including, Chernotsky/Geller, McGowan, and Walleri have examined this.[45] Additionally, economic dependence has been measured in terms of three aspects, viz. trade, aid, and export concentration.[46] Thus, if a government uses different strategies such as using aid in one condition, trade in another, or multinational corporations in third situation, then employing these procedures individually may obscure a systematic relationship. It is observable that the purpose of this aid is mostly finance designated for increasing investment and thereby accelerate development. However, it has another effect especially when low-income countries are faced with problems of capital shortages problem. This creates many arguments around foreign aid. The assistance received by low-income countries are not proportional to their economic and welfare needs. Again, the major donors have largely engaged in bilateral programs rather than through international agencies, nations, or the International Bank for Reconstruction and Development. And also, this aid is not given on a humanitarian basis, rather it is given to serve Western interest in low-income countries. The main issue or concern is that aid is much more related to the interests of the donor than to the needs of the recipient. However, this does not suggest that it has been systematic in any efficient way.[47]

Kremer, van Lieshout, and Went further state that, "[a]nother change which has occurred is that the historical distinction between development and emergency, or humanitarian aid is not nearly as clear-cut as is commonly thought."[48] Today, development aid project

---

[45] Richard Vengroff, "Dependency and Underdevelopment in Black Africa: an Empirical Test," *The Journal of Modern African Studies* 15, no. 4 (1977): 613-630.

[46] Barbara Stallings, "Economic Dependency in Africa and Latin America," (1972).

[47] McKinlay and Little, "A Foreign-Policy Model of the Distribution," 314.

[48] Kremer, Monique, Peter van Lieshout, and Robert Went. "Doing Good or Doing Better." *Development Policies in a Globalizing World* (2009).

expenditures are primarily concerned with saving lives. Even though most of these emergency aid project expenditures focus on reconstruction and rebuilding livelihoods, they do not end up achieving their purpose. This is noticeable during disasters. People need help and the aid is not even used to save lives.[49] In spite of this evidence, Easterly suggests that there are opportunities for adjustment, mostly in areas such as public health. He explains in his book that preventing children from death is not costly. All it needs is proper management of money. For instance, the successful story about the mosquito nets. Providing bed nets, to protect people from malarial mosquitoes' bites while they sleep, significantly lowers malaria infections and deaths.[50]

McKinla and Little point out that aid programs founded on a strong local base and through local agencies have a considerably success rate than those imposed from outside. Thus, some donors argue that aid should be given in different forms, either to individuals to provide them with the tools to enable them to be employed, and thus escape from poverty. Alternatively, donors should not only provide aid to help address humanitarian problems, but they should also provide aid to help meet immediate basic needs of the poor. In essence, humanitarian aid has been criticized for several reasons. For instance, variations in the amounts of aid received by low-income countries do not correspond to the variations in their levels of need. The major donors largely retain bilateral control over the aid programs. They would refuse to increase the supply of aid substantially through multilateral agencies. Furthermore, it is now generally acknowledged that aid provides the donor with an element of control or leverage over the recipient. Proponents of this position view foreign aid and technical assistance as a tool for manipulation. This does not generate a culture of independence.[51] Finally, it is frequently asserted that the aid program of the United States has only been maintained because of rivalry and competition among the

---

[49] Ibid.
[50] Easterly, *The White Man's Burden*, 13.
[51] McLeish, *Key Ideas in Human Thoughts*, 193.

superpowers.[52] Additionally, aid assigned to countries with inadequate infrastructures or investment structures may not use effectively. Instead, countries need technology as well as investment in their human capital and in their infrastructure to have a chance of transforming their economies to produce value-added goods.

However, donor agencies essentially want to give aid to poor countries, not to rich ones. Also, the rich countries push donor agencies to give mostly to the government in the recipient country. The implication of this is that, were all poor countries to have bad governments, then donor agencies will have to give aid only to bad governments.[53] However, the ideal thing would be to get aid from the rich of rich countries to the poor of poor countries. Again, the reality is that aid shifts money from being spent by the best governments in the world to money being spent by the worst. One wonders how much of these billions benefits the poor people. Boone found that aid has zero effect on investment as well as on growth. Additionally, "Boone addressed the problem of reverse causality by using political factors to predict which countries got aid—usually rich countries gave aid to poor countries that were their political allies, or with which they had a colonial association."[54] Here, another criterion arises, i.e. the benefits derived by donor and recipient countries.

In 1996, for instance, sub-Saharan Africa received $17 billion in aid. This accounted for almost one-third of all official aid provided in that year. Indeed, over the past decades, Sub-Saharan Africa has received a lion's share of all official aid. This amount jumped from 19 percent of total aid in the mid-1970s to a whopping 22 percent by 1980. It was estimated to reach 30 percent by the end of the 1980s. Moreover, Easterly found that although foreign aid claimed to exist for entirely homegrown reasons, foreign aid received does not produce these successes. However, he suggests that the poorest countries can grow and develop on their own. Perhaps, if this is the situation, these poor countries will not accept foreign aid and will not

---

[52] Robert D. McKinlay, and Richard Little. "A Foreign Policy Model of US Bilateral Aid Allocation." *World Politics* 30, no. 1 (1977): 58-86, accessed January 9, 2018, http://www.jstor.org/stable/2010075.

[53] Easterly, *The White Man's Burden*, 133.

[54] Ibid., 45.

depend on these kinds of donations. Further still, among the poorest countries, there were individual poor countries that failed to grow. As Easterly's book indicates, Chad had zero growth from 1950 to 2001.[55]

It must however be noted that low-income countries with higher levels of economic development and better levels of performance are economically more stable. Greater economic stability provides the basis from which other donor interests (such as trade or investment) may develop. Furthermore, economic stability is a necessary condition for political stability. Any kind of external financial flow changes would act as incentives to recipient government officials and their citizens, regardless of the precise nature of donor practices.[56] According to previous studies, a large-scale transfer of income within most developing countries are 'politically unlikely' to occur. Thus, policies to alleviate poverty need to focus on access to resources and fair distribution of assets. These studies further indicate that substantial increases in aid influx over a sustained period could have a harmful effect on institutional development in sub-Saharan Africa. Although, in yet another study by Remmer, he reflects on the impact of aid in different countries, there were concerns within the government. Any effort to explain government issues around the globe needs to address the subject of aid flow.[57]

Yet, the mechanisms adopted by foreign aid programs to track and monitor aid flows are very demanding in terms of recipient capacity. They impose detailed conditions identifying the amount of money, the purpose, the cost of administering the projects and the payback period. In addition, the project achieved by their contracted workers with high transaction costs, means that recipient countries will not receive the technology and will not get these jobs opportunities for its people. That is what results in diminishing the effectiveness of aid. Moreover, the downside of having excessive foreign aid over long periods is that it can weaken institutions. This

---

[55] Ibid., 40.

[56] Moss, Gelander, and Walle, "An Aid-Institutions Paradox? 13.

[57] Karen L. Remmer, "Does Foreign Aid Promote the Expansion of Government?" *American Journal of Political Science* 48, no. 1 (2004): 77-92, accessed December 14, 2017, doi:10.2307/1519898.

seems to be the case in Africa, where high levels of foreign aid are associated with declines in the quality of governance. Such declines also depend on parameters such as the way the aid is provided, the motives behind it, what it is used for, the domestic policies, interventions to guide it, and the quality of political leadership.[58] There are, nonetheless, some alternative explanations of the ineffectiveness of foreign aid. The purchase of goods and, services from donor country consultants may prevent the aid from bringing about growth to the recipient country. Another probability is that the donor country gives the aid for political reasons, which may again limit the aid's effectiveness.[59] Even though high levels of aid can work against improving governance, they also have the potential to spur good governance according to the World Bank publication, *Assessing Aid - What Works, What Doesn't, and Why*.[60] Notwithstanding, the publication is a devastating multi-country study of the failures of donor conditionality. It shows the aid given to countries is ineffective in having them voluntarily pursue good policies[61]. Furthermore, the potential to improve will be in cases where high levels of aid are channeled to governments with clear development agendas to improve the quality of the civil service, strengthen policy and planning capacity, as well as establish strong central institutions. Yet the way large amounts of aid are delivered can prove to have adverse effects. They weaken institutions rather than build them.[62]

Most writing on aid stated that aid would promote development, fight hunger, and support democracy and human rights. These claims are similar to those made by both The International Monetary Fund and The World Bank. Therefore, the failures of aid need more effort by concerned people to reform the aid system. It is important to

---

[58] John W McArthur, and Eric Werker, "Developing countries and international organizations: Introduction to the special issue," (2016): 155-169, accessed February 9, 2018,
https://link.springer.com/content/pdf/10.1007%2Fs11558-016-9251-2.pdf.

[59] Easterly, *The White Man's Burden*, 49.

[60] Accessed, July 19, 2018.
http://documents.worldbank.org/curated/en/612481468764422935/Assessing-aid-what-works-what-doesnt-and-why.

[61] Mallaby, *The World's Banker*, 253.

[62] Brautigam and Knack, "Foreign Aid, Institutions, and Governance," 260.

mention that transparency is the element most regularly missing from institutional aid. Considering the fact that African countries are among those receiving the most foreign aid per capita, the issue now facing many of these African countries becomes how to consolidate and extend these reforms with less external support. However, Goldsmith analyses the relationship between the amount of development assistance given to sub-Saharan countries in the 1990s, and changes in their political systems. He suggests a positive correlation between development assistance and democratization in the 1990s. Moreover, his paper indicates that democratization is more than a false front put up for donors.[63]

In the context of aid, the best single indicator of relative need is the population and the per capita GDP. Scholars used a country's GDP as the best single indicator of the degree of reliance or dependency. As population increases and per capita GDP declines, the relative need for aid rises. An aid recipient's dependency on a particular donor is operationalized by expressing its bilateral aid receipt as a percentage of its GDP. Moreover, the size of the recipient's population and its per capita GDP are important as a requirement to the foreign policy. Consequently, the influence of population supports the significance of power politics as a source of policy on aid. Conversely, using the population as an indication of humanitarian aid will influence the country's aid program. McKinlay and Little, in "A Foreign Policy Model of US Bilateral Aid Allocation," analyze the humanitarian vision. Their work emphasizes the economic assistance utility, suggesting that the provision of aid is designed to promote economic development in low-income countries, while the foreign policy view emphasizes the instrumental utility of aid and suggests that its provision is designed to promote the foreign policy interests of the donor.[64] It is in this regard that theoreticians of soft power lay claims that such powers have found their way into the political life of nations to the point where

---

[63] Arthur A. Goldsmith, "Donors, Dictators and Democrats in Africa." *The Journal of Modern African Studies* 39, no. 3 (2001): 411-36, accessed December 14, 2017, http://www.jstor.org/stable/3557318.

[64] McKinlay and Little, "A Foreign Policy Model of US," 58.

"…countries can get some (smaller) [aid recipient] states to change their behavior on certain issues by applying "pressure" which is often economic—withdrawal of aid, severing ties, or sanctioning elites."[65] These kinds of actions have been the rallying point for dependency theorists.

According to McKinlay and Little (1978), the United Kingdom does not pay much attention to countries' trading or security ties with to the Communist bloc. Thus, in comparison to the USA, the United Kingdom is not concerned with any global conception of security and absolute commitment of aid. One wonders if these benefits are not used as a mechanism for containment. However, the distribution of dependency established through the U.K.'s aid also conforms to the general foreign policy interpretation. While the pattern of dependency has its own distinctive points of emphasis, the central interests structuring this pattern are consistent with those underlying the distribution of absolute and relative commitment.[66] Remarkably, McKinlay and Little studied the importance of the commitment. A commitment identifies an attempt by one state to register its support for another. Three main utilities may be associated with commitment; they account for the willingness of high-income countries to demonstrate a commitment to a low-income country. They include the following positions; the commitment may be used to prevent intervention by a hostile state. Also, it may be a tool to discourage a developing state from jumping ship and getting out of the sphere of influence a developed state. And finally, even when a developing country is non- aligned, there may still be a desire on the part of a developed state to demonstrate commitment to it, if only to discourage it from moving into a rival's sphere of influence.

---

[65] Magu, *Peace Corp and Citizen Diplomacy*, 45.
[66] McKinlay and Little, "A Foreign-Policy Model of the Distribution," 324.

Bibliography

Books

Brown, Michael Barrat. *After Imperialism*. Humanities Press Intl, 1970.

Carmody, Padraig Risteard. *The New Scramble for Africa*. Polity Press, 2016.

Dollar, David and Lant Pritchett. *Assessing Aid - What Works, What Doesn't, and Why (English)*. World Bank Policy Research Report. Washington, D.C.: The World Bank, 1998. Accessed, July 19, 2018.
http://documents.worldbank.org/curated/en/61248146876442 2935/Assessing-aid-what-works-what-doesnt-and-why

Easterly, William, and William Russell Easterly. *The White Man's Burden: Why the West's Afforts to Aid the Rest have done so much ill and so little good*. Westminster, UK: Penguin Books, 2006.

Habermas, Jürgen. *Theory of Communicative Action*, (Translated by Thomas McCarthy). Boston: Beacon Press, 1985.

http://documents.worldbank.org/curated/en/61248146876442293 5/Assessing-aid-what-works-what-doesnt-and-why.

Magu, Stephen. *Peace Corp and Citizen Diplomacy: Soft Power Strategies in US Foreign Policy*, Lanham: Lexington, 2018.

Mallaby, Sebastian. *The World's Banker: A Story of Failed States, Financial Crises, and the Wealth and Poverty of Nations*. Canada, HC: Penguin Books, 2004.

McLeish, Kenneth. *Key Ideas in Human Thoughts*. Rocklin, CA: Prima Publishing, 1995.

Ndi, Bill F. *Secrets, Silences, and Betrayals*, Mankon-Bamenda: Langaa Research and Publishing, 2015.

Scott, James C. *Domination and the Art of Resistance: Hidden Transcripts*. New Haven, CT: Yale University Press, 1990.

Journal Articles

Alesina, Alberto and David Dollar, "Who Gives Foreign Aid to Whom and Why?" in *Journal of Economic Growth*, 5, No. 1 (2000): 34. Accessed January 15, 2018.

https://dash.harvard.edu/bitstream/handle/1/4553020/alesina_whogives.pdf.

Asiedu, E. "On the Determinants of Foreign Direct Investment to Developing Countries: is Africa Different?" *World Development*, *30*(1), (2002): 107-119. Accessed January 19, 2018. http://people.ku.edu/~asiedu/FDI-in-Africa-WD.pdf.

Brautigam, Deborah A., and Stephen Knack. "Foreign Aid, Institutions, and Governance in Sub-Saharan Africa." *Economic Development and Cultural Change* 52, no. 2 (2004): 255-285. Accessed January 8, 2018. http://www.jstor.org/stable/10.1086/380592.

Dichter, Thomas. "Hype and Hope: The Worrisome State of the Microcredit Movement." *The Microfinance Gateway* (2006). Accessed December 9, 2008. http:// www.microfinancegateway.org/content/article/detail/31747?print=1.

Goldsmith, Arthur A. "Donors, Dictators and Democrats in Africa." *The Journal of Modern African Studies* 39, no. 3 (2001): 411-36. Accessed December 14, 2017. http://www.jstor.org/stable/3557318.

Herfkens, Eveline, and Mandeep Bains. "Reaching Our Development Goals, Why Does Aid Effectiveness Matter." *United Nations Millennium Campaign and Organization for Economic Co-operation and Development* (2008).

Kremer, Monique, Peter van Lieshout, and Robert Went. "Doing Good or Doing Better." *Development Policies in a Globalizing World* (2009).

McArthur, John W., and Eric Werker. "Developing Countries and International Organizations: Introduction to the Special Issue." (2016): 155-169. Accessed February 9, 2018. https://link.springer.com/content/pdf/10.1007%2Fs11558-016-9251-2.pdf.

McKinlay, Robert D., and Richard Little. "A Foreign Policy Model of US Bilateral Aid Allocation." *World Politics* 30, no. 1 (1977): 58-86. Accessed January 9, 2018.

http://www.jstor.org/stable/2010075.

_____. "A Foreign-Policy Model of the Distribution of British Bilateral Aid, 1960–70." *British Journal of Political Science* 8, no. 3 (1978): 313-331. Accessed January 11, 2018. http://www.jstor.org/stable/193645.

Moss, T. J., G. Pettersson Gelander, and N. Van de Walle. "An Aid-Institutions Paradox? A Review Essay on Aid Dependency and State Building in Sub-Saharan Africa." The Mario Einaudi Center for International Studies, Working Paper 11-05 (2006). Accessed January 11, 2018. https://www.cgdev.org/sites/default/files/5646_file_WP_74.pdf.

Perez, Louis A. "Dependency." *The Journal of American History* 77, no. 1 (1990): 133-142. Accessed January 21, 2018. http://www.jstor.org/stable/2078645.

Remmer, Karen L. "Does Foreign Aid Promote the Expansion of Government?" *American Journal of Political Science* 48, no. 1 (2004): 77-92. Accessed December 14, 2017. doi: 10.2307/1519898.

Riddell, Roger C. "The End of Foreign Aid to Africa? Concerns about Donor Policies." *African Affairs* 98, no. 392 (1999): 309-335. Accessed January 9, 2018. http://www.jstor.org/stable/723522.

_____ . "3 Does Foreign Aid Work?" in *Doing Good or Doing Better* (2009)

Stallings, Barbara. "Economic Dependency in Africa and Latin America." (1972).

Accessed January 19, 2018. http://www.jstor.org/stable/159582.

Vengroff, Richard. "Dependency and Underdevelopment in Black Africa: An Empirical Test." *The Journal of Modern African Studies* 15, no. 4 (1977): 613-630.

Accessed January 21, 2018. http://www.jstor.org/stable/159582.

Chapter 10

Bate Besong's *Disgrace: Autobiographical Narcissus and Emanya-nkpe Collected Poems*[1]: Unmasking Francophone Cameroons' Epistemicide

Hassan Yosimbom
University of Yaoundé

In Cameroonian State Universities, the knowledge produced by weltanschauung arising from the Anglophone region is considered "inferior" in relation to the "superior" knowledge produced by Francophones who arrogate the status of being the canon of thought for the production of Cameroonian knowledges. The eight State Universities are classified into the six Francophone-culture-orientated universities (Yaoundé 1, Soa, Douala, Dschang Ngaoundere and Maroua) found in the Francophone region and two Anglo Saxon-culture-orientated Universities (Buea and Bamenda) found in the Anglophone zone. The dominant language of instruction in the Francophone-culture-orientated universities is French while that in the two Anglo Saxon-culture-orientated Universities is English. Anglophone epistemologies are those that originate from the Anglophone zone and are shards of the Anglo-Saxon culture; Francophone epistemologies are those originating from the Francophone zone and are fragments of the Francophone culture. The knowledges produced from the minoritarian socio-historical experiences and weltanschauung of Anglophones, also known as "non-Francophone," are considered "inferior" and not part of the canon of Cameroonian thought. Moreover, knowledge produced by the two Anglo Saxon Universities of Buea (UB) and Bamenda (UBa) is also regarded as "inferior" and "outcast" from the Francophone canon of thought. The foundational structures of

---

[1] My citations from BB's poems will ignore the stanzaic form and focus on coupling poetic ideas that unmask Epistemicide in contemporary Cameroons.

knowledge of the Westernized, Francophone-dominated six state universities are simultaneously epistemically regionalist and have created and sustained a Francophone/Anglophone asymmetry. In *Disgrace*, Bate Besong (BB) thus portrays the asymmetrical relationship between Anglophones and Francophones as sustained by a Francophone knowledge owing its hegemony to its discrediting of rival Anglophone knowledges by suggesting that they are incomparable to the Francophone culture in terms of efficiency, coherence, and scientificity. The differences between Francophones and Anglophones are not merely political but also relate to what matters as relevant knowledge (Santos, 2006: 13). As a perpetrator/benefactor of that asymmetry, the Francophone culture seems to relish in the destruction or marginalization of Anglophone knowledges. This destruction/marginalization of knowledges is what I call epistemicide and argue that in *Disgrace*, BB proposes two processes for combatting Francophone epistemicidization of Anglophone knowledges: the *sociology of absences (SA)* and the *sociology of emergences (SE)* (Santos, 2002a, 2004, 2005, and 2006 and Santos and Rodríguez-Garavito 2005).

The Santosian Conception of the Sociologies of Absences and Emergences

According to Santos (2006: 15-18), the *SA* "consists of an enquiry that aims to explain that what does not exist is in fact actively produced as non-existent, that is – as a non-credible alternative to what exists" (15). In this vein, "the objective of the [SA] is to transform impossible into possible objects, absent into present objects, invisible or non-credible subjects into visible and credible subjects" (15). It does so by countering Santosian *five monocultures* (MK, MLT, MND, MU, and MCP) and their resultant *five principal social forms of non-existence* produced by hegemonic epistemology and rationality i.e. the ignorant, the residual, the inferior, the local and the non-productive with *five ecologies:* the ecologies of knowledges, temporalities, recognitions, trans-scales, and productivities. In line with Santos (2006), this chapter argues that the Francophone/Anglophone asymmetry has created five

218

monoculture. The Monoculture of Knowledge *(MK)* i.e. the "manufactured" Francophone high culture thus recognized or legitimated as the canon considers the Anglophone zone to be nonexistent because it is ignorant or backward [*the ignorant Anglophone*]. With *MLT* the Francophone zone sees history as a unique and well-knowledge meaning and direction that excludes the Anglophone zone and produces it as non-existent by describing it as backward [*the residual Anglophone*]. *MND* allows the Francophone zone to institutionalize social classification, to naturalize hierarchies and categorize the Anglophone zone as substandard [*the inferior Anglophone*]. Through *MU*, the Francophone zone becomes dominant on the scale and the Anglophone zone becomes the subservient. It makes the Francophone zone the "universal" ignoring specific contexts as the "global" that has continued to dominate Cameroonian thinking and privilege activities or entities that widen their scope to the whole globe [*the local Anglophone*]. Through *MCP*, all labor from the Francophone zone is converted into productive force for the Cameroonian economy, while labor from the Anglophone zone that cannot be converted and is regarded as non-productive and therefore non-existent [**the non-productive Anglophone**] (15-18). The creation of the ignorant, residual, inferior, local, and non-productive Anglophone means that the SA proceeds by confronting each of the modes of the production of Anglophone absence through nonconformity, the struggle for credibility and the practices of transgressive freedom, that is, practices of transformative action and transformative knowledge (18).

The *SA* works by replacing *monocultures* with *ecologies* (18-28). The *EK* confronts the logic of the MK with the identification of other knowledges and criteria of rigor that operate credibly in social practices by asserting incompleteness of all knowledges as a precondition for an epistemological dialogue and debate among the different knowledges. Also, *ET* confronts the logic of the MLT with the idea that linear time is only one among many conceptions of time, thus encouraging multitemporality through multitemporal literacy. On its part, *ER* confronts the logic of social classification by encouraging social and cultural diversity of the collective subjects at the local, national and transnational levels of human struggle. Furthermore, *ETR* confronts the logic of abstract universalism and global scale by arguing that "the world, rather than converging or reconverging, is diverging or rediverging" and so, "there is no globalization without localization, and as there are alternative globalizations there are also alternative localizations" (24-5). Lastly, *EP* counters the MCP by "recuperating and valorizing alternative systems of production, popular economic organizations, workers' cooperatives, self-managed enterprises, solidary production, etc., which have been hidden or discredited by the capitalist orthodoxy of productivity" (27). This essay also contends that the ecologies foster a version of Cameroonian realism that includes the realities rendered absent by Francophone suppression and marginalization of Anglophones. Unmasking epistemicide therefore involves a double-pronged Santosian process of a deconstruction that assumes the five forms un-thinking, de-residualizing, de-racializing, de-localizing and de-producing, and a reconstruction that comprises the five ecologies mentioned above. Santos (29-32), contends that the second manner of combatting epistemicide, the SE, is also called the epistemology of subaltern cosmopolitan legality. To him, "whereas the goal of the SA is to identify and valorize social experiences available in the world, although declared non-existent by hegemonic rationality and knowledge, the SE aims to identify and enlarge the signs of possible future experiences under the guise of tendencies and latencies that are actively ignored by hegemonic rationality and knowledge" (29). The SE is thus an enquiry into the alternatives contained in the horizon of concrete possibilities. Using potentialities and capacities as its point of departure, the SE attempts to undertake "a symbolic enlargement of knowledges, practices and agents in order to identify therein the tendencies of the future in which it is possible to intervene so as to maximize the probability of hope vis-à-vis the probability of frustration" (30). Whereas the SA deals with alternatives available in the present, the SE is nonconformist and deals with possible future alternatives. Whereas the SA acts in the field of social experiences, the SE acts in the field of social expectations and so the SE is a continuation of the SA.

Despite the diversity of BB's oeuvre as playwright, poet and essayist, *Disgrace* has been chosen for this essay because in its collection of 56 poems, the first sixteen titled "Disgrace: Autobiographical Narcissus", are borne out of BB's experience with the university system in The Cameroons and thus set the anti-epistemicide tone of this essay. Part one of the essay focuses on the *SA* from five perspectives entitled: "The MK and the EK"; "The MLT and the ET"; "The MND and the ER"; "The MU and the ETR"; and "The MCP and the EP". The second part centers on the *SE* as an embodiment of signals, clues or traces of future possibilities of Cameroonian knowledges and argues that in order to achieve epistemological understandings, interactions, and coalitions at points of difference with Francophones, Anglophones need to decolonialize their own minds. This would lead to a "transepistemo-Cameroonization" which would neither be a clone of Francophone officialized culture nor a narcissistic nationalization of Anglophone knowledges. It would have to be independent/critical SA and SE, based on careful differentiating and empathic grasping of particular values and sensibilities born in particular historical and cultural contexts of Cameroonian borderlands (Tlostanova 203). The SA and SE enable a radical understanding of "situated [Cameroonian] knowledges" (Haraway 1998), questioning Cameroonian knowledge itself, its contexts, and the universities where it is produced, as well as the Francophone/Anglophone micro-levels which generate other knowledges (Tlostanova 204). The essay advocates transepistemic democratic iterations involving contestations and re/contextualizations of universalist knowledge claims/projects (Benhabib 16); and "egalitarian reciprocity" in which Francophone and Anglophone participants all have equal rights to suggest and criticize topics of transepistemic conversations. The monocultures that constitute the epistemicides of this essay's caption are not discussed as fragments; they are interrelated and of each other and constitutive of The Cameroons' epistemic/transepistemic structures.

The Monoculture of Knowledge/Rigor of Knowledge and the Ecology of Knowledges

Most Cameroonians, especially Francophones, conceptualize the Cameroonian world through the myth of Francophone objectivist/universalist knowledges which is tied to Francophonecentric forms of thinking and knowledge production (Grosfoguel and Cervantes-Rodriguez, 2002: xi). "Francophonism", or the liturgy about the socio-economic, cultural and political superiority of the Francophones, has been the common denominator of the relationship between Francophones and Anglophones. Francophonism, and its corresponding mythologies, serve the function of concealing the root causes of Francophone hegemonic power and privilege Francophone systems in the national hierarchy of The Cameroons and the oppressive designs upon which they have been erected. Francophonism has also been efficient in silencing the Anglophone "Other"; in the more than 50 years of The Cameroons' independence. The myth of "objectivist/universalist knowledges" has perniciously controlled the Cameroonian imagination and eclipsed representations of alternative ways of life, political options, and epistemologies (xi). This section identifies the following as MK: this myth and its links to the Francophonecentric forms of thinking and knowledge; the liturgy about the Francophone superiority; and the pernicious control of the Cameroonian imagination and the eclipsing of Cameroonian representations of alternative ways of life, political options, and epistemologies. As a monoculture, the myth of objectivist and universalist knowledges attempts to prevent people from recognizing that "we always speak from a specific site in the gender, class, racial, and sexual hierarchies of a given region in the modern/colonial world-system". Our knowledges, as Haraway (1988) contends, are always already "situated" (xii).

In this section, I argue that Ribeiro's notion of "subaltern knowledges" as well as Foucault's (1976) "subjugated knowledges," reminds us that the colonial experience leads to complex translocal scenarios that shape the production and dissemination of knowledge, including "subaltern knowledges." The notions of "subjugated knowledges," "subaltern knowledges," and "border thinking" (Mignolo 2000) eloquently illustrate the point that knowledges are not produced in a universal neutral Francophone location. I acknowledge the provincialism and epistemic regionalism that constitute The Cameroons' foundational epistemic structures as a result of the genocidal/epistemicidal Francophone hegemony. Such structures initiate a break with the uni-versalism where one ("uni") Francophone epistemology defines for the rest and recommend epistemic diversity which creates a pluri-verse of meanings and concepts where the Francophone/Anglophone inter-epistemic conversations produce re-definitions of concepts and pluriversal concepts. (Grosfoguel 89).

BB's opening poem, "The foolishness of trusting in tribal gods", initiates the debate that in Cameroonian universities, bourgeois political capitalism has created a hollow gap of epistemic tribalism/regionalism and challenges progressive intellectuals/politicians to fill the void with substantially new forms of trans-epistemic dialogues (TD). The poem criticizes university administrations, the Ministry of Higher Education, and the government for the oppressive manner in which they are wont to handle university crises. If the general belief that in traditional societies tribal gods are the major source of knowledge and cosmogonic wisdom is tenable, then BB's use of "tribal gods" in this poem is a metaphor for any unicentric/monoculturecentric reliance on a particular regional source of knowledge production. Given that art is a prefiguring of the future; a laboratory for new models and a clarion call, the poem is also a transepistemic call for blind views on knowledge production/acquisition. BB introduces the poem with three accusations: "You have not renewed the walls, or sought to restore the ruined houses"; "You have taken all the fat which covered the internal organs of the warthog... and offered to the tribal adders in the corn barn"; and "My daughters have endured the suffering that should have been mine... when I gave voice... inveighing the injustices and assassinations in the bruised homestead; I, too, interrogated [by] the Abouem à Tchoyi Commission [(ATC)]" (3).

223

The lack of a culture of maintenance (captured through the image of the walls not renewed and the ruined houses); the promotion of ethnicism/regionalism (portrayed through the internal organs, offered to the tribal adders); the institutionalization of repression (seen in the suffering of the daughters); and the use of intimidation against revolutionary intellectuals (depicted through the ATC's interrogations) contain elements of epistemicidization that foster the MK. The image of the tribal adders in the corn barn reminds one of a special form of ethnicization – the "nativization" of South Westerners as autocthonous sons-of-the-soil and the "alienization" of North Westerners as foreign come-no-goes in the UB in particular and the Higher Education System in The Cameroons in general. In an explanatory/confirmatory note to the ATC, BB makes five claims that could enhance one's understanding of the MK in the university system in The Cameroons. To BB, "by May 2005, the UB [harboured] the bitterest hatreds [and] divide-and-rule"; [this led] to President Biya's ATC (117) [because the UB] campus was rocked "by ethnicity, opportunism, sycophancy, hate and envy [yet the] ATC prove[d] to be myopically restrictive" (117).

The reminder that the ATC, commissioned to probe into a purely Anglo-Saxon crisis, created by Presidential Decree, symbolizes the fetishization of Francophone knowledges in The Cameroons. The contention here is not a blatant epistemicide propaganda that Francophone-culture-groomed administrators lack the ability to investigate issues that concern Anglophones. If Francophone-culture-groomed administrators were to develop the capability to disinterestedly investigate Anglo Saxon issues and Anglophone-culture-groomed administrators were to develop the capacity to effectively investigate Francophone based issues, The Cameroons would become the locus for TDs. Rather, the argument is that in a country that has seasoned Anglo Saxon scholars who possess the appropriate knowledge to resolve Anglo Saxon crises, the creation of the ATC was a travesty of epistemology because like most of such commissions, it proved to be myopic and hegemonically Francophonecentric. The creation of the commission ignored Haraway's (1988) assertion about "situated knowledges" and

224

confirmed the idea of *the ignorant Anglophone* whose epistemological capability is limited to producing "subaltern knowledges". If one takes seriously Castells' (2009) notion that Cameroonians live in "a global knowledge economy and in a society based on processing information" (1), then the quality, effectiveness and relevance of the university system will be directly related to the ability of people, society and institutions to develop. Thus, the ATC was an MK par excellence because its Francophonized Presidential Decree creation ignored the ability of the Anglophone people/institutions to nurture strategies/strategists for conflict resolution. As a Francophonecentric political organ imposed on an Anglophonecentric academic community, the commission monoculturally epistemicidized the UB's potential as a critical source of equalization of chances and democratization of society. The university's creation of trans-epistemic opportunities to protest against epistemicide through countering knowledges of intimidation and political intrigue were stifled by the commission.

BB's repeated use of the pronoun "you" to refer to these agents of epistemicide is a technique of multiple-referentiality that captures epistemicidal plurality at its widest sense. The speaker complains that "*You* have made the minds of your autocrats dull, their ears deaf, and their eyes blind, so that they cannot see or hear or understand" (4). He also asserts that "*You* have never been one to remove the chains of oppression, or let the oppressed go free; never been one to dismantle the yoke of injustices, or listen when the prophet presents his case" (4). Finally, he laments that "*You* dare not bind the cormorants with chains... *you* and regime collaborators will receive the legend of honour from the local party Corruptibility" (4). These "***you***" agents include the university administrators, the Ministry of Higher Education, the government and the ATC. The poem garners its verisimilitude by testifying that the epistemicidization of Anglophone knowledges is carried out by some Anglophones, co-opted into the Francophonecentric administrative machinery and Francophones, blinded by their insatiable quest for Francophone epistemic hegemony. Both have failed to recognize the UB's and the UBa's abilities to develop a new culture as the sources of cultural renewal and innovation. They continue to promote universities that are corporatist and bureaucratic, defending their own interests, and extremely rigid administratively.

Furthermore, the *"you"* in "You have made the minds dull...." refers to university administrators and some co-opted lecturers who have failed in their mission to edify Cameroonian leaders. BB's reference to the senses of hearing, sight, and understanding in the poem is not accidental because they are the major senses for knowledge acquisition. BB's argument is that the universities that should define the scope of political/leadership knowledge are failing because they are being politicized. Epistemological debates over the analysis and sources of leadership knowledge have been replaced by political malignancy characterized by the binding of cormorants with chains and the reception of legends of honour from the local party corruptibility (4). The *"you"* in "You have never been one to remove the chains of oppression...." refers to university lecturers, administrators and political leaders such as Governor Abouem à Tchoyi who have failed to nurture a philosophy of liberation and listen to prophets such as BB. It is therefore not surprising that the speaker in "The foolishness of trusting in tribal gods" concludes that among the revelers of the Pontiff Sovereign there is no one who can open the eyes of the blind; free those who sit in the dark prisons; give strength to hands that are tired and knees that tremble with weakness; turn the darkness of Babylonia to light or level every mountain (5) of an MK.

The gross irresponsibility of the "Pontiff Sovereign" and his "revelers" indicates that the idea of a single epistemological process emanating from a few Francophone dominant centres remains prevalent in the Cameroons. Given that Francophone epistemicide is a cultural project of ordering the Cameroonian world according to rational principles from the perspective of a Francophonecentric consciousness, BB proposes a rethink of knowledge production in Cameroonian universities by advocating an EK through the poems "Post-mortem intellectual" – a rebuke on a once polyvalent intellectual who has suddenly withdrawn into the cocoon of the MK; and "The playwright & the campus giants" – a celebration of a defiant playwright who has defied all odds and risks to continue to nurture EKs. In "Post-mortem intellectual" the speaker rebukes the intellectual, presumably a university don, for his/her shocking lackluster academic performance: "Your itinerary does not show that you work night and day... against mimic monstrosities [that] have pinioned the state as game to be hunted and eaten" (6). To the speaker, the intellectual has disappointed both himself and the university as well as the entire nation. The speaker says: "We thought you would always soar into the sky like Mandelan meteor, exalt, your luminosity into the Spartans risking their lives on a daily basis to give voice to those on the margin [... and] unravel the hidden meanings of the parables of the ensigns & magis from Bobo-Dioulasso" (6). The images of a Mandelan meteor, the Spartans and the ensigns and magis from Bobo-Dioulasso, capture the shepherd/flock relationship that was supposed to exist between the intellectual and those on the margin. Furthermore, the poet's allusion to the history of Mandelan and Spartan determinations confirm that besides questioning discourses of epistemicide, Cameroonians need polyvalent intellectuals who can develop new multi-epistemic trends that pay attention to the epistemic potential of local histories embedded in, or arising from, the Francophone/Anglophone asymmetry thereby leading the country from an MK into an EK.

"The playwright & the campus giants" stresses the importance of local histories. The speaker records the university administration's attempts to kill local histories with defiance: "We are not worried on account of the bureaucratic obfuscators; sorcerers of Staff Development Grants; necromancers of thousand Mission Warrants who gloat over the erasure of memory [and] plot against the playwright" (13). These local histories and epistemologies advocated by Anglophone intellectuals such as the playwright have remained largely invisible in Francophonecentric discourse precisely because they have been actively produced as nonexistent – as noncredible alternatives to what exists – through what Santos (2006) calls SA. This SA is seen through the speaker's numerous expressions insisting that the campus' "academic history has been written in blood"; "playwrights suffer persecution"; "intellectual flabbiness is anointed

227

behind a montage of petrol bonds", administrators rely on "Prime Ministerial & Presidential Decrees of ease", sell their own "compeers for a grotesque medal" and become stupid mules which must be controlled with a bit & bridle (14, 15). The poem thus calls for a SE that enables the identification and enlargement of the range of knowledges that could be considered credible alternatives. It is devoted to the SE by foregrounding the contributions of intellectuals like playwrights. It envisions knowledge as embedded in local contentious practices and in larger historical struggles. It thus credits the knowledge being produced in dialogue, tension and interaction with other groups.

To borrow from Santos (2002b: 46-47) BB's EK argument in the poem is that "all [epistemologies] are incomplete and problematic in their conceptions of [Cameroonian] dignity. The incompleteness derives from the very fact that there is a plurality of [epistemologies] and this is best visible from the outside, from the perspective of another [epistemology]." If the Francophone epistemology were as complete as it claims to be, there would be just one single Cameroonian epistemology. Thus, to raise the consciousness of epistemological incompleteness to its possible maximum is one of the most crucial tasks in the construction of a multicultural conception of The Cameroons. The construction of such a singular multicultural "Cameroon" is at hand because the speaker in the poem optimistically warns Cameroonian epistemiciders that they "will soon disappear like harmattan grass that dries up [or] die like plants that vanish the Kalahari" (15), and concludes: "Playwrights and scholars will possess this campus and enjoy intellectual prosperity & peace" (16).

The Monoculture of Linear Time and the Ecology of Temporalities

The MLT is based on the Francophone's epistemicidal assumption that The Cameroons' history has a unique and well-known meaning and direction. The meaning and direction of that history have been formulated in different ways since independence:

the new deal, national integration, rigor and moralization, emergence in 2035, and globalization. These formulations subscribe to a linear Cameroonian time at whose cutting edge is the core Francophones, their dominant knowledges, institutions and forms of sociability. This logic produces non-existence by describing as backward whatever is asymmetrical vis-à-vis whatever is declared Francophone. The socio-economic and politico-cultural encounters between the Anglophones and Francophones illustrate this condition because they continue to meet simultaneously but are not considered contemporaneous. Non-existence assumes the form of a residuum, which in turn has assumed many designations such as the primitive, traditional, obsolete, underdeveloped and as this section argues, the *incapable-of-politicking* Anglophone. In this light, BB's critique of the MLT is built on democratization and elections in "Ntarikon, massacre, 1990" and "Election results".

"Ntarikon, massacre, 1990" summarizes the pogrom that the CPDM government unleashed on Anglophones for breaking out of the cocoon of monopartyism and launching the SDF party in 1990. That launch was an attempt to tackle politics of the Cameroons from a different angle by arguing that politics does not constitute a linear movement towards Francophone political ideas and ideologies symbolized by the CPDM. The launchers introduced a different temporality into a Cameroonian politics saddled with the hegemony of the French culture's political epistemologies. The SDF party aimed at tackling politics from below rather from within. The aim was not to solve The Cameroons' political problems "objectively", once and for all. There were very strong Anglophone and subjective aspects to the party's enterprise, as there is for all those who advocate change. But there was also a very pragmatic side: at its simplest, to provide new insights into Cameroonian politics by articulating a politics of being for the construction of an Anglophone identity of belonging, to build Anglophone/Francophone reciprocity of believing, with focus on Anglophone agency; and a politics of partaking that would defend Anglophone/Francophone subjects.

Thus, the launching of the SDF was a counter-hegemonic epistemology/temporality that demanded a broad definition of objectives and a pluralistic conception of emancipatory goals for all Cameroonians. Through its slogan, "Power to the People", it seemed to argue that the "accelerated transformation of political and ideological landscapes required that [epistemic] transversality be brought about through constant analytical vigilance and strategic flexibility" (Santos, 2006: 39). Unfortunately, the government sought to stifle Anglophone temporality by killing and wounding some people, thus raising doubts as to whether democracy was being consolidated or dissipated. The successful launch of the SDF attested that even if the regime wanted to prevent democratic change and consequently the creation of an ET, it could not succeed because of the mounting illegitimacy of the one-party state and the pro-democracy movements.

Furthermore, "Election results" affirms that the "collective pain" of a people whose election results were manipulated, especially in the 1992 multiparty presidential elections, indicates widespread abuse of power. To a large extent the Biya CPDM regime has been greatly credited with legalizing multiparty politics; something the Ahidjo CNU regime could not do. There has undeniably been widespread and significant change in the nature of the political institutions in place. Since the launching of the SDF, The Cameroons has moved away from a single-party political system and has organized multiparty elections in 1992, 1997, 2004, and 2011 but in line with BB's argument in "Shame". These MLT elections have failed to recognize that a politician is a creator, an initiator who should never dream of moving into the turbid void of his own desires and dreams (Gramsci 172). Cameroonian politicians in "Shame" are not creators/initiators and the regime has continued to be mired into the "shame" of geriatric politics in "the Ngoa-Ekele House of Prodigal Illusion" (34). BB laments that "as in a dirge/Carnation placed on the coco-nut head of the father of the Nation/without good judgment; is a gold ring affixed in a bush pig's snout/like the Foumban referendum lamp flickering out in the charnel power of an incestuous lure" (33).

BB's likening of the Foumban referendum that "united" Francophone and Anglophone Cameroons to an "incestuous lure"

230

confirms that since then, Cameroonian politics has been focused on a MLT that moves only towards French culture. He condemns the referendum's epistemicidization policy by arguing that:

> Only diplomatic missions with zero luminence and foolishly misguided would think that redeemers who fill their houses with loot in *Ghana-must-go-bags* and parade themselves/in the handsome turban of parliamentary immunity plebiscited by the *macarana'a* Labrado of Francois Xavier Mbouyoum's National Electoral Observatory, have gained, an honourable reputation (34).

To avoid the "shame" of loot, the misuse of political and administrative power, Cameroonians need to build narratives that rearticulate national designs by/from local histories while valorizing the perspective of the subaltern; and remapping the Francophone/Anglophone colonial experiences towards a culture that remaps their respective weltanschauung without being either of them.

Given Mignolo's (329) argument that "there is nothing outside of totality [because] totality is always projected from a given local history," it becomes possible for Francophones/Anglophones to think of "other local histories producing either alternative totalities or an alternative to totality". Such alternatives would not play on the "residual Anglophone/core Francophone" couplet inherent to Francophone epistemicide. They would rather build on a transepistemicism relation centred on the local histories in which Francophone national designs are necessarily transformed, thus transforming also the local histories that created them. Unlike epistemicide, such a move towards TD would bring to the fore the manifold local histories that, in questioning national designs envisage "cultures of transcience" that go against the cultural homogeneity fostered by such designs. The consolidation of such a debate would sharpen the cleavages in epistemic strategies and political action and defend epistemo-diversity by borrowing from Santos' (2006) "demo-diversity" to advocate the valorization of liberal, inter-cultural, and consensus epistemologies. The point would not be to accept uncritically any of these forms of epistemology, but rather to make possible their inclusion in the transepistemic debates about the deepening and radicalization of Cameroonian knowledges.

From an ET perspective, the SDF was fashioned to be a Mignoloian (2000) "border thinking" (38), "border epistemology" (26) and "pluritopic hermeneutics" (16) asserting the need "for a kind of thinking that moves along the diversity of historical processes" (40). The ET is not just a question of changing the contents, but the very terms of the transepistemic conversation between Francophones and Anglophones. It is not a question of replacing existing Francophone and Anglophone epistemologies either; these will certainly continue to exist and as such remain viable as spaces for transepistemic critique. Instead, the ET through "Ntarikon massacre, 1990", "Election results" and "Shame" opens up the space for an epistemology that comes from the Anglophone border and aims toward transepistemic political and ethical transformations of democratization and election results. While BB acknowledges the continued importance of the monotopic critique of epistemicide by Anglophone critical discourses (such as the SDF), he suggests that this has to be put into dialogue with the critique(s) arising from the multicultural difference that constitutes The Cameroons' border thinking: "A sensible person does not become a pariah; among his own people by hiding behind the iron curtain of PARTY DISCIPLINE" (35). The result is a "pluritopic hermeneutics", a possibility of thinking/politicking from different Cameroonian spaces which finally break away from Francophonecentrism as the sole Cameroonian epistemological perspective. This is a double critique of epistemicide from the perspective of ET—from the exterior of the Francophone world system.

Like border thinking, the ET entails both "displacement and departure" (308), a critique and positive affirmation of alternative orderings of the Cameroonian political correctness. Also, like border thinking, the ET points towards a different kind of epistemic hegemony, a multiple one. To reformulate Mignolo (2000), "the 'Francophone and the rest of the Cameroonians... provide the model to overcome epistemicide, as the "rest" becomes the sites where the

ET emerges in its diversity, where transepistemicism creates new local histories remaking and readapting Francophone/Anglophone national designs and transforming local (Cameroonian) histories from where such designs emerged. "Interdependence" may be the word that summarizes the break from the idea of epistemic *totality* and brings about epistemic *networks* whose articulation will require epistemological principles of the ET that promote "diversality as a universal project," implying that Cameroonian communities have the right to be epistemically different precisely because "they" are all epistemic equals (310, 311).

The Monoculture of the Naturalization of Difference and the Ecology of Recognitions

The absence of epistemic interdependence and *networks*, the persistence of epistemic *totality* and uni-versality, the systematic abrogation of the Anglophone right to be epistemically different precisely because they are epistemic residuals have resulted in the MND. This in turn has resulted in the categorization of the Anglophone as substandard and epistemic inferiors. The MND is thus a standardization of Francophone epistemic boundaries that proclaim hegemonic epistemic identity and stand ready to repel Anglophone epistemic difference. That is, the guardians of the "Berlin Wall" of Francophone epistemic hegemony have been as much concerned to keep Francophone epistemic indigenes and conversely keep Anglophone epistemic foreigners out. In this section, I argue that though a boundary-keeper, Francophone epistemology has also been a great boundary-defier that continues to seek to epistemicidize Anglophone epistemology. That is, Cameroonian social practices will never be democratized enough if the knowledge guiding them is not democratized. Anti-democratic repression will always include the disqualification of the ways of knowing of the repressed Anglophone because just as there is no democracy without popular education, there is no democracy of practices without democracy of knowledges, without an ER.

"Appointments in UB" decries the absence of the right to epistemic difference. With an Anglo-Saxon institution, the persona would have expected that the administrators in UB be elected through deliberative democracy/epistemology. Unfortunately, the Francophone-epistemology-inclined Ministry of Higher Education appoints administrators without recourse to any criteria. A deliberative epistemological ideal for electing university administrators should have started from the premise that administrative preferences will conflict and that the purpose of deliberative epistemic institutions must be to resolve such conflicts by encouraging open and unforced discussions to strike the fairest compromise between the competing points of view. But conversely, BB tells us that in UB, lecturers have become numbers "in the Gaullist galley system *Where Good is Bad and Bad is Good* [because they are] in an academy constructed on the muzzling of dissident voices... by the preposterous fiction of the ATC" (22). The argument here is not that a deliberative epistemology is faultless; neither is it that all the administrators who have been appointed by the ministry have been incompetent. Some appointees of the ministry do a wonderful job in steering the university's epistemic ship in the right direction. However, by suppressing the Anglo-Saxon tradition of election of university administrators with a Francophone tradition of appointments that follow the "us/them"; "indigene/foreigner"; "son-of-the soil/come-no-go"; "loyalist/dissident" binaries, the ministry renders itself guilty of the MND and consequently, epistemicide.

Furthermore, the images "the ATC" and especially that of a "Gaullist galley system" with its historical connotations of the French leader, Charles de Gaulle, and a small ship rowed by French-controlled prisoners and slaves, gives the university the image of an epistemological slave to French epistemology. BB laments that because of epistemicidal appointments, "Materialistic pursuits govern the lives of yesteryears trade Union leaders" (23). BB then calls on the university community to rise up against the "foulest treachery" and the "raucous greed" (24) of the appointees whom he calls "freak messiahs" (23) who spend their tenures of office amplifying the "*lapiro-refrain*: SILENCE, SUBMISSION, COLLABORATION" (24). The "foulest treachery", "raucous greed" and the "*lapiro-refrain*" are shards of an MND that help in creating the *inferior Anglophone* or manufacturing the *superior Francophone*.

BB's reference to the "lapiro-refrain" reminds one of the Cameroonian musician Lambo Sandjo Pierre Roger (Lapiro de Mbanga) who died in New York on March 16, 2014, after having spent his entire musical career fighting against all forms of oppression in The Cameroons. In 2008, he was imprisoned after criticizing the government of The Cameroons in the song "Constitution constipée" ("Constipated Constitution"). Born in the Francophone zone (Mbanga, Littoral Region) and bred in both the Francophone and Anglophone zones, Lapiro became a perfect symbol of TD. He sang in local Pidjin English, mixed with French, English and Douala, a multilanguaging Lapiro himself called *Mboko talk*. Most of his songs, like most of the poems in *Disgrace*, started from the premise that the recognition of the epistemological diversity of The Cameroons must be at the core of national resistance against capitalism and of the formulation of alternative forms of sociability. Through his heterolingual *Mboko talk,* Lapiro proposed an alternative epistemology that, far from rejecting either the Francophone or the Anglophone, placed both in the context of the diversity of knowledges existing in Cameroonian.

Starting from the assumption that cultural diversity and epistemological diversity are reciprocally embedded, both BB and Lapiro argue that the reinvention of social emancipation is premised upon replacing the MND by an ER. The ER "promotes non-relativistic dialogues among knowledges, granting equal of opportunities to the different kinds of knowledge engaged in epistemological disputes, and decolonizing knowledge and power on university campuses. When these opportunities are granted the *persona* in "Why we laugh at politicians and give them names" will no longer lament that "[i]n our 'White Collar Delinquent's Democracy, the monopoly of power is the birthright of [crooks and] elections are won under Monsieur Chirac's distillery" (25). The speaker in

"Camouflage" will no longer bother about "armed robbers in the guise of Provincial Governors" (28). However, BB concludes that TD requires patience because "[g]reat tidings often have small and humble beginnings; but they survive, grow steadily, and flower" (29).

Following Mignolo's (2000) idea of border thinking as "thinking from another place, imagining another language, arguing from another logic" (313), BB's argument that the administrators of UB should be deliberatively elected, just like Lapiro's condemnation of "silence, submission and collaboration" in the face of epistemic hubris, constitutes subaltern knowledge conceived from the borders of a UB world that strives to break away from, or force dialogue with the dominance of the five Francophone Universities world. Just as border thinking refers to "the moments in which the imaginary of the world system cracks" (Mignolo, 2000: 23), the ER represents "an epistemology of and from the border" (52), a kind of "double critique" (Khatibi) that is critical of both Francophonecentrism and of the excluded Anglophone epistemological traditions themselves; an ability that stems from UB's location in the borderlands of The Cameroons' State Universities system. The ER is an ethical way of thinking because, in its assumed marginality to the commandeering Francophone centre, it has no ethnocidal, Francophobic or Anglophonemaniac dimension that characterizes the Ministry's epistemicidal appointments. Its aim is not to correct the MND's lies and tell the ER's truth, but "to think otherwise, to move toward 'another logic' – to change the terms, not just the content of the conversation" (70).

Thus, *Disgrace* has optimism-inducing poems such as "Year of restoration" (37); "Eve of an apocalypse i & ii" (75); and "Resurrection" (78); all of which metaphorically announce the demise of all forms of hegemony as a "champagne party [that] will end" (90). This optimism enables a new view of the diversity and alterity of The Cameroons that does not fall into the traps of an essentialist rhetoric, but rather highlights the irreducible differences that cannot be appropriated by the monotopic critique of Francophonecentrism, and that does not conceive of difference as antithesis in search of revanchism. BB's ER sees the SA as a kind of

236

deconstruction that moves towards a fragmented, plural transepistemic project instead of reproducing the abstract universals of Francophonecentrism. It is an attempt to move beyond the current mono-epistemic Francophonemania by revealing the coloniality of Anglophone knowledges embedded in the geopolitics of The Cameroons epistemology – a necessary and already ongoing step in order to "undo the subalternization of [Anglophone] knowledge and look for ways of thinking beyond the categories of [Francophone] thought" (Mignolo, 2000: 326).

The Monoculture of the Universal and of the Global and the Ecology of Trans-scales

Given that the MK raises Francophone knowledges over Anglophone knowledges; the MLT limits The Cameroons' history and progress to Francophone progress; and that the MND raises the Francophone to the superior other, one could argue that the three monocultures all combine to elevate the Francophone scale as the primordial, thereby declaring the irrelevance of all other competitors. In *Disgrace*, the dominant Francophone scale appears under two different forms: the universal and national. Under the MU, Francophone universalism becomes the national scale of the entities or realities that prevail regardless of specific Francophone or Anglophone contexts (Santos 17), and privileges entities or realities that widen the Francophone scope to the whole country, assuming the prerogative to designate rival Anglophone entities as local. This section contends that dialogues between scales/trans-scales may lead to Cameroonian universalisms constructed from below - subaltern cosmopolitism. That is, the end of the monoculture of Francophone universals which is also the beginning of the ETR, starts from the recognition of the presence of a plurality of knowledges and of distinctive conceptions of human dignity and of the Cameroonian world. In the construction of the SA, the merits of the different Cameroonian scales and conceptions need to be assessed, with the critical consciousness that the future of Cameroonian knowledges is found at the crossroads of TDs. The section further argues that since the epistemic diversity of the Cameroonian world is open, with all knowledges situated; there are neither pure nor complete scales/knowledges, but constellations of Cameroonian scales/knowledges.

"Their champagne party will end" laments domination: "our middlemen… have sworn… to bankrupt our national coffers; our workers died of chronic shortages [and] repulsive old creeps… give their champagne parties in open defiance" (88). BB captures the twin Gramscian (1971) issues of domination and leadership through the expressions "victims they had exploited wretched" and "our middlemen" respectively. The Gramscian/BBian conceptions of power as "domination/ [victims of exploitation]" and as "intellectual and moral leadership/[our middlemen]" imply that power is a combination of consent and coercion. BB further concurs with the Gramscian postulation that the grey area that lies between coercion and consent is occupied by "corruption" and "fraud" (Gramsci 80n). Thus, in the poem, the middlemen who were supposed to be the leaders have been bought over by the MU that refuses to punish those who bankrupt the nation. In the eighth stanza of the poem, the speaker explains that "during the golden epoch there was much talk of *Unity, Reconciliation, Self-Reliance* somewhere up in the fringes of their Integration" (89). The golden epoch reminds one of the broken promises that were made during epochal events such as the union between Southern Cameroons and East Cameroon in 1961 and the legalization of multiparty politics in the 90s. This is not to say that the government has been completely indifferent to acts of socio-economic and politico-cultural epistemicide.

The New Deal Government has been trying to combat the MU through measures such as: the promotion of transparency and the fight against corruption epitomized by President Paul Biya's book, *Communal Liberalism*; "Operation Antelope" (that identified and erased hundreds of ghost workers from government payroll), and "Operation Sparrow Hawk" (that arrested untouchable embezzlers like Edouard Ekoto, Ondong Ndong Gerald, Urbain Oleguena Owono). Thus, the poet's identification of unity, reconciliation and self-reliance as "shit" reminds one of the regime's inability to achieve lasting TD between Francophone majoritarian epistemologies represented by the champagne party of the middlemen who erect white elephant structures and the Anglophone minoritarian epistemologies represented by the men of courage and conscience who speak too inconveniently and are invited into gallows. The speaker in the poem makes his lamentation clearer by adding that Southern/Anglophone Cameroonians have watched their "oil bonuses spreading, along their cobbled façades;/the posh suburbs neighbouring the foreign multinational warehouse on the coast/where, the arrivist-factor looking frightened behind the wheel of his chocolate cotroën-maserati hurries home to his plastic daughter" (89).

The misuse of oil bonuses to purchase expensive cotroën-maseratis is a perennial Third World problem that reminds one that the largely Frenchified capitalist system that The Cameroons inherited from her colonial master(s) is characterized by economy-crippling consumerism. It also reminds one of the situation in The Cameroons where even though the National Oil Refinery (SONARA) is found in Anglophone part of the country, the Anglophone cry has been that it is predominantly run by a few Francophones and Anglophones do not enjoy oil bonuses because the capitalist system has resulted in the paradoxical increasing oil wealth and the impoverishment of the citizens (165). The implication is not that most Francophones enjoy those bonuses or that competent Francophones should not be given deserving positions/duties in the SONARA simply because it is found in the Anglophone part of the country. BB's argument is that since independence, the epistemology that governs SONARA is still hegemonically Francophone. That is, from a SA perspective, the few Francophones who seem to have deprived Anglophones of the oil bonuses have been epistemicidizing Anglophone knowledges that question their rationalized irrationality thereby turning the New Deal Government into a Raw Deal. Such epistemicidization is confirmed in "Professor", a poem in which BB records the failure of a university professor to be the gadfly of his society because of the professor's partisan political inclinations. BB calls such a professor a "politically

239

partisan mameluke", "an Establishment mole" and an inventor of lies (16). As the highest symbol of knowledge production, one would have expected the professor to stand for the truth, especially with regards to issues like the distribution of oil bonuses but unfortunately, the professor has sacrificed his calling on the altar of the politics of his stomach. One would have expected that the Professor would, through his lectures, propagate a counter-hegemonic politics focused on the struggles against social exclusion and sensitize his students on the social need for equal power relations and a redistributive ethos (Santos, 2005: 29). Ironically, the professor epistemicidally decides to stifle research in the faculty by promising to stifle research and send subversive poets to innermost prisons (17).

The professor's decision to stifle research on the grounds that it is dissident to his Francophone abstract universalism represents what Ngugi (2009) calls "dismemberment". In this context Anglophone dismemberment captures not only the physical fragmentation caused the professor's "establishment of his power by organizing the ignorance of the faculty" (16) and his readiness "to besmirch the prescient and phoenix spirit on campus" (17) but also by the epistemological colonisation as well as the "cultural decapitation" that has resulted in deep forms of alienation among Cameroonian universities (Ngugi, 2009: 2). Through the ETR, BB, in "The mimic academic passes on", confronts this logic of abstract universalism by warning the professor that the Cameroonian world, rather than converging is rediverging and so, there is no Francophonization /universalization without localization/Anglophonization, and as there are alternative universalizations there are also alternative localizations (Santos 24-5). The disempowerment of the Anglophone "local" represented by the professor's mistreatment of his colleagues – their being reduced to the expression of an impact – derives from its imprisonment in a Francophone scale that prevents it from moving beyond impact and aspiring to nationalize/globalize itself. The SA operates here by denationalizing/deglobalizing the Anglophone local vis-à-vis Francophone hegemonic epistemologies – by identifying what is there in the Anglophone "local" which is not reducible to the effect of the impact – and by exploring the possibility of renationalizing/reglobalizing it as a counter-hegemonic epistemology (26). True to the tenets of TD, the mimic academic passes on because as a "clay-pot professor he ploughs leanness in undergraduate psyches; assassinates Amilcar Cabral's militants who tried to walk within UB with a non-sectarian heart; has changed his research zeal into the similitude of an ox; and his idols are silver and gold" (30-31). When the mimic academic passes on, his colleagues (viewed here as different scales) will delink themselves from the inert series of Francophone impacts and relink themselves as sites of resistance and generation of alternative epistemologies. This inter-colleague/inter-scale movement will establish what this section identifies as the ETR.

The Monoculture of Criteria of Capitalist Productivity and Efficiency and the Ecology of Productivities

The fifth logic of non-existence, the logic of productivity privileges growth through market forces. It applies both to nature and to human labor and argues that productive nature is nature at its maximum fertility whereas productive labor is labor that maximizes generating profit (Santos, 2006: 16). It asserts that non-existence is produced in the form of non-productiveness. Applied to nature, "non-productiveness is sterility; applied to labor, 'discardable populations', laziness, professional disqualification, lack of skills" (17). In this section, I contend that BB's poetic vision suggests that in The Cameroons, there exists an MCP through which labor from the Francophone zone is converted into productive force for the Cameroonian economy, while labor from the Anglophone zone is discarded as non-productive and non-existent. In "Confidence placed in the party comes to nothing" BB paints a pathetic picture of a female Anglophone who is mercilessly relieved of her duties because the party/government on which she has always placed her confidence suddenly considers her non-productive. The speaker mocks her: "whenever she entered the Elig Edzoa Hotel & Towers: Pro Consuls, Professors, Heads of Division, Albino and Contractors lay down in reverence to her … Secretary General of the Party

Praesidium ... at the champagne party of chronic carnivores, in the firmament of power" (27). Despite her slavish commitment to the party, the party hierarchy did not hesitate to fire her when they suddenly considered her non-productive; and her somnambulant trophy, ... a/badly and hurriedly buried corpse; whose ambulant legs stick out from the Faculty cemetery where the wicked are everywhere, and everyone praises what is evil" (27). This poem focuses on the role of the Cameroonian intellectual in Cameroonian politics. Since independence, Cameroonian intellectuals, like other African intellectuals, have played a major role in shaping societal visions. Through the once-cordial-but-suddenly-turned-turbulent relationship between the intellectual and party hierarchy, BB demonstrates that the relationship between Cameroonian intellectuals and politics/leadership has been frustratingly symbiotic. Given the selfish intentions of the powers that be, heroic attempts to be intellectually relevant have often proven forlorn for the critical/organic intellectuals like BB and quixotic for fawning/cosmetic intellectuals like the lady in the poem. The critical/organic intellectuals have struggled to tear down the barriers to TDs by insisting on an EP whereas the cosmetic intellectuals have been the flag bearers of the government's MCP thus promoting epistemicide.

BB explains that Pro Consuls, Professors, Heads of Division, Albino and Contractors revered her (27). She behaved like the Secretary General of the Party Praesidium at the champagne party of chronic carnivores (27). As an intellectual, especially one in an Anglo-Saxon institution, she failed to learn that contemporary Cameroonian politics is one of generalized monopolies. Intellectual autonomy has shrunk irredeemably, with intellectuals becoming subcontractors of the leaderships' epistemic monopolies. She thus has no control over her relationship with the leadership and so the one o'clock Etoudi radio announcement (27) can hire and fire her at will. The radio announcement is BB's warning to intellectuals that the media is the handmaiden of epistemicide. It is used to declare the non-productivity of someone who has worshipped the party all her life. Etoudi, the seat of the government of The Cameroons, reminds one of the notorious ATC discussed earlier. Like the ATC that turned out to be a veritable Trojan horse, the announcement engenders epistemicide because the rudimentary conceptual apparatus used by the leadership to analyze the productivity/non-productivity of intellectuals/epistemologies seems to have lost the capacity to prevent political deliquescence. BB argues that the opportunism, sycophancy and collaboration of cosmetic intellectuals allows tyranny to become entrenched in The Cameroons. They help Cameroonian dictators legitimize their regimes by buying off and co-opting The Cameroons' academics for a pittance. The university strike that orchestrated the hegemonic ATC in "The foolishness of trusting in tribal gods"; the launching of the SDF party and killings that followed suit in "Ntarikon massacre, 1990"; the manipulation of election results in "Election results"; and the misuse of unity, reconciliation and self-reliance in "Their champagne party will end" have all been products of intellectual opportunism. They cannot simply be understood in terms of a single supreme epistemology on the consequences of colonial rule, reunification, ethnicity, electioneering, or the throes of democratization. The history of these issues is far more complex and organic academics cannot account for all these events within one epistemology, but within TDs that remind both Francophone and Anglophone cosmetic intelligentsia that the history and politics of The Cameroons are as intricate as their comprehension.

From an EP perspective, the relationship between intellectuals and the leadership of The Cameroons requires what Holloway (2010: 253) calls an "eriugenic somersault". That is, the institution of TDs that see "all the forms of social relations [as] form-processes", view "all categories [as] swollen ec-statically with their own negation, or simply, that each obedience contains a disobedience which it cannot contain" (253). This somersault is not an academic invention, but simply part of a shift in the flow of the anti-MCP struggle; it is the emergence and growth of the fight against the Francophone's declarations of non-productivity as the essence of the fight against epistemicide (254). The EP will disclose and give credit to the diversity of Cameroonian social practices and credit them against the exclusive credibility of hegemonic practices. By criticizing both the intellectual subservience to party and its epistemic manipulation, BB argues that the reality of productivity cannot be reduced to what exists; it should amount to an ample version of realism obliterated by silence, suppression and marginalization. BB's poetic method is that of a Hollowayian (2010) "crack", a crisis that wishes to understand the MCP not from its solidity but from its EP cracks. Cameroonian academicians need to understand epistemicide not only as domination but also from the perspective of its crisis, contradictions and weaknesses, and how Anglophone intellectuals react to those contradictions. An EP that recognizes the differences and possible symbiosis between Francophone and Anglophone epistemologies becomes what Holloway (2010: 9) calls a "crisis theory" of the MCP's own "misfitting". *Disgrace* testifies that Cameroonians do not fit into the system, or, if they do manage to squeeze themselves on to the MCP's "ever-tightening Procrustean bed", they do so "at the cost of leaving fragments of themselves behind, to haunt" (9) them and their kind and render them vulnerable to Etoudi radio announcements and ATCs. In "Dining with the devil", BB paints a graphic picture of what happened to someone who once forced himself into that bed. When the commissar rigged and usurped the people's votes, the mob "placed a used tyre around his neck at the Commissariat of the people's revolution, on Voting Day" (18) and he fell like "an overripe cucumber" (18).

The Sociology of Emergences as an Embodiment of Signals, Clues or Traces of Future Possibilities of Cameroonian Knowledges

The SE is for the second epistemological operation depicted in *Disgrace*. Whereas in the first part of this essay I have argued that the goal of BB's SA is to identify and valorize social experiences/knowledges available in the Anglophone Cameroon world, although declared non-existent by a Francophone hegemonic rationality and knowledge, the BBian SE identifies and enlarges the signs of possible future Cameroonian experiences, "under the guise

244

of tendencies and latencies that are actively ignored by [the Francophone] hegemonic rationality and knowledge" (Santos, 2006: 29). This section enquires into the alternatives that are contained in the BBian horizon of concrete possibilities by identifying a symbolic BBian enlargement of Cameroonian "knowledges, practices and agents in order to identify therein the tendencies of the future (the Not Yet) in which it is possible to intervene so as to maximize the probability of hope vis-à-vis the probability of [epistemicidal] frustration" (31). The enlargement is a Cameroonian "sociological imagination with a double aim: to know better the conditions of the possibility of hope; [and] to define principles of action that favour the fulfilment of those conditions" (31). It is an epistemology of resistance that reinvents epistemic emancipation and democratizes the production of knowledges. Here I explore the use of the imagination to confront epistemicide and affirm the possibility of transepistemic worlds void of *disgrace*.

Even though most of the poems in *Disgrace* subscribes to the SE, "Scholar" and "Poetry is" grapple with the litmus test of an organic scholar and committed poetry respectively, and thus focus on the producer and production of knowledges rerspectively. In "Scholar" BB defines a scholar as "a tree that grows beside a stream [and gains fame] according to how he has lifted up the axes upon the thick trees and the dark places of the earth that are full of graven and molten images" (38). BB further says that a scholar "is sure-footed as a deer; is avatar of encyclopedic memory; makes the syllabus his chariot; he walketh upon the tarmac of cassia and oil upon the séances of old Wagadougou strings, ... as of sabbatical fire in a jubilee of bookshelves" (38). In "Poetry is", he argues that poetry is "All vines and multi-tangerines; Bosom of honeypoles; Nectar, baked pheasants; Sunshine & moonwreaths; Cycles of redemption; Phoenix of Ujama; Soyinka and Peace now" (108). To him, poetry is "not Hitler, not Hiroshima; Nyerere not Marshall Amin Reggae, not irate Marxist slogans; Not hatchet-swinging mallams; Not Gulag; Poetry is Jua voice of Anglophone Universe" (108). The BBian definitions of a scholar and poetry have images of Santosian possibilities (potentiality) and capacities (potency); *want, tendencies* and *latencies*; and *clues*. These images include: a tree that grows beside a stream, the lifting up of axes upon the thick trees and the dark places of the earth, the sure-footedness of a deer, the avatar of encyclopedic memory, the syllabus his chariot, walking upon the tarmac of cassia, oil upon the séances of old Wagadougou strings, and a jubilee of bookshelves in "Scholar". In "Poetry is", they are: vines and multi-tangerines, bosom of honeypoles, nectar, baked pheasants, sunshine & moonwreaths, cycles of redemption, phoenix of Ujama, Soyinka, peace, Nyerere, reggae, and Jua voice of Anglophone Universe. Given that these images speak of an epistemic rejuvenation or renaissance, they valorize *clues* as pathways towards discussing and arguing for a concrete alternative epistemology – replacing the "MKs" with "EKs" – that places Francophones and Anglophones in a diversity of knowledges that maximize unhierarchized contributions towards building a transepistemic Cameroonian world where another knowledge is always possible beyond Francophone and Anglophone epistemologies. Furthermore, BB's submission that "Poetry is Jua voice of Anglophone Universe" could be confirmation that the success of TDs will depend on the type of intellectuals that the Seven State Universities will continue to produce. BB recommends that they should be molded after the famous Anglo Saxon-culture-orientated politician who was the voice of the Anglophone universe. BB later explains in "The Grain of Bobe Augustine Ngom Jua" that "the time has come to return from the mountain shore the cavalier floods of the immortal Mungo or we shall find again tomorrow Bobe's seed, gone, with the drought" (103) of Francophone epistemicide.

BB further draws a parallelism between the functions of a scholar and those of a poet. A scholar "will pull you out of the dangerous obelisk, out of the deadly quicksand, at the call of the world-wide web…./he delights himself with the statues of diurnal talcum of the prescient Okomfo Anokye; his amphitheatre rings with the hieroglyphics of Cheikh Anta Diop/Spanning the millennia of time" (38, 39). Similarly, "The poet is solemn like the Spartan fakirs/In vision, more erratic – *if tuned so* – than Aro inmate" (108). The pulling out of people from a dangerous obelisk and the erratic vision implies that scholars and poets should respectively, be servants and visionaries of their people. It is precisely because Cameroonian scholars and poets have ignored that function that they aid in the production of hegemonic epistemologies: Francophonized Anglophonisms and Anglophonized Francophonisms. With the Francophone center specializing in Francophonized Anglophonisms, the Anglophone periphery is being forced to specialize in Anglophonized Francophonisms. Transepistemicism as a mode of production of knowledge thus refers to the nationalization of resistance against Francophonized localisms and localized Anglophonisms. BB's scholar, poetry and poet therefore represent the horizon of concrete possibilities and the hope of transepistemicism. To paraphrase Santos' (2006: 7-8), transepistemicism would be a new social, economic, cultural and political phenomenon. Transepistemicism would not be an event; nor a mere succession of epistemological events. It would not be a social movement, even though it would often designate itself as the movement of epistemological movements. Although it presents itself as an agent of social change, transepistemicism would reject the concept of a historical Francophone/Anglophone subject and confer no priority on any specific social actor in this process of social change. It would hold no clearly defined ideology, in defining either the epistemologies it rejects or the ones it asserts. Its modes of struggle would be extremely diverse and appear to be spread over a continuum between the poles of epistemic institutionality and transepistemic insurgency. No one person or group of persons would represent it or speak in its name, let alone make decisions, even though it would see itself as a forum that facilitates the decisions of the movements and organizations that take part in epistemic pluriversality.

Conclusion

In this chapter, the essay has tried to argue that the exercise of the SA is counterfactual and that for it to be carried out, it demands both epistemological and democratic imaginations which allow for the recognition of different Cameroonian "knowledges, perspectives and scales of identification, analysis and evaluation of practices" (Santos, 2006: 28) and that this presupposes the recognition of different Anglophone and Francophone practices and social agents respectively. In part one, it established that both the epistemological and democratic imaginations have a deconstructive and a reconstructive dimension that results in TDs. It has examined deconstruction from five perspectives, corresponding to the critique of the five logics of Francophone hegemonic rationality, namely *un-thinking* the ignorant Anglophone; *de-residualizing* the residual Anglophone; de-*inferiorizing* the inferior Anglophone; *de-localizing* the local Anglophone; and *de-producing* the non-productive Anglophone; and grappled with reconstruction through five Santosian ecologies – *the EK, the ET, the ER, the ETR, and the EP*. In part two, the essay demonstrated that the transepistemic knowledge of the SE is a process of ongoing critical interpretation that engenders a power-sensitive conversation. The essay has asserted that transepistemicism is a paradigmatic model, not of closure, but of that which is contestable and contested; that it is the Cameroonian myth of epistemological accountability and responsibility for solidarities linking the cacophonous visions and visionary voices of Anglophones and Francophones that characterize the knowledges of The Cameroons. All in all, transepistemicism is a subaltern cry that the geopolitics of Cameroonian knowledges shows the limits of any abstract universal, and so, The Cameroons is not unthinkable beyond Francophone epistemology.

Works Cited

Benhabib, Seyla. *Dignity in Adversity: Human Rights in Turbulent Times*. Polity Press, 2011.

Besong, Bate. *Disgrace: Autobiographical Narcissus and Emanya-nkpe Collected Poems*. Design House, 2007.

Castells, Manuel. (2009). "Lecture on Higher Education." Delivered at the University of the Western Cape. 7 Aug. 2009.

Foucault, Michel. *Power/Knowledge: Selected Interviews and Other Writings 1972-1977*, edited by Colin Gordon, Translated by.Colin Gordon, Leo Marshall, John Mepham, and Kate Soper. Pantheon Books, 1976.

Gramsci, Antonio. *Selections from the Prison Notebooks*, edited and translated by Ouintin Hoare and Geoffrey Nowell Smith. International Publishers, 1971.

Grosfoguel, Ramón. "The Structure of Knowledge in Westernized Universities: Epistemic Racism/Sexism and

the Four Genocides/Epistemicides of the Long 16th Century." *Human Architecture: Journal of the Sociology of Self- Knowledge*: vol. 11, no.1, 2013.

Grosfoguel, Ramón, and Ana Margarita Cervantes-Rodriguez, editors. "Introduction: Unthinking Twentieth-Century Eurocentric Mythologies: Universalist Knowledges, Decolonization, and Developmentalism." *The Modern/Colonial/Capitalist World-System in the Twentieth Century: Global Processes, Antisystemic Movements, and the Geopolitics of Knowledge*. Greenwood, 2002.

Haraway, Donna. "Situated Knowledges: The Science Question in Feminism and the Privilege of Partial Perspective." *Feminist Studies*, vol. 14, no. 3, Fall 1988, pp. 575 - 599.

Mignolo, Walter. (2000). *Local Histories/Global Designs: Coloniality, Subaltern Knonwledges and Border Thinking*. Princeton UP, 2000.

- - -.. "The Geopolitics of Knowledge and the Colonial Difference." *The South Atlantic Quarterly*, vol. 101, no.1, Winter 2002.

Ngugi wa Thiong'o. *Re-membering Africa.*: East African Educational Publishers, 2009

Santos, Boaventura. "Toward an Epistemology of Blindness: Why the New Forms of 'Ceremonial

Adequacy' Neither Regulate nor Emancipate." *European Journal of Social Theory*, vol.4, no.3, 2001, pp. 251–79.

- - -.. *Toward a New Legal Common Sense: Law, Globalisation and Emancipation* Butterworths, 2002a.

- - -. "Toward a Multicultural Conception of Human rights." *Moral Imperialism: A Critical Anthology*, edited by Berta Hernandez-Truyol, New York UP, 2002b.

- - -.. "A Critique of Lazy Reason: Against the Waste of Experience." *The Modern World-System in the Long Durée*, edited by Immanuel Wallerstein, Paradigm, 2004.

- - -.."Beyond neoliberal governance: the World Social Forum as Subaltern Cosmopolitan Politics and Legality."

Law and Counter-Hegemonic Globalization: Toward a Subaltern Cosmopolitan Legality, edited by Boaventura de Sousa Santos and César A. Rodríguez-Garavito. Cambridge UP, 2005.

- - -..*The Rise of the Global Left: The World Social Forum and Beyond.* London: Zed Books, 2006.

Santos, Boaventura, and César A. Rodríguez-Garavito."Law, Politics, and the Subaltern in Counter-Hegemonic

Globalization.". *Law and Counter-Hegemonic Globalization: Toward a Subaltern Cosmopolitan Legality*, edited by Boaventura de Sousa Santos and César A. Rodríguez-Garavito. Cambridge UP, 2005.

Tlostanova, Madina. (*Gender Epistemologies and Eurasian Borderlands.* Pelgrave Macmillan, 2010.

Chapter 11

Classical Studies at the University of Malawi 1982-2018: Evolving (In)dependence

Richard Evans
Tuskegee University

Beyond its theoretical aim to problematize the concept of imported, colonial languages in Africa as languages of oppression, this essay is, in several aspects, distinctly and significantly autobiographical: I personally participated in the establishment of a new Classics Department at the University of Malawi in the early 1980's i.e., 1985-1987. The establishment of a Department of Classics in 1982 occurred only slightly later after the foundation of Dr. Kamuzu Banda's now famous/infamous Classical school, Kamuzu Academy, in 1981, which has been painted as the epitome of neocolonial cultural imperialism (Nyamnjoh, "Potted Plants..." and wa Thiong'o *Decolonising the Mind*). From my participation, I can make accurate comments from direct, personal knowledge on the observations, opinions and motives of colleagues on the ground at the time of these foundations. Additionally, collaboration in developing a Classics Department in Africa has informed my later theoretical interests and current views as a classical scholar and literary researcher: Classics and Africa produce a spicy intellectual soup.

During the time I worked in Malawi, I reflected about the efficacy of laying out a full, university-level Classics program in a largely rural and poverty-ridden country. I was also challenged by some of my colleagues directly on this point. I recall a conversation with a German Africanist about why a Classics Department was a good idea at the University of Malawi. My answer then had something to do with the ability of an African university to compete with its European and American counterparts. His response puzzled me since I was naive about the issues of neocolonialism and cultural imperialism in the educational programs of Africa. He asked why an African university should need to look like universities in Europe or the United States in terms of its curriculum. The very question has been articulated by wa Thiong'o in *Decolonising the Mind,* and more recently by Francis Nyamnjoh in an article in the *Journal of Asian and African Studies*, "'Potted Plants in Greenhouses': A Critical Reflection on the Resilience of Colonial Education in Africa". At that time, I was, of course, seeing the development of African higher education from the perspective of its historical connections to the colonizers, their languages and their educational traditions, not in the light of an African linguistic revolution, an "African Renaissance" proposed by Ngugi wa Thiongo in *Something Torn and New*. To be fair to my perspective, in the mid-1980's Malawi, the local language, Chichewa, the native language of my students, had not been developed (so I was informed) to a point that incorporated a written literature and vocabulary sufficient to cope successfully with accelerating global science and technology. As a result, Malawi could hardly consider replacing English wholly as the language of higher education. Given the historical context of Malawi, British and American models of higher education appeared the most natural direction for institutional patterns and the language of instruction. This is the very educational direction and ideology contested by Ngugi wa Thiong'o and Francis Nyamnjoh, as one central problem of enduring, cultural neocolonialism all over Africa.

In this essay, as well as reporting my participation at the beginning of the Classics Department at the University of Malawi. On the one hand, I will address some significant theoretical questions about language in general and whether languages, specifically Latin or Greek, but also English and French, can serve as totalizing neo-colonist instruments of oppression. On the other hand, I would explore whether languages, those of colonizers as well as the local languages of the colonized, carry within themselves, by their internal dialogic nature, the ability to liberate the individuals who use them from attempted, oppressive manipulation.

When I arrived in Malawi at Chancellor College, early in January of 1985, as a new lecturer in Classics, I had come to assist a developing department, recently founded by its first lecturer and head, Caroline Alexander, and operating for about two years when I came onto the scene. My particular contribution to the department was meant to be the strengthening of the ancient Greek curriculum since I was an avid and a traditional Hellenist, working on a dissertation at Columbia University which focused on oral formulae in Attic judicial oratory. I was excited about the prospects of imposing my purist, old fashion, philological orientation on the new department. My idea was that there should be fewer courses in translation and more of the authentic, hard-core classes in original Greek texts. I did not envision my intentions as political at all, neither in terms of academic politics since I was an empirical positivist in research method. Also, in terms of geo-political perspective, I was unaware that a native African leader could be what is now labeled as neocolonialist. Neocolonialism was not part of my political vocabulary or of my political scope of concerns. I did understand, however, the concept of *dictator* and that Malawi's then President-for-Life, Dr. Kamuzu Banda, was clearly such as political animal, but he had, in my view, the redeeming feature of being a strong supporter of the study of Classics. I thought to myself how could reading Homer, Plato, Thucydides, Vergil, Cicero or Tacitus, those sorts of texts that traditional Classical education privileged, effect anything less than the cultivation and liberation of the mind: *Cultura animi philosphia est.* Perhaps this African dictator had some benevolent angle with a strong educational program in the back of his mind behind his obvious iron fist.

My first two semesters in Malawi were busy with adjusting to teaching and to administrative duties in a world very different from my own. Caroline Alexander, who had come to Chancellor College two years prior to my arrival and whom I succeeded as interim head of department, had done expeditiously much of the tedious labor of writing the overall program plan and individual course syllabi. Alexander, as far as I could see from our conversations, did not see her work as an endeavor in cultural imperialism but more a kind of personal academic entrepreneurship as she later suggests in a 1995 article written for the *Inquirer*:

I taught Latin, tutored a theology student in Greek and lectured my students on "classical civilization". I had a four-year degree programme[sic] to develop, a library and slide collection to build, textbooks to buy. Malawi is one of the poorest countries in the world, and money that had been pledged did not often materialized. *But where else in the world would I have been asked to establish a brand new classics department.* [my italics] (web)

Among members of the faculty, we both progressed in a negative aura of elitism, sparked by remarks Dr. Banda had made at the graduation ceremony in 1982. Just prior to the arrival of Alexander that December, Banda had stated bluntly, to the chagrin and annoyance of many present, that "first, no person was truly educated unless he knew Latin and Geek" and, second, an institution could not claim to be a real university unless it had a department of Classics". This exaggerated and perverse claim for the total superiority of Classical education (which was no longer true in Europe and had never been true for China, India or Africa) I attributed to proud, academic elitism based on his own educational experience. Since Dr. Banda had been educated in the U.S. and the U.K., where else was he to turn for models of university excellence for structuring higher education in a former British colony with an English-language educational system and already tuned toward Euro-American patterns. Most great universities in the U.S. and Britain, in fact, did have Classics departments. Thus, I did not perceive in his over-the-top remark any commitment on Banda's part to deprive Malawi of its native languages or culture by replacing them with Latin or Greek, a wholly unrealistic goal in any case. I did, however, feel a certain secret pleasure at the brash elitism of Banda's pronouncement in favor of his (and my) pet subject as I reflected on my own undergraduate days when I was one of only two Latin majors to graduate in a class of 999 and had tolerated many snide remarks about the foolishness of my area of study and the coming dire financial consequences of my poor choice of study. So I tended to revel privately in Banda's snobbish comments as a kind of poetic revenge for my personal denigration by boors and philistines. How amazing, as well as bizarre, that in poor Malawi the dictator regarded a Classical education so highly that could create *by fiat* a Classics program at the University of Malawi. I fantasized that if I were made dictator somewhere, I would do the same. My only qualm of conscience, however, was the expenditure for a luxury subject at the University of Malawi in face of the obvious poverty that I saw around me everywhere in the rest of the country. But, there could be no reasonable person to find a justifiable explanation for the new Classics Department at Chancellor College.

The official reason that I had been given by the Vice Chancellor for the establishment and deployment of a university Classics curriculum in 1983 was to provide educational continuity for those pupils who would be coming up from the recently rolled out Kamuzu Academy, a classical school on the model of British public schools. The Academy, founded by Banda in 1981, was purported to be fully funded by the President from his own private funds and was his particular, personal project. During my time at Chancellor College, the Academy overshadowed the College Classics Department in every way. It was clearly better funded; it had more faculty with significantly higher salaries than their university counterparts and many more students; in fact, when we lack texts at the College, we had textbooks sent to us from the Academy with Kamuzu Academy book stamps. I believed that such a dynamic and unusual Classical project at the secondary level, privately funded and initially successful, deserved an appropriate university reception since I believed that Classical education developed well-furnished, critical minds regardless of the continent on which it was provided. In my thinking, the personal funding of the Academy by Banda offset limited expenditure for the three Classics lecturers at the university. After all, there were also some donations from foreign governments. Most library books had been donated by the government of Greece. The U.S. government sent out a Fulbright professor to help staff the department fully. Additionally, we were expecting a healthy number of students coming up from Kamuzu Academy who would wish to continue their Classical studies in our newly established department.

To my regret and disappointment, this caravan of eager students never arrived at Chancellor College.

Moreover, the problem of a luxury school in a country of real poverty legitimately reemerged in the face of later revelations about the Banda government. Alexander reports that it has come to light that the Academy was not personally funded from Banda's private fortune in the way that was publically advertised:

> From its inception, the Academy had been touted as Banda's personal gift to the national. Other African leaders might crown themselves emperor or build the largest Cathedral in the world, bur Banda had - or so it was supposed - provided pounds 10m from his own pocket to set up an institution of permanent social worth, with another large sum put in trust to cover the annual running costs of about 1.3m. But when the new government [post Banda] took over and did some basic auditing, it quickly discovered that annual expenses had been lifted directly from the national educational budget. (Web).

Beside financial concerns, the Kamuzu Academy, since its foundation in 1981, has been the focus of general unease in Malawi as well as a target for much anti-neocolonialist rhetoric, mounted against the so-called cultural imperialism of Western educational ideology from critics of Neocolonialism. Although the Academy was autonomous and distinct from the University, whatever local hostility attached itself to Classics at the Academy passed on, at least indirectly, to entire project of Classics in Malawi. The University Classics department shared certain elements that were targeted as neocolonial features of Banda's Eton of the bush: imported foreign lecturers, teaching in English, financial support from non-African governments, and emphasis of "dead" European languages. Even the supporters of the Academy sometimes offered tepid or cautious praise for an obviously peculiar educational exercise.

From a general, non-ideological and non-political perspective, the founding headmaster of Kamuzu Academy expressed his view of the somewhat uneasy connection of intense Classics instruction at the Academy to the state of economic development in Malawi:

All about them [the students] is a world where a stream or a river is more likely a source of personal hygiene than Archimedes' bathtub and where a knowledge of Greek and Latin is less a survival aid than is a hoe. "It is," the Scottish headmaster, John Chaplin, said, "incongruous." (Cowell, Web.)

I, at times, had this same feeling about Classics at the University as well. Because Classics is cultural subject which examines ancient Mediterranean societies, it may seem to many less directly related to the African bush than perhaps biology or mathematics. Yet the same could be said, I realize, for the study of Latin in the Australian Outback or in a small Western town in the U.S. The Scottish headmaster reveals more, perhaps, about his own feelings of displacement from home and his personal intellectual connections to Europe than he reveals about the relevance of Classical languages to the lives of his pupils. But the remark, neither hostile nor particularly ideological in tone, does display a certain sense of psychological uneasiness concerning how an elite British educational institution might *not* fit very well with quotidian life in Africa. Academic critics who theorize neocolonialist Africa have more forceful and well-articulated views of the disconnection between Banda's Classical school and African life.

Ngugi wa Thiong'o offers no doubts about the ideological negativity of Banda's "own monument," commenting about both the emphasis on English and teaching "dead" foreign languages:

> For good measure, no Malawian is allowed to teach at the academy – none is good enough - and all the teaching staff has been recruited from Britain. A Malawian might lower the standards, or rather, the purity of the English language. Can you get a more telling example of the hatred of what is national, and a servile worship of what is foreign even though dead. (*Decolonising...* 19)

With genuine respect for wa Thiong'o's realistic concern over developing African languages toward literary and educational purposes (*Decolonising* [sic] *the Mind*), nonetheless I suggest that there

257

may have been sound reasons behind the initial hiring British teachers for Banda's Classical school other than some kind of hatred of the local. No doubt, snobbism was involved in the importation of British teachers; however, pragmatically for Malawi in 1981, there would have been few, outside of Christian ministers, who would have had training in Latin and Greek sufficient to teach those subjects to A/level. Moreover, Classical schools elsewhere typically advertise for teachers who themselves had early educational exposure to Latin to be instructors in the school. And finally, an important question must be posed: Why must the learning of Latin and Greek necessarily exclude or disrespect the development of native languages at a national level? The Kamuzu Academy was only one, unique school with free tuition for those who attended; its curriculum was not a national curriculum. In fact, we have a record of Banda's stated motivation for founding the Kamuzu Academy in an interview he had with Dr. Caroline Alexander at the time of his legal process for political murders during his presidency and that motivation does not seem to suggest the suppression of African languages or cultures at the national level:

> During the course of the interview with Banda, before we got round to Caesar, I had asked him about his school [Kamazu Academy]. He said that he had built it so that young people could receive the kind of education in Malawi that he had been forced to seek abroad. "Some appreciate it, some don't. But that was my idea." (Web)

Is there any reason to disbelieve Banda's self-professed motive for founding his school? He had a personal interest in the Classics and felt that a Classical education had supported his intellectual development. In addition, in his younger years, he had even considered studying to become a Classics professor (Alexander, web). Certainly, later as a medical doctor, he saw the strong connection between classical languages and the vocabulary of medical science, one of the major pragmatic reasons often put forward for the study of Latin in Occidental societies. Are these not plausible motives, with no anti-African sentiment, for a classical school?

From the critique of neocolonialism and cultural imperialism in academic circles, geo-political, economic, sociological, strategic and racial motives find immediate acceptance as realistic reasons for various imperialistic projects and their postcolonial continuations. The hermeneutics of suspicion, linked to the realistic historical contexts of colonial exploitation, offers a fertile field for cultivation of much genuinely righteous and self-righteous rhetoric directed against continuing neocolonial manipulation and interference in African education. Perhaps, a less unpleasant, anti-African motivation lies behind the foundation of the Kamuzu Academy. Could it be simply one dictator's desire to make available a type of education that he admired *regardless* of its European and elitist associations?

Personally, I can believe Banda's professed statement based my own educational background in Classics. I studied Latin for three years in high school; Greek was not available. When I went to university, I was distressed to find out that students who had attended British public schools had years of study of both Greek and Latin, and at a much high standard than my high school Latin. I also remember how I later admired the curriculum of the Italian *Liceo Classico* and wished that I could have got such deep, humanistic preparation for my university studies. I even contemplated how I might found a school on the model of the *Liceo Classico* as a private institution in the United States. There was certainly no idea of colonizing or Italian cultural domination of the United States in my thinking; rather I had a desire to translate for those few, who might wish it, a system that effectively imparted, at the high school level, classical humanities to a most excellent standard. Nonetheless, since there is no avoiding the unpleasantness of colonialism in the history of Africa, Banda's planting of a replica of the King's College of Our Lady of Eaton beside Windsor in the Malawi bush reeked, to many observers, of blatant cultural and class hegemony as well as unabashed neocolonialism.

The Kamuzu Academy, as recently as 2012, continues to draw intense academic fire as a classic example (pun intended) of Euro-American intellectual imperialism in the area of African education. Francis Nyamnjoh in his article "'Potted Plants in Greenhouses'" comments:

> Even when the finances are there, there is no guarantee that African political and intellectual leaders will do what is right for African education [center it in relevant African epistemologies]. By way of example yet again, at the Kamuzu Academy, where the neo-Etonians were trained to recite Shakespeare and glorify the classic philosophers of the metropolis, the library that housed the classics was deliberately designed in the image of the Library of Congress in the USA. From it, students imbibed an awful lot of Latin, classical music, western history and etiquette and consumed a lot of McDonalized entertainment television. (Nyamnjoh 142)

Nyamnjoh's objection to the Westernized curriculum is not so much that Classics and Shakespeare are bad in themselves nor unworthy of study in their own proper contexts, but that in the imposition of Occidental educational values and curriculum are irrelevant to indigenous African languages, social life and local epistemologies that should form the center of African education:

> Education in Africa has been and mostly remains a journey fueled by an exogenously induced and internalized sense of inadequacy in Africans, and one endowed with a mission of devaluation or annihilation of African creativity, agency and value systems. (Nyamnjoh 138)

One must agree that the suppression of local languages and traditional arts, where that has happened, is not a good thing. Additionally, humanist scholars might readily align themselves with Nyamnjoh's critique of what amounts to the religion of science (locked to Western educational systems of the 19th, 20th and 21st centuries) which imposes on the pedagogy and research in humanistic disciplines the iron logic of quantification over qualitative and philosophic evaluation (Nyamnjoh 130-131). Yet, at least, some humanists might not consider offering African students insight into the European mind-set through Classical languages a force for annihilating local languages, for wrecking African minds or for "[e]ducation as [c]ultural [v]iolence" (Nyamnjoh 132).

Barbara Goff provides a more congenial view of Classical education in Africa. Her recently edited collection of essays on the intersection of the field of Classics and colonialism, (the uses of Classics in Africa for colonial domination but also for local liberation), pits the Kamuzu Academy, in opposition to Nyamnjoh's view. For her, it is an exemplar of the assertion of the African drive for educational independence in the face of continued, external economic pressures for technical and scientific development. Situated in the middle of illustrations of colonial plundering such as the affair of the Elgin Marbles and numerous direct educational impositions from metropolitan nations, Banda's Academy becomes, on Goff's view, " ... a quite different institution in which Africans can be seen to assert an independent claim to classical culture without having it imposed... on them." (Goff 10) Since the establishment of Kamuzu Academy was the choice of a local African leader and its educational program was humanistic and non-technical, the institution required private or local government monies and did not conform to the typical pragmatic directions forwarded by well-funded, technical development schemes of foreign governments (Goff 10). Goff suggests that such a local educational direction and financial backing, particularly if that choice moves away from the immediate pressure of the economic development agenda of first-world nations, illustrates refreshing African intellectual and economic independence from former colonizers. The same liberationist views could be envisioned for the establishment of a full Classics department at the University of Malawi since a determination to add a traditional humanistic discipline into a mix more technical subjects ran in the face of pragmatic sentiment, both domestic and foreign. Although the Academy provided a demonstration of an African nation (or its leader) emphasizing Western, humanistic education in ideas over pragmatic training in techniques, Goff admits that overall "[c]classics in the education of Africans, as a contested inheritance from the days of colonialism, has been and remains a highly contentious issue..." (Goff 11).

One central problem that emerges in anti-colonialist critiques of Classical education in Africa is the issue of imposed languages. Greek and Latin were imported as part of an English or French education system in which the two ancient languages were taught in the languages of the colonizers. I remember being aware that my students at the University of Malawi were true polyglots when they studied Greek and Latin in English which was not their mother tongue. I might add here that students at the University did speak African languages along with English in daily activities; and I recall no stigma attached to speaking African languages. More, there was no animus against local languages in the Department of Classics. One of our part-time members was an Anglican missionary who regularly celebrate liturgies in Chichewa. However, English, one of the official languages of Malawi, not Chichewa, *was* the language of instruction and examination at the University although I was told that Chichewa was the language of instruction in Malawi through primary schools when a transition to English was required because of the limitations of Chichewan vocabulary in academic vocabulary. Lucretius and Cicero, also, had problem with the lack of philosophical vocabulary in Latin, and for several centuries both history and philosophy were Greek subjects among the Romans who indulged in them, so I found no special neocolonialist issue with the use of English as a university language. Other views of colonial development have produced a different reaction to the question of languages in colonial and postcolonial education. This language problem is the central concern, in fact, of Ngugi wa Thiong'o's *Decolonising the Mind*.

Intellectual colonization, after military and economic control, extends domination of the metropolitan agents over African education, literature and hence, mentality, through the imposition of non-native, European languages according to wa Thiong'o. In *Decolonising the Mind,* he angrily narrates his own story of education in Kenyan colonial schools where his mother tongue, Gikuyu, was repressed and where pupils were forced linguistically, at least, into foreign skins:

> But since the new, imposed languages could never completely break the native languages as spoken, their [colonial powers] most effective area of domination was ... the written. The language of an African child's formal education was foreign. The language of the books he read was foreign. The language of conceptualization was foreign. Thought in him took the visible form of a foreign language. So the written language of the child's upbringing in school (even his spoken language within the school compound) became divorced from his language at home. (wa Thiong'o 17)

Ngugi wa Thiong'o's poignant description narrates not only his personal experience, but also the psychological experience of every schooled pupil in Western Europe from the fall of the Roman Empire through the Renaissance and even later since all formal instruction was in Latin. Of course, in the Middle Ages, there was no linguistic manipulation from outside governments and the use of Latin in school was not connected to political domination. But surely, in the words of wa Thiongo, "[t]here was often not the slightest relationship between the child's written world, which was also the language of schooling, and world of his immediate environment in the family and in the community (17)." In the Medieval period, this disassociation between the language of school and the languages of daily life world would have been even more pronounced in European areas that did not speak local dialects derived from Latin.

The point I making here is not that colonialist imposition of foreign languages is in any way politically justified or wholesome, only that unintended result may be an advantageous, multilingual consciousness for the polyglot, colonial student. Ngugi wa Thiobng'o himself is an excellent example of this comparative linguistic consciousness at work. His appreciation of the tension between the thought world of his native African language and the (colonial) language of his schooling, only possible for the multilingual individual, is detailed in *Decolonizing the Mind*. In fact, he became, by accident, a comparatist through his schooling in a language other than his native one. wa Thiong'o developed the ability to see the competing ideological systems of different languages and the clash of values represented by this competition.

The key to this multilinguistic consciousness is the fact that regardless of how colonizing authorities tried to create unitary thought world of authoritarian domination of through a particular language, (French, Portuguese, English or Spanish), any language of intended domination builds the potential of intellectual rebellion into itself through *heteroglossia*. The concept of heteroglossia, theorized by Mikhail Bakhtin, is the notion that any natural language always carries within itself varying levels of history, style, competing ideologies. Bakhtin writes:

> Thus at any given moment of its historical existence, language is heteroglot from top to bottom: it represents the co-existence of socio-ideological contradictions between the present and the past, between differing epochs of the past, between different socio-ideological groups in the present... (Bakhtin 291).

These varying ideological layers within any language, or between languages, are available to an astute user of the language(s) as linguistic consciousness, an animated vision of ideational competition and ideological opposition within the language(s). In the speaker's mind, a given language becomes *dialogized*. No longer, can that speaker be confined to a thought system programmed for control and domination; language itself offers a means to think out of the limitations of attempted control.

This dialogized linguistic consciousness is especially enhanced for the bilingual or polyglot because of potential interanimation of the various languages in the mind of the polyglot. wa Thiong'o suggests the chink in the armor of colonial, monolinguistic domination: "... the new, imposed [colonial] languages could never completely break the native languages as spoken..." (*Decolonising ...* 17): As long as local languages were spoken at home, in the marketplace, on the back paths or in the villages, linguistic domination remained impossible. (As examples, Irish and Welsh, almost exterminated by English pressure and local disuse are remaking a slow, if not dramatic recovery from almost extinction.) Thus, the linguistic situation of the colonial and postcolonial zones is fertile for multilingual practice and communication. Bakhtin illustrates the nature of "socio-ideological language consciousness as it becomes creative by an example of a multilingual, Russian peasant:

> Thus an illiterate peasant, miles away from any urban center naively immersed in an unmoving and for him unshakeable everyday world, nevertheless lived in several language systems: he prayed to God in one language (Church Slavonic), sung songs in another, spoke to his family in a third, and when he began to dictate petitions to the local authorities through a scribe, he tried speaking yet a fourth language (the official-literate language, "paper" language). (Bakhtin 297-298)

Bakhtin's point here is that the peasant is uneducated, in fact illiterate. He has not been forced to have schooling in a foreign language or any language, and he is analytically unaware of the ideological differences in the languages of his daily life. His linguistic consciously is not yet dialogized. A change comes when the peasant, for whatever reason, sees that he uses ideologically distinct and varied languages in different contexts; he has to actively choose his language according to the occasion and need:

> As soon as a critical interanimation of language began to occur in the consciousness of our peasant, as soon as it became clear that all these were not only various different languages but even internally variegated languages, that the ideological systems and approaches to the world that were indissolubly connected with these languages contradicted each other and in no way could live in peace and quiet with each other... the necessity of choosing one's orientation among them began, (Bahktin 296)

In *Decolonizing the Mind,* the trenchant analysis of the psychology of the colonial schoolchild's linguistic alienation, in school and through English, from her local language and immediate world offers a forceful example "that the ideological systems and approaches to the world that were indissolubly connected with these languages contradicted each other...." (Bakhtin 296). wa Thiong'o's capability of analyzing deeply and emotionally the ideational and psychological disjunction in the mind of the schoolchild, forced to use language for school that was remote from his local roots, is the direct result of his own multilinguistic consciousness. No monoglot could readily produce such a detailed and heart-felt rendering of this sort of language situation.

Paradoxically then, the very imposition of colonial languages that wa Thiong'o is protesting serves as the basis for dialogized, polyglot consciousness that makes his protest possible. One could wonder if the boys of Medieval Europe also felt such great angst and anomie at being schooled in Latin as wa Thiong'o suggests for colonial children being schooled in French or English. Of course, Latin was not the language of an oppressive colonizing power in the Middle Ages but the universal language of the Church and education. Nonetheless, Latin was not the language of daily life, except in monasteries, and surely pupils knew that it was not their mother tongue. It is an interesting question whether immersion in Latin at school or in the monastery imposed on schoolboys a sense of psychological alienation from their mother tongues.

Greek and Latin students in Malawi, although taught Latin and Greek through English, were certain to obtain the benefits of multi-linguistic consciousness, dialogized polyglossia, which is one of the particular aims of an education in Classical languages which cultivates an active sense of the historical evolution of Latin language and literature from its Greek roots. The appropriation and naturalization of Greek literary genres, style and themes by the Romans for their own Latin literature, a standard trope of Roman literary history, illustrates the deployment of the word as "a two-sided act". V. N. Volosinov in *Marxism and the Philosophy of Language* explains:

> Orientation of the word toward the addressee has an extremely high significance. In point of fact, *the word is a two-side act*. It is

determined equally by *whose* word it is and *for whom* it is meant. As word, it is precisely *the product of the reciprocal relationship between speaker and listener, addresser and addressee.* Each and every word expresses the "one" in relationship to "the" other. I give myself verbal shape from another's point of view.... A word is a bridge thrown between myself and another. (86)

Over the past fifty years, the literary appropriation of the Classics in Africa, (especially Greek tragedy), for purposes of protest against forces of colonialism point to the two-sidedness of Classical texts and the modern languages in which they have been taught, ancient and foreign in origin on one side, but contemporary and living on the other side. As parts of the Classical literary tradition have been absorbed, naturalized and nativized in Africa, objections to "... a servile worship of what is foreign even though dead..."(wa Thiong'o 19) become less pragmatically urgent and theoretically operative.

Here it should be noted and emphasized, on the linguistic theory of Bakhtin and Volosinov, that the objection to the imported languages of colonial oppressors as *languages of oppression* is not a realistic or comprehensive view of any natural language, ancient or modern. Colonial oppressors attempted to control local, colonized populations through the colonizers' languages, but such an attempt was bound to fail because of the inherent, but possibly unrecognized, dialogic nature of those languages. Local populations who employed the colonizers' languages appropriated those languages for their own use since every word "*the product of the reciprocal relationship between speaker and listener, addresser and addressee*" (Volosinov 86). Classical literary texts, dialogically positioned as recent scholarship has revealed, have offered special avenues for African literary and linguistic appropriation against the outside ideological domination of colonial and postcolonial forces.

For example, a close reading of Chapter Six in Goff's *Classics and Colonialism*, "Greek Tragedies in West African Adaptations", by Felix Budelmann, reveals important works of important African playwrights who derive their plays from ancient Greek drama. They use canonical Greek models as "counter-discourse" in the face of

Eurocentric neocolonialism. Ola Rotimi, *The Gods Are Not to Blame*, from *Oedipus Rex*; Wole Soyinka, *The Bacchae of Euripides: A Communion Rite*; Jacqueline LeLoup, *Guiedo*, from *Oedipus Rex*; Femi Osofisan, *Tegonni: An African Antigone; The Trojan Women or the Women of Owu* are pertinent examples of such works. An analysis of these plays shed light on how they present the Greeks from an African perspective and, it also how they reveal a significant, recent development in the discipline of Classical Studies. This expansion leads to considering these contemporaneous classical inspired plays as a significant aspect of Classical scholarship. Over and above, it brings to light contemporary receptions of those primary texts that philologists study. The connection of critical reflection by classicists on reception of Classical texts in Africa relates a traditional discipline, once considered totally Eurocentric, to political and literary concerns of another continent and presents the analysis of classical texts as much an African matter as a European matter. In other words, what elements of the Greek text allow African playwright to read contemporary African issues back into an ancient play and what does that retrojection of issues tell us about the significance of the ancient play?

Further, during the past thirty years to forty years or so, research and investigation in Classical Studies has been expanding from its traditional and canonical, Eurocentric limitations both chronologically and geographically, bringing Late Antiquity and more of the Near East and Africa into focus for serious scholarly consideration. For example, the noted Oxford scholar of Homer and Hesiod, Martin West, in the introduction to his commentary on *The Theogony*, made the bold but totally defensible claim that "Greece is part of Asia; Greek literature is a Near Eastern Literature" (West 31). West's commentary on Hesiod's *Theogony* was published in 1966. At present, the discipline of Classical Studies looks considerably less Eurocentric than it did in 1966 when West suggested a Near Eastern literature in place what most had labeled quintessentially and fundamentally European. Contemporary Classics has much of direct relevance to offer the African student beyond anti-African, Occidental intellectual imperialism. Many contemporary cultural turns, incorporated into academe in general, such as feminism, multiculturalism, reception theory, new historicism, and the challenge of marginalized voices to the Western canon, have entered into the discipline of Classics and opened up new topics and avenues for research. Importantly and directly in respect to Africa was the publication and the succeeding vociferous debate surrounding Martin Bernal's *Black Athena*. Hotly argued but generally dismissed as largely inaccurate in details and conclusions by Classical scholars, *Black Athena*, notwithstanding the rejection by specialists of its Afro-centric biases, brought the African side of ancient Mediterranean cultures into the spotlight. The *Black Athena* debate pushed classicists to scrutinize more closely the male-dominated and Eurocentric ideologies of 19th and early 20th century upon which Classical scholarship had been built, thereby aiding the broadening of ideological perspectives in the discipline (Goff 16).

Even the strident critic of Eurocentrism and European language domination in postcolonial Africa, Ngugi wa Thiongo suggests how knowledge of the Occidental Classical tradition could be fruitful for the developing African experience. One could find many examples, no doubt, but wa Thiongo's illustration in *Something Torn and New: An African Renaissance* is important since it is developed as part of his critique of independent Africa's domination by European languages. Constructing an analogy to the hegemony of Latin in Europe at the beginning of the European Renaissance, wa Thiong'o traces out the emergence of the national languages of Europe from the "shadow of Latin" (87):

> The European Renaissance involved not only exploration of new frontiers of thought but also a reconnection with the European's memory, the roots of which lay in ancient Greece and Rome. In practice, this reconnection involved disengagement from the tyranny of hegemonic Latin and the discovery of European's own tongues. (*Something Torn and New* 123)

In a parallel fashion, wa Thiong'o proposes that Africans abandon the hegemony of European languages and return to their native linguistic roots as a way to promote their own "Renaissance".

This somewhat unusual application of Western intellectual history to Africa is an apt example of how the study of European history, including Classical history, can be a true benefit to African students. In wa Thing'o's analogy, English or French would be the "hegemonic Latin" that requires disengagement. A closer examination of the fading of Latin and the rise of vernaculars will show that the analogy is not exact but somewhat problematic. Latin at the dawn of the Renaissance was a living tongue, although nobody's mother tongue. Medieval Latin had created a growing vocabulary to cope with new concepts that its users encountered in their intellectual development. In the 15th Century in Italy, there arose a neo-Ciceronian movement that promulgated strict imitation of Cicero in style and vocabulary. This stylistic fad, adopted by important Renaissance intellectuals, actually diminished the flexibility of Latin as a growing, living instrument that during the Middle Ages had been adapted to describe new conceptions. In other words, Latin became, in style and vocabulary, focused in its own Roman past, trapped in the ancient world, and was surpassed by more flexible vernaculars that lived in the present. Contemporary French, and especially contemporary English, do not suffer any such stagnation as did Latin under purist Ciceronism in the European Renaissance. Through the unfortunate history of colonialism, European languages were imported into Africa so that they are there now as part of the intellectual history of Africa. As African nations move forward to build and support their own local languages, why should they extirpate the linguistic riches left behind by an ugly phase in their history? Can't good clothes arrive in an ugly suitcase?

Returning to the reception and application of Classical languages and literatures in the contemporary African intellectual milieu, we can find that the Classics at the University of Malawi in the 21st Century is turning to reception theory and comparative education for new directions. Thirty-four years after its foundation, the Department of Classics produced, in 2016, its first Ph.D. with a dissertation,

Contextualising Classics Teaching in Malawi: A Comparative Study (Nyamilandu, web). Examining ways to present Classical Studies as more pertinent to the cultural horizons of contemporary Malawian undergraduates, Steven Nyamilandu, a Classics lecturer at Chancellor College, investigated the current structure and strategies of Classics programs in Great Britain, the U.S., Africa and Asia. Further, he capitalizes on cultural connections already establish through African adaptation and redirection of Classical literary works, particularly Greek drama. The principal pedagogical suggestions from Nyamilandu's study focus on raising awareness among Malawian students of naturalization of Classical texts to the African context. African students would approach Classics within the broadest framework possible, i.e., ancient history, philosophy, art and archaeology, digital Classics, as well as Greek and Latin languages. They would search out apt comparisons of the cultural position of Classical study in countries around the world with the cultural conditions in contemporary Malawi. These new directions for contextualizing Classics in Malawi can easily be linked to the previously referenced geographical and ideological expansion of Classical Studies toward Africa and the Near East, the Afrocentric/Eurocentric ideological debate triggered by Bernal as well as the application of multiple critical theories to Classical texts.

Although traditional philology of the type prevalent when the Classics Department was inaugurated at the University of Malawi promoted a hermeneutics of trust which struggles to shape a descriptive, critical language focusing on the immediately obvious form and content of literary texts, new philology adds to the mix a hermeneutics of suspicion which offers much wider scope for ideological debate, political contestation, comparative study and the interrogation of marginalized voices. From the dialogic perspective of Bakhin/Volosinov, the study of Classical languages and literatures was always potentially open to a wider vision of ideas that, in point of fact, has been emerging in the past thirty to forty years. Bakhtin has formulated the following description of the heteroglot state of natural languages, writing,

271

Thus at any given moment of its historical existence, language is heteroglot from top to bottom: it represents the co-existence of socio-ideological contradictions between the present and the past, between differing epochs of the past.... These "languages" of heteroglossia intersect each other in a variety of ways, forming new socially typifying "languages". (Bakhtin 291).

The contemporary African student, then, has sufficient space within such a dialogic view of language to accommodate the study of Greek and Latin, in English, French or local African languages, without the specter of neocolonial linguistic domination. Multilinguistic consciousness produces a form of intellectual liberation.

Works Cited

Alexander, Caroline. "A Classic Dictator." *The Independent,* 7 October 1995, www.indepedent.co.uk/arts-entertainment/a-classic-dictator1576491. Html

Bakhtin, M.M. *The Dialogic Imagination.* Trans. Caryl Emerson and Michael Holquist, University of Texas Press, 1981.

Bernal, Martin. *Black Athena: Afroasiatic Roots of Classical Civilization, Vol. I: The Fabrication of Ancient Greece, 1985-1985.* Rutgers UP, 1989.

Budelmann, Felix. "Greek Tragedies in West African Adaptations." *Classics Colonialism,* Ed. Barbara Goff, Duckworth, 2005, pp. 118-146

Cowell, Alan. "Malawi's Elite Academy: The Very Model of Eton." *The New York Times,* 04 May 1983, www.nytimes.com/1983/07/04/world/malawi-s-elite-academy-the-model-of-eton.html

Goff, Barbara. Introduction, *Classics and Colonialism,* Ed. Barbara Goff, Duckworth, 2005. pp 1-14.

Nyamilandu, Steve Evans McRester Trinta. *Contextualising Teaching Classics in Malawi: A Comparative Study.* Dissertation, University of St. Andrews and University of Malawi, 2016. http://hdl.handle.net./10023/9427

Nyamnjoh, Francis B. "'Potted Plants in Greenhouses': A Critical Reflection on the Resilience of Colonial Education in Africa." *Journal of Asian and African Studies,* vol. 47, no. 2, 2012, pp. 128-154.

Volosinov, V. N. *Marxism and the Philosophy of Language.* Trans. L. Matejka and I. R. Titunik, Harvard University Press, 1973.

wa Thiong'o, Ngugi. *Decolonizing the Mind: The Politics of Language in African Literature.* James Currey, 1986.

_____. *Something Torn and New: An African Renaissance.* Civitas, New York, 2009.

West. M.L. (Ed.). *Hesiod: Theogony.* Oxford UP, 1966.

273

INDEX

Mok, 139, 158

Moraña, 22, 26, 27

Mozambique, 191, 194

MPLA, 40

Muholi, Zanele, 30, 47, 51

Mulgan, 17, 26

Murray, Stephen O., 45, 51, 154, 159

Museveni, Yoweri, 46, 47

Muste, A.J., 33, 35, 37, 39, 51

N

NAACP, 32

Nadin, 139, 158

nature, 63, 64

Ndlovu, 16, 18, 20, 27

Ndunduyenge, 154, 159

Netting, 101, 102, 110, 119

Ngugi, 64, 76, 228, 236, 239, 244, 248, 249, 255, 258

Nigeria, 30, 36, 44, 61, 62, 90, 91, 121, 124, 125, 128-132, 183

Nkengasong, Nkemngong John, 7, 27, 58, 76

Nkrumah, Kwame, 36

Nussbaum, 110, 119

Nyamilandu, 256, 258

Nyamnjoh

Francis, B., 1, 5, 7, 25-27, 58, 238, 239, 246, 247, 258

Nyerere, 233

O

Oakerson, 114, 119

Okpewho, 137, 159

Olupona, 137, 138, 158, 159

Orjiako, 154, 155, 159

Osofisan, Femi, 253

Ostrom, 98, 101, 102, 106, 113, 119

P

Pan-Africanism, 29, 44

Pargament, 141, 142, 144, 152, 159, 160

T

U

V